IMAGES
of America

Chinese in St. Louis

1857–2007

On the cover: Please see page 36. (St. Louis Mercantile Library.)

IMAGES
of America

CHINESE IN ST. LOUIS
1857–2007

Huping Ling, Ph.D.

ARCADIA
PUBLISHING

ISBN 978-0-7385-5145-6

Published by Arcadia Publishing
Charleston, South Carolina

Printed in the United States of America

Library of Congress Catalog Card Number: 2007920838

For all general information contact Arcadia Publishing at:
Telephone 843-853-2070
Fax 843-853-0044
E-mail sales@arcadiapublishing.com
For customer service and orders:
Toll-Free 1-888-313-2665

Visit us on the Internet at www.arcadiapublishing.com

To the Chinese Americans in St. Louis,
whose struggle and success have inspired this book.

Contents

ACKNOWLEDGMENTS

I am grateful to the individuals who have most generously shared their life histories with me and or provided access to the images and permissions for publication: Haiyan Cai, Kin Cai, James Chi, Edwin Chiu, Jean Chiu, Mimi Chou, Miller Chow, Anna Crosslin, Ngoc Doan, Hung-Gay Fong, Tony Gao, Richard Ho, Lillie Hong, Mu-Lien Hsueh, Eric Huang, Wen Hwang, Xinsheng Jiang, Ann Ko, Don Ko, Lily Ko, Walter Ko, Yee M. Kwong, Harold Law, Hong L. Le, Annie Leong, Chung Kok Li, Jerry Li, Zhihai Liang, Sherwin Liou, Grace Shen Lo, Grace Yin Lo, Lo Kang, Chris Lu, Jenny Lu, Andrew Luh, Rose Luh, Samuel Pan, Dachung Pat Peng, Tzy C. Peng, Eliot F. Porter Jr., Hong Sit, Yuan-Sheng Sui, Bin Sun, Ching-Ling Tai, William K. Y. Tao, Tong Wang, Nelson Wu, Hsinyi Yang, James Yeh, Patricia L. Yeh, Grace Chen Yin, Guanzheng Yu, Francis Yueh, May Yueh, James Zhang, Peter Zhang, Zheng Guojin, Anning Zhu, and Wubing Zong. I am also grateful to May and Francis Yueh for their continued support of my research and writing on Chinese in St. Louis. Special thanks also go to Marjorie Cheung for encouragement and for tirelessly verifying the captions of her family photographs.

I give my heartfelt thanks to the following agencies and institutions that have provided access and or permissions for publication of the images and artifacts: St. Louis Chinese American News; St. Louis Chinese Journal; St. Louis Chinese Association; St. Louis Chinese Academy; St. Louis Chinese Language School; St. Louis Modern Chinese School; Missouri Historical Society Library and Research Center; Missouri History Museum; Mercantile Library; Olin Library and West Campus Library at Washington University; St. Louis Public Library; the Recorder of Deeds at St. Louis City Hall; National Archives-Central Plains Region, Kansas City, Missouri; National Archives-Pacific Sierra Region-San Bruno, California; the International Institute of Metro St. Louis; and Valhalla Cemetery.

Some information in this book is derived from my book *Chinese St. Louis: From Enclave to Cultural Community* published by Temple University Press in 2004. Interested readers may consult the latter for more expansive information on Chinese Americans in St. Louis.

My family has been the most steadfast support of my long-term research on Chinese Americans. I am forever indebted to them.

INTRODUCTION

In 1857, Alla Lee, a 24-year-old native of Ningbo, China, seeking a better life, came to St. Louis, where he opened a small shop on North Tenth Street selling tea and coffee. Lee first arrived in California as interpreter of a missionary. With the assistance of church and business networks, Lee traveled to the East Coast, and in 1857 arrived in St. Louis. A decade later, Lee was joined by several hundred of his countrymen from San Francisco and New York who were seeking jobs in mines and factories in and around St. Louis. The stories of Lee and the Chinese workers reflect an important factor in the early Chinese settlement in St. Louis: many were migrants who sought opportunities in other parts of the country when their situations deteriorated in California. The rather hostile socioeconomic climate in the United States forced these immigrants to keep moving to survive. Their paths to the Mound City, St. Louis's nickname as the earlier Native American inhabitants left many enormous burial mounds nearby, were largely determined by religious connections, recruitment efforts of the capitalists, and kinship networks.

Most of these Chinese workers lived in boarding houses located near a small street called Hop Alley. In time, Chinese hand laundries, merchandise stores, herb shops, restaurants, and clan association headquarters sprang up in and around that street. In St. Louis, Hop Alley became synonymous with Chinatown. Hop Alley, like many Chinese communities in other parts of the country, has been stereotyped as a mysterious and dangerous place, often associated with opium dens, tong wars, and murder.

Despite prejudice and discrimination, Hop Alley survived with remarkable resilience and energy. St. Louis Chinatown was not simply a ghetto plagued by urban problems of crowded, unsanitary living and working conditions and crimes. In fact, it was a lively commercial, residential, and recreational center for the Chinese. The hand laundries, grocery stores, restaurants, and tea shops were essential businesses enabling the survival, and in some cases, remarkable success of the early Chinese settlers. These businesses, especially the hand laundries, were also indispensable to the larger St. Louis communities that readily utilized the much needed services. The elbow grease of the Chinese laundrymen certainly made the industrial machine of St. Louis run smoother and better. No matter how small the Chinese population became from time to time, its members contributed disproportionately—less than 0.1 percent of the total general population providing 60 percent of the laundry services for the city.

While the laundries provided services to the larger community, Chinese grocery stores, restaurants, and tea shops primarily sustained the survival of Chinese residents. The importance of these businesses not only lies in their supply of merchandise and services essential for the daily existence of the Chinese, but also in their absorption of Chinese immigrant laborers who were excluded from the general labor market. Moreover, these businesses contributed to the metropolitan atmosphere that the city boosters were eagerly pursuing.

Like other urban Chinese immigrant communities, Hop Alley developed a self-protective and self-governing structure, the On Leong Merchants and Laborers Association, commonly known as On Leong. Since its founding in the beginning of the 20th century, it had been the dominant community organization in St. Louis Chinatown, serving as an unofficial local government of Chinese immigrants in America. A powerful economic force within the Chinese community, On Leong provided useful social services to its members and families.

The lack of family life among early Chinese immigrants had been used first as evidence of Chinese cultural peculiarity, sojourning mentality, and incapability for Americanization, and later as an excuse for Chinese exclusion. Hop Alley, however, depicts a different picture, in which Chinese family lives existed and many Chinese immigrants made efforts to settle and even assimilate into the host society. For those who had family and children, Hop Alley was their home and community. For those who could not have family with them due to Chinese exclusion laws, financial difficulties, and Chinese cultural restraints, Hop Alley was a necessary substitute for family life and an emotional outlet. Interactions with community members on Sundays restored the energy drained by a week of toil. Hop Alley, to a certain degree, normalized their "abnormal" immigrant life in America.

The postwar prosperity brought the urban renewal movement, which intended to improve the look of the city and further promote its economy. The urban renewal projects included the clearing and reconstruction of the downtown district that consequently dismantled Hop Alley, thus ending the history of the century-old Chinatown in 1966.

The decades of the 1960s to 1980s saw two major shifts take place among the Chinese St. Louisans. The first was the transformation of Chinese from the predominantly Chinatown residents to suburban dwellers scattering throughout West County, the suburban municipalities west of the city. Meanwhile, the continued urban removal movement thwarted the community's effort to construct a new Chinatown. The Chinese professionals, either new arrivals or American-born, also found less dependence, both occupationally and recreationally, on an ethnic commercial and residential district. Also the Chinese economy changed from laundry business to food service and related retailing industries. At the same time, the professional Chinese were employed by the mainstream economy.

Although the Chinese population in St. Louis has increased substantially, one cannot easily spot either a commercial or residential Chinese district. Signs of Chinese American presence, however, are clear. More than half of the city's modern buildings and structures have involved the engineering design of a Chinese American consulting firm, William Tao and Associates. Two weekly Chinese language newspapers vie to serve the community. Three Chinese language schools offer classes of Chinese language, arts, and culture. A dozen Chinese religious institutions have substantial memberships. More than 40 community organizations independently or jointly sponsor a wide array of community activities ranging from cultural gatherings to the annual Chinese Culture Days held in the Missouri Botanical Gardens that draws more than 10,000 visitors. More than 500 Chinese restaurants cater to the St. Louisans who are fond of ethnic cuisine.

The establishment and development of Chinese community organizations, Chinese churches, and Chinese language schools between the 1960s and 1980s signified the formation of a Chinese American cultural community in St. Louis. Without physical boundaries, the cultural community proves to be a functional, cohesive, and tightly knit ethnic community structure. Without geographical concentrations, the myriad community organizations and cultural institutions have created a visible and indispensable ethnic community. Through its wide array of activities and events, the cultural community effectively bound its members together and rendered them invaluable social and emotional services. The cultural community has exhibited an alternative ethnic community model when a physical ethnic concentration is absent and a geographical ethnic community is difficult to construct.

One

Coming to America

The 1882 Chinese Exclusion Act banned the entry of Chinese laborers while it exempted Chinese merchants. Some Chinese laborers, in order to bring their families to America, changed their status from laborer to merchant by faking a partnership in a grocery store. Others were smuggled by train or boat from Canada, Mexico, and the Caribbean. Immigration authorities responded by assuming all Chinese immigrants were guilty of fraudulent entry until proven otherwise and singled them out for prolonged detention and interrogation at entry points. During the period when the Angel Island Immigration Station was operating (1910–1940), immigration officials climbed aboard and inspected the passengers' documents each time a ship arrived in San Francisco. They allowed those with satisfactory papers to go ashore. The remainder were transferred to a small steamer and ferried to the immigration station on Angel Island to await hearings on their application for entry. Although a few whites and other Asians were held at the detention center, the majority of the detainees were Chinese. The immigration detention center on Angel Island was a two-story wooden structure, where men and women were held separately. The duration of imprisonment was often months. Immigrants were first taken to a hospital for medical examinations. Those afflicted with parasitic diseases such as trachoma, hookworm, and liver fluke were excluded and deported. The rest were sent back to their dormitories to await the hearing on their application. Regardless of the validity of the Chinese arrival's legal documents for entry, a Chinese woman had to go through an extensive cross-interrogation on family, home life, and native village. An applicant's testimony could largely determine the result of his or her application. Under such practice, a felon could gain admission as long as he or she and the witnesses were prepared to produce the same testimony, while a bona fide applicant could be denied if he or she failed to provide expected testimony.

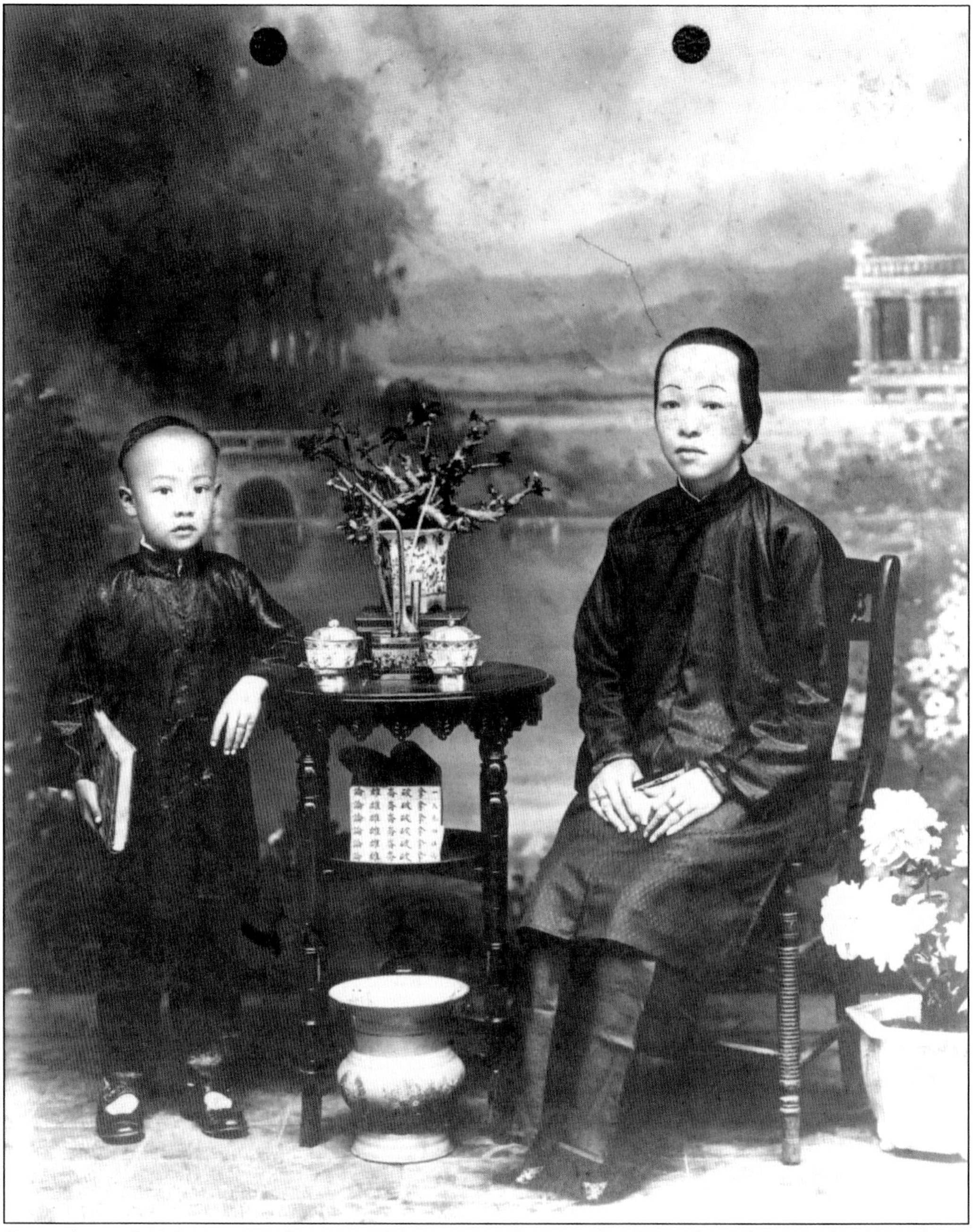

Since the mid-19th century, the natural disasters and internal upheaval in China pushed hundreds of thousands of Chinese immigrants to leave their wives and children behind and sail overseas. The discovery of gold in California in 1848 and the construction of the Transcontinental Railroad in 1869 also lured the Chinese laborers to come to America in search of fortunes, thus being called *Gam Saan Haak*, or "gold mountain guest." Pictured in 1918 are Young Ng She and Young Sum Wood, wife and child of Chinese merchant Young Hoy of Hawaii. (National Archives-Pacific Sierra Region, San Bruno, California.)

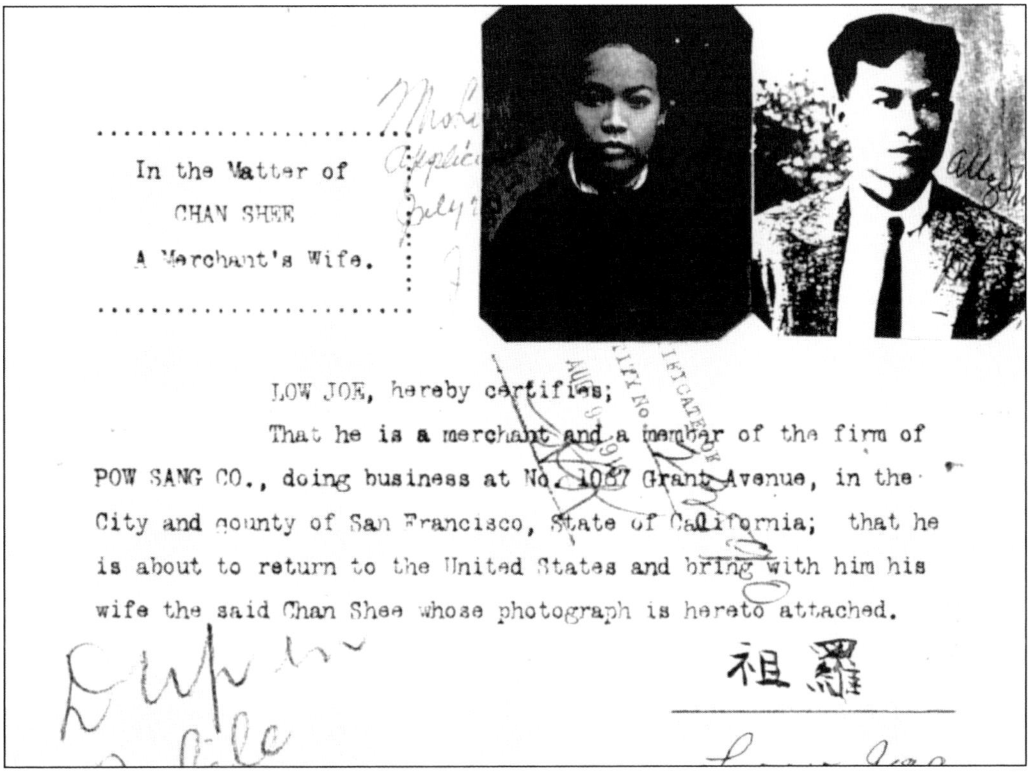

In the Matter of

CHAN SHEE

A Merchant's Wife.

LOW JOE, hereby certifies;

That he is a merchant and a member of the firm of POW SANG CO., doing business at No. 1087 Grant Avenue, in the City and county of San Francisco, State of California; that he is about to return to the United States and bring with him his wife the said Chan Shee whose photograph is hereto attached.

祖羅

Low Joe, a Chinese merchant living and working in San Francisco, is pictured with his wife Chan Shee in 1916. The 1882 Chinese Exclusion Act prohibited the entry of Chinese laborers but exempted Chinese merchants and U.S. citizens. All Chinese immigrants had to provide documentation indicating their status as merchants or family members of merchants or U.S. citizens. As indicated here, when the couple entered the United States, Low Joe had to present to the immigration authorities a certificate to prove his merchant status in order to apply for admission of his wife to America. (National Archives-Pacific Sierra Region, San Bruno, California.)

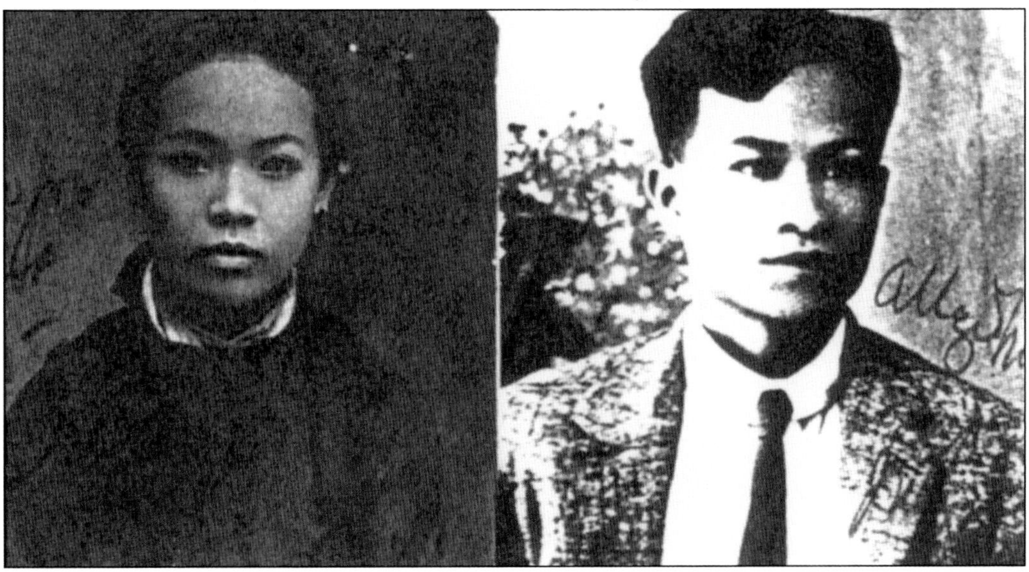

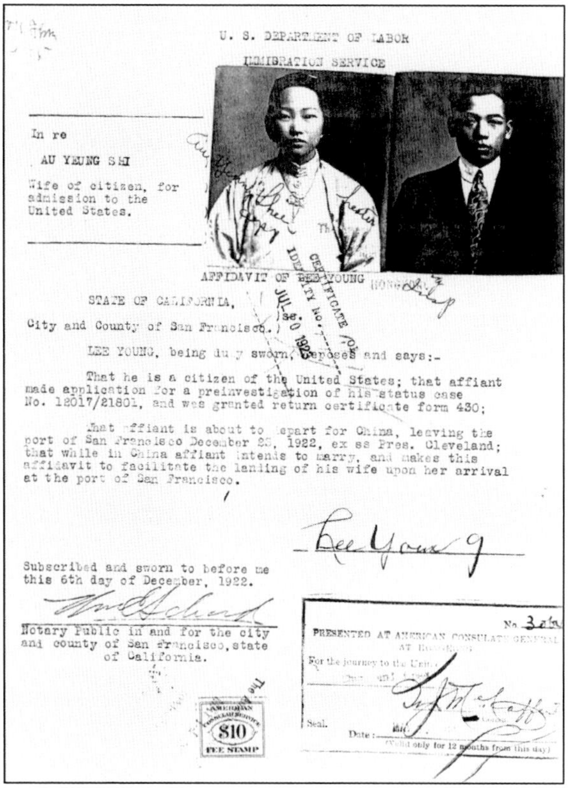

U. S. DEPARTMENT OF LABOR
IMMIGRATION SERVICE

In re
AU YEUNG SHI
Wife of citizen, for admission to the United States.

AFFIDAVIT OF LEE YOUNG

STATE OF CALIFORNIA,
City and County of San Francisco.) ss.

LEE YOUNG, being duly sworn, deposes and says:-

That he is a citizen of the United States; that affiant made application for a preinvestigation of his status case No. 12017/21801, and was granted return certificate form 430;

That affiant is about to depart for China, leaving the port of San Francisco December 23, 1922, ex ss Pres. Cleveland; that while in China affiant intends to marry, and makes this affidavit to facilitate the landing of his wife upon her arrival at the port of San Francisco.

Lee Young

Subscribed and sworn to before me this 6th day of December, 1922.

Notary Public in and for the city and county of San Francisco, state of California.

PRESENTED AT AMERICAN CONSULATE GENERAL

$10
FEE STAMP

Lee Young, a U.S. citizen, is pictured with his wife, Au Yeung Shi, in 1923. Due to the uneven gender ratio, many America-born Chinese males had to go to their ancestral land for brides. In December 1922, Lee Young left for China to marry his bride there and returned to the United States the following year. To ensure the entry of his bride, Lee Young had to obtain an affidavit to prove his citizenship prior to his departure for China. (National Archives-Pacific Sierra Region, San Bruno, California.)

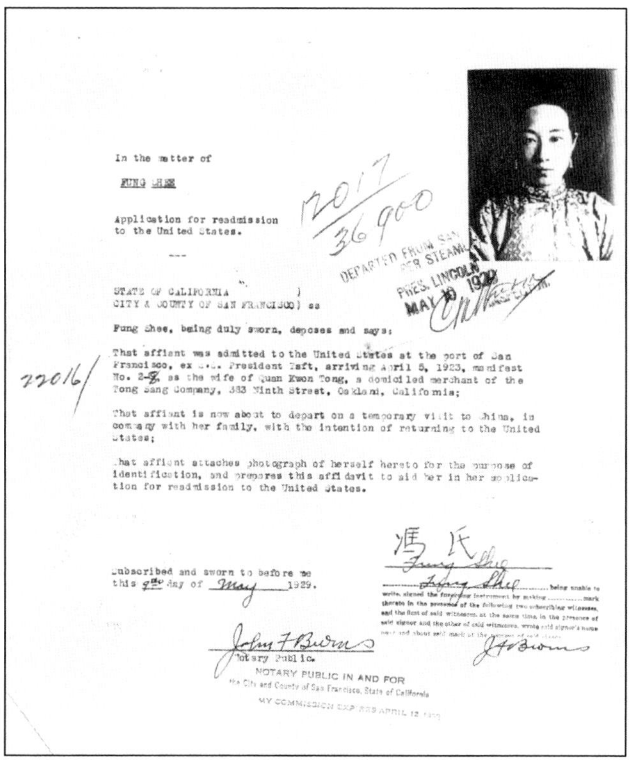

In the matter of
FUNG SHEE

Application for readmission to the United States.

STATE OF CALIFORNIA)
CITY & COUNTY OF SAN FRANCISCO) ss

Fung Shee, being duly sworn, deposes and says:

That affiant was admitted to the United States at the port of San Francisco, ex S.S. President Taft, arriving April 5, 1923, manifest No. 2-8, as the wife of Quan Kwon Tong, a domiciled merchant of the Tong Sang Company, 383 Ninth Street, Oakland, California;

That affiant is now about to depart on a temporary visit to China, in company with her family, with the intention of returning to the United States;

That affiant attaches photograph of herself hereto for the purpose of identification, and prepares this affidavit to aid her in her application for readmission to the United States.

Subscribed and sworn to before me this 9th day of May 1929.

馮氏
Fung Shee

Notary Public.
NOTARY PUBLIC IN AND FOR the City and County of San Francisco, State of California

Fung Shee, wife of Quan Kwon Tong, a Chinese merchant at the Tong Sang Company in San Francisco, came to join her husband from China in 1923. In 1929, she went to China for a visit but had to apply for her readmission to the United States prior to her departure for China. (National Archives-Pacific Sierra Region, San Bruno, California.)

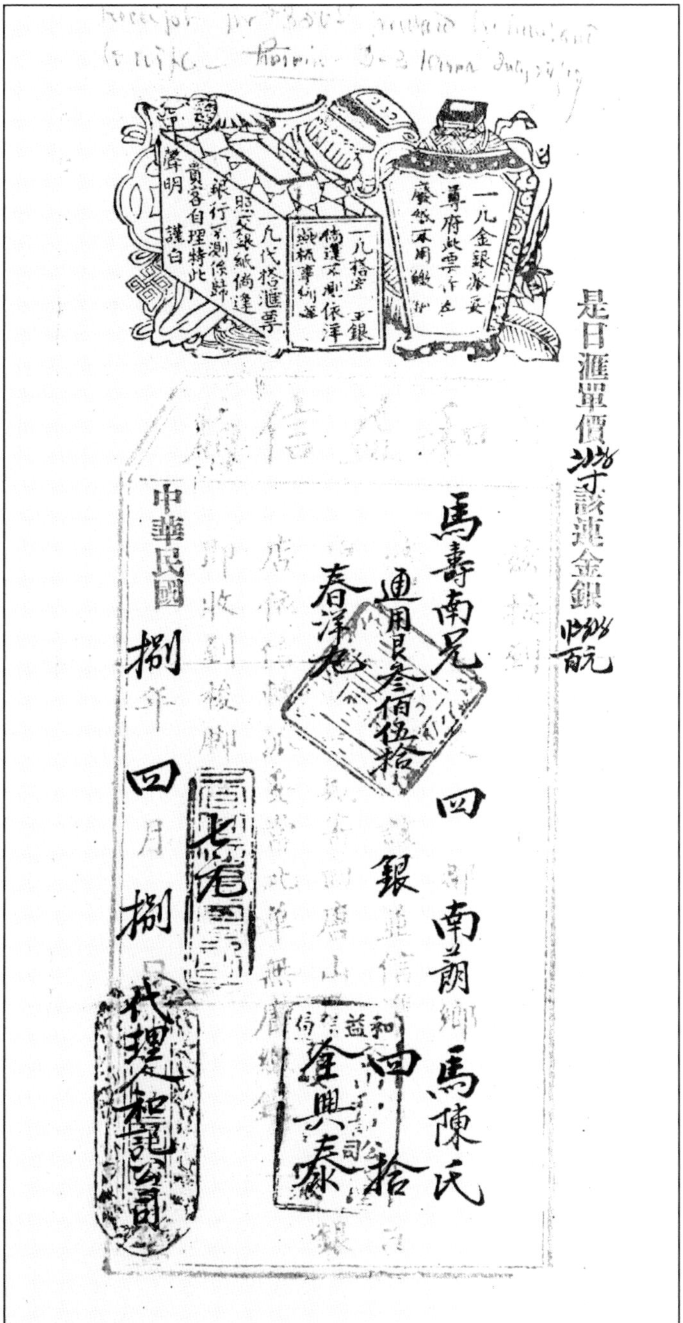

The strong desire for family reunions and hope for a better life encouraged many Chinese women to overcome traditional ideologies that prohibited a women from leaving their home village and the physical handicap of bound feet to sail across the Pacific Ocean to join their husbands in America. The money made by the Gam Saan Haak in America was remitted home to enable the wife to purchase a ticket for a steamship. The image here shows a money order of $350 mailed by Chinese immigrant Kun Shau Ma to his wife, Chan Shee, in Hong Kong on April 8, 1919. (National Archives-Pacific Sierra Region, San Bruno, California.)

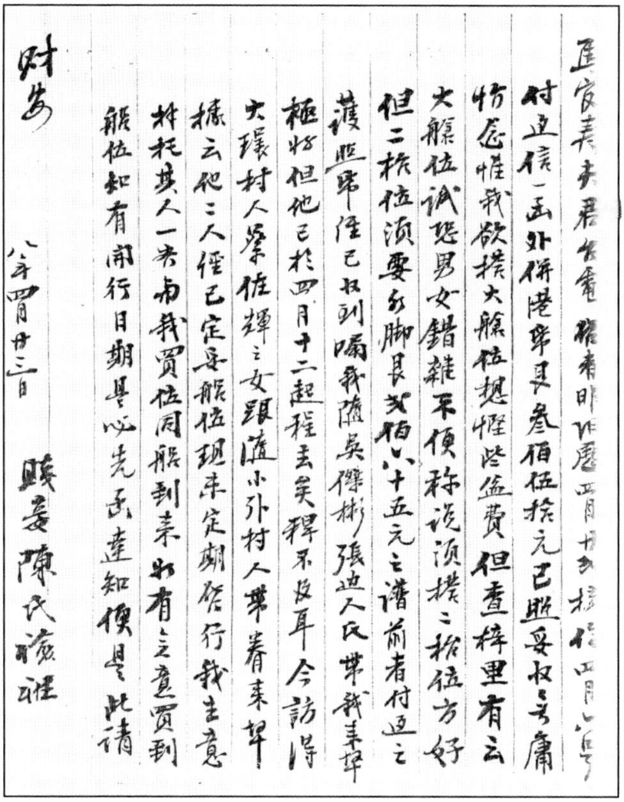

This is the original letter from Chan Shee to her husband, Kun Shau Ma, in Chinese and its English translation, dated April 23, 1919. The passage from Hong Kong to the Pacific West Coast of America was lengthy and difficult. Most Chinese immigrants purchased third- or steerage-class tickets and endured odor, crowdedness, and seasickness for over a month. However, what waited for them ahead was more uncertainty and hardship. (National Archives-Pacific Sierra Region, San Bruno, California.)

April 23, 1919

Dear Husband,
Mr. Kun Shau.

Received your letter of the April 6th. and Hongkong money paper $350.00 on the date of April 22 in Chinese calendar. I desire to take the third class ticket, for it cost little money, but I heard someone said third class is not very comfortable for lady. and it is better to take the second class. It shoud cost about $265.00, I has received the passport and glad come with Ng Get Bun, but he sail on April 12. I know that Choy Jor Fay's girl of the Tai Wan village come with a man and his farmily of the Shew Yan village. The two men has been ordered steamship ticket. but did't know whan the time for sail. I beg them to buy a ticket for me and come with them on the same steamer. If I has my ticket, and know what day does the steamer sail. I will write you and let you know.

Your Wife,

Chan Shee.

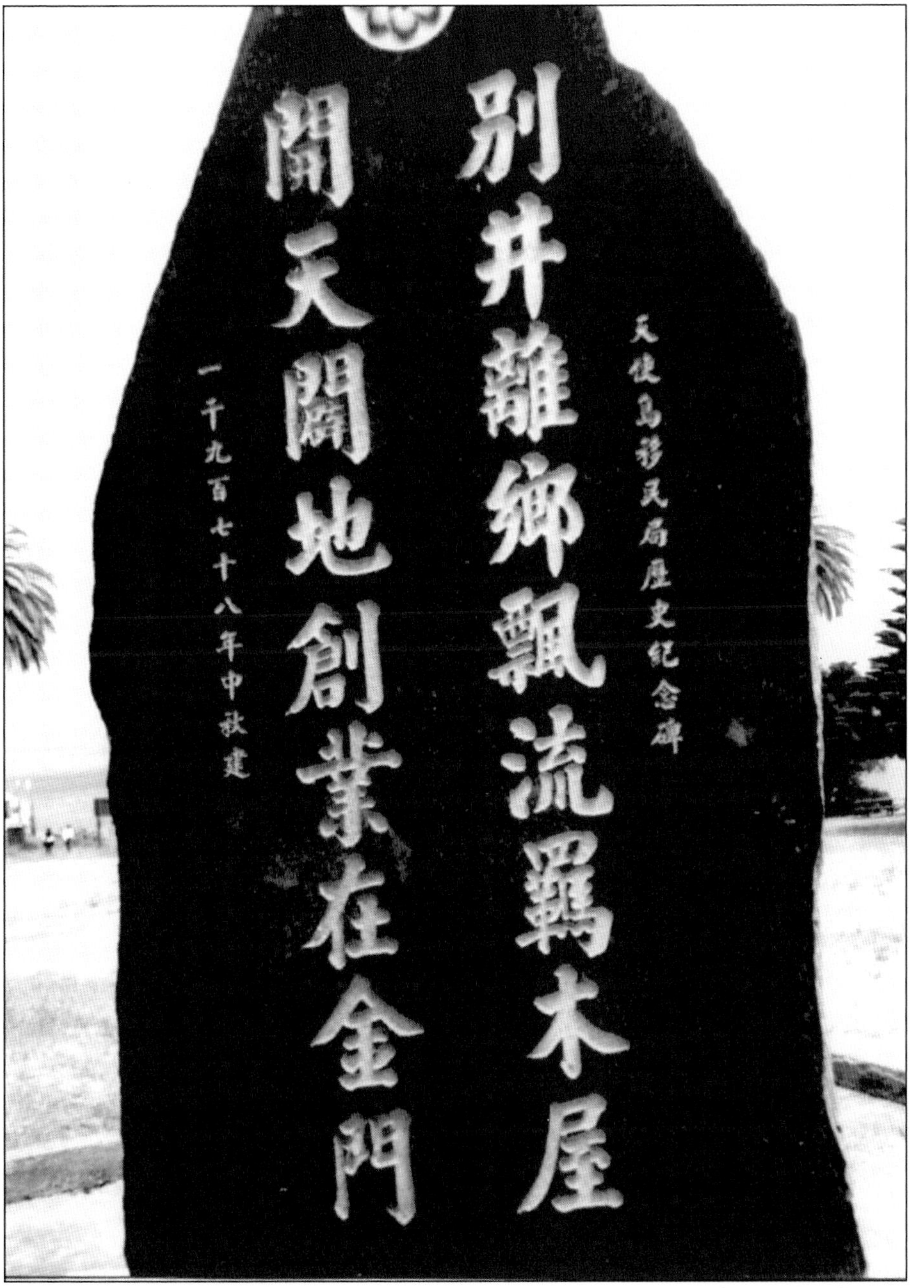

This plaque in front of the immigrant station on Angel Island was erected in 1978. The engraved Chinese characters say "Leaving home behind and being detained in wooden shed, looking for new life by the Golden Gate" (translation by author). The Angle Island Immigrant Station was in operation from 1910 to 1940. It was called the Ellis Island of the West, in comparison with Ellis Island located on Hudson River that processed European immigrants. The two immigration stations differed in their specific functions. While Ellis Island was merely a way station, as the processing of a vast majority of European immigrants took only between three to five hours, Angle Island was set up as a detention center for Asian, mainly Chinese, immigrants. (Photograph by Huping Ling.)

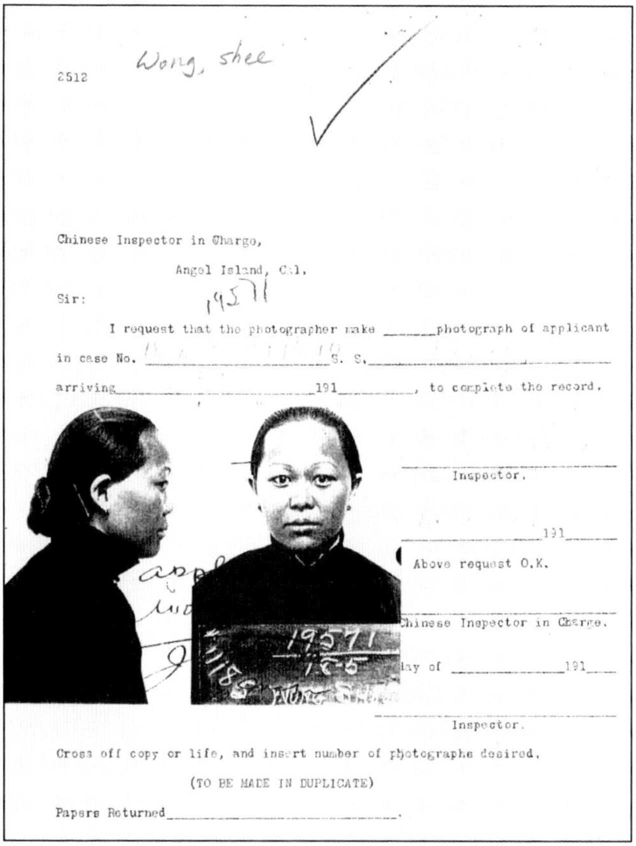

2512 Wong, shee

Chinese Inspector in Charge,

Angel Island, Cal.

Sir: 19571

I request that the photographer make ______photograph of applicant in case No. ____________S. S.____________ arriving____________191________, to complete the record.

____
Inspector.

____________191______

Above request O.K.

____
Chinese Inspector in Charge.

____day of ____________191____

____
Inspector.

Cross off copy or life, and insert number of photographs desired.

(TO BE MADE IN DUPLICATE)

Papers Returned____________.

At the immigrant station, an immigrant was photographed and given a case number as indicated in the images. An immigrant family was split as men and women were detained in separated quarters for cross interrogation. (National Archives-Pacific Sierra Region, San Bruno, California.)

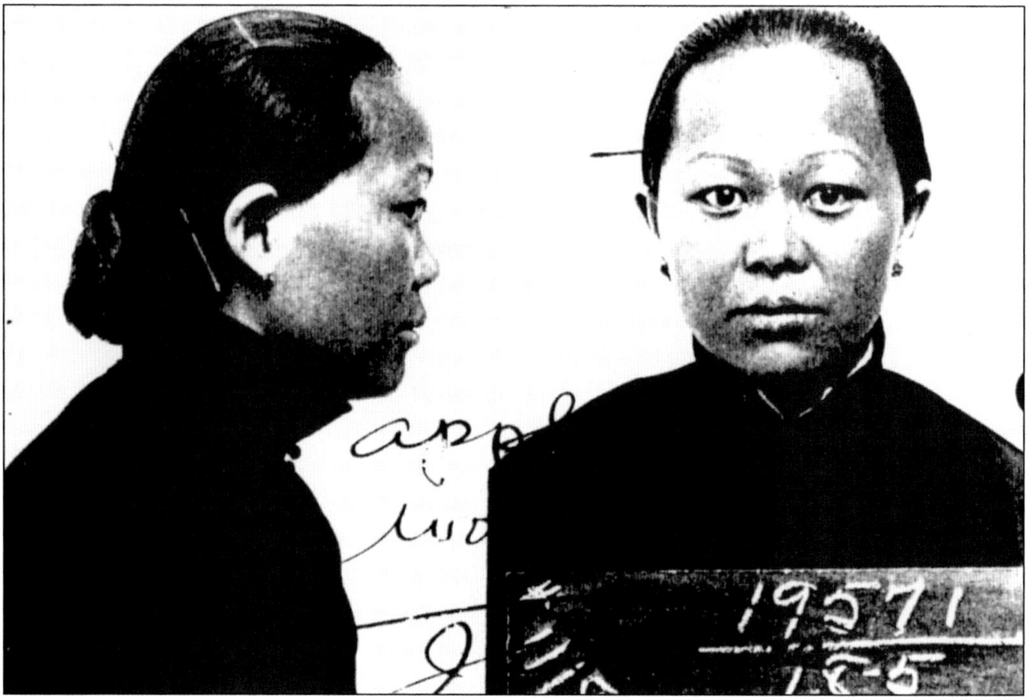

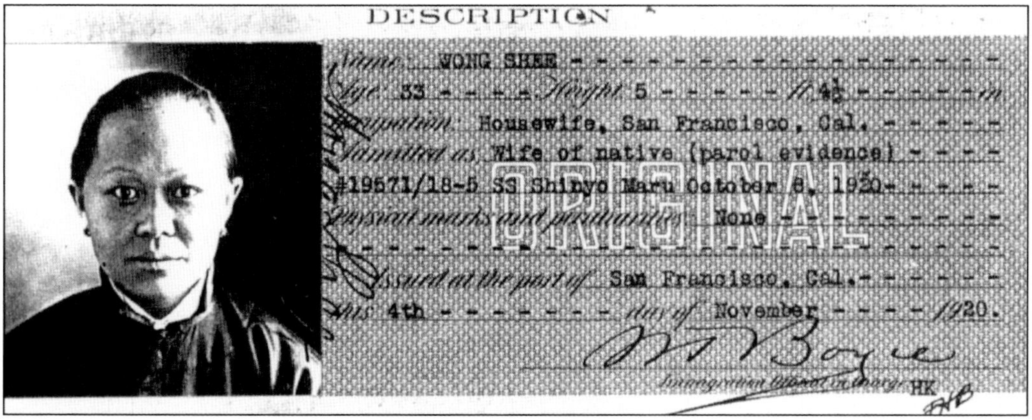

DESCRIPTION

Name WONG SHEE
Age 33 Height 5 ft. 4½ in
Occupation Housewife, San Francisco, Cal.
Admitted as Wife of native (parol evidence)
#19571/18-5 SS Shinyo Maru October 8, 1920
Physical marks and peculiarities None
Issued at the port of San Francisco, Cal.
this 4th day of November 1920.
Immigration Officer in Charge HK

ORIGINAL

Each detainee was given a description card indicating his or her name, age, gender, height, immigrant status, name of the steamship, ship ticket number, departing port, landing port, and the date of entry. (National Archives-Pacific Sierra Region, San Bruno, California.)

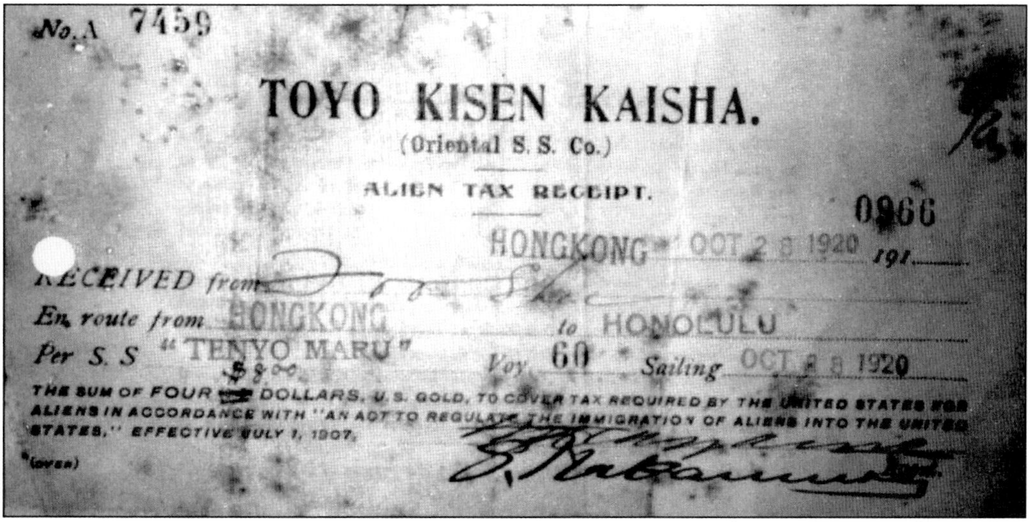

No. A 7459

TOYO KISEN KAISHA.

(Oriental S. S. Co.)

ALIEN TAX RECEIPT.

0966

HONGKONG OCT 28 1920 191

RECEIVED from

En route from HONGKONG to HONOLULU

Per S. S "TENYO MARU" Voy. 60 Sailing OCT 28 1920

THE SUM OF FOUR DOLLARS, U. S. GOLD, TO COVER TAX REQUIRED BY THE UNITED STATES FOR ALIENS IN ACCORDANCE WITH "AN ACT TO REGULATE THE IMMIGRATION OF ALIENS INTO THE UNITED STATES," EFFECTIVE JULY 1, 1907.

(over)

The 1920 steamship ticket of Chinese merchant wife Foa Shee is pictured here. At the immigration station, all documentations provided by the detainees were kept for cross examination. (National Archives-Pacific Sierra Region, San Bruno, California.)

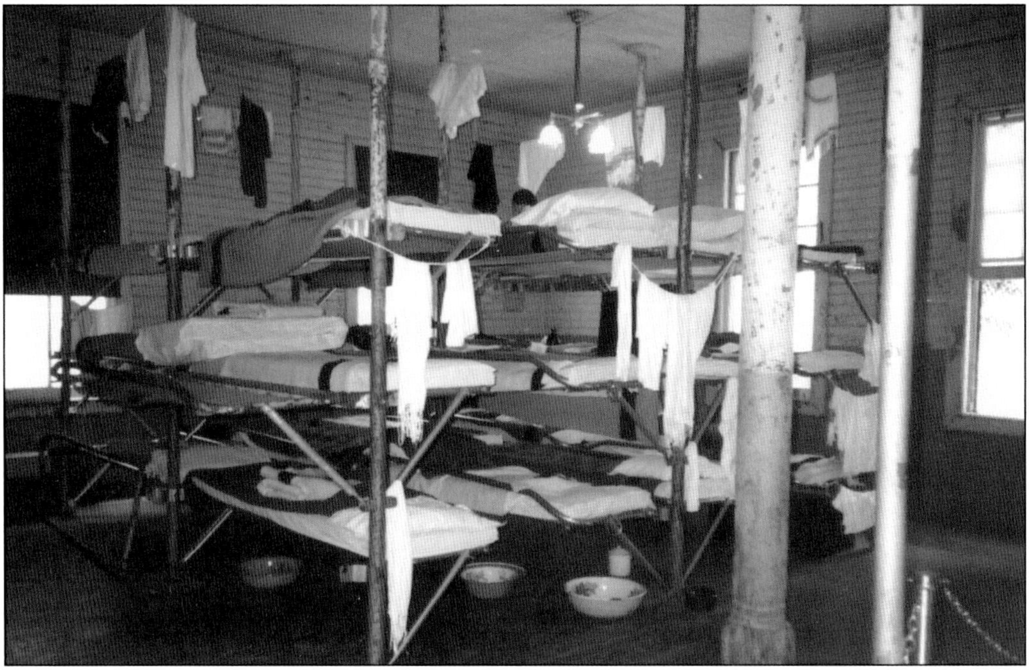

The immigration detention center on Angel Island was a two-story wooden structure. The duration of imprisonment was often months. While detained, Chinese immigrant women were separated from their husbands and sons (only children under 12 could stay with their mothers). Not knowing what would happen to them, many women became stressed and ill. Some Chinese women, unable to cope with the stress and desperation, committed suicide in the bathroom. To deal with the depressed and irritated detainees, the immigration station on Angel Island set up an isolation room, a nine square foot, tiny room without windows. The offensive inmates were locked in this room for hours until they managed to "calm down." (Photographs by Huping Ling.)

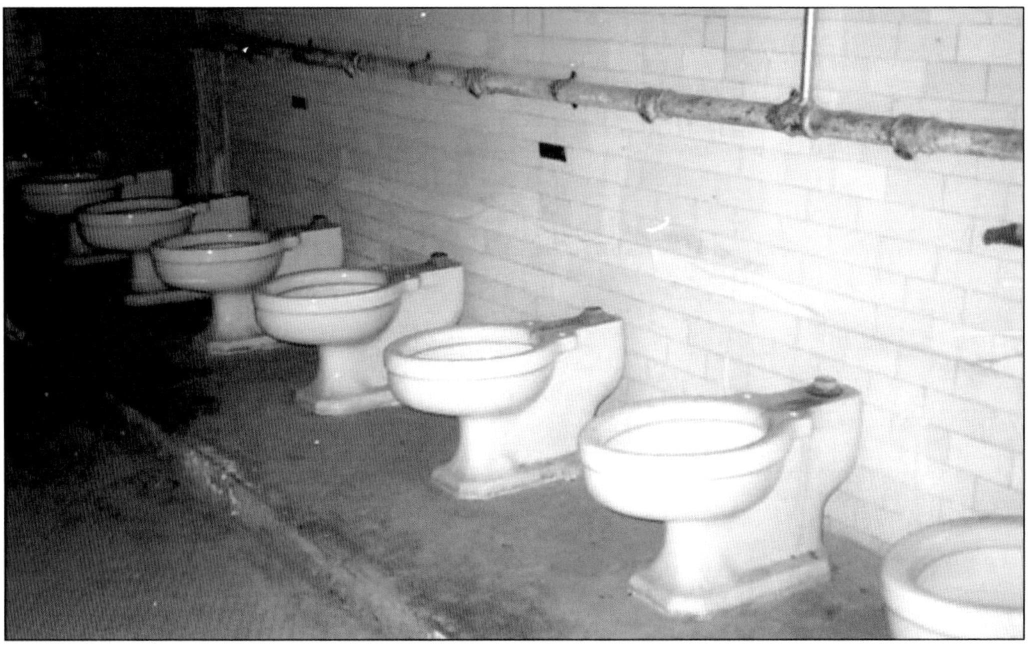

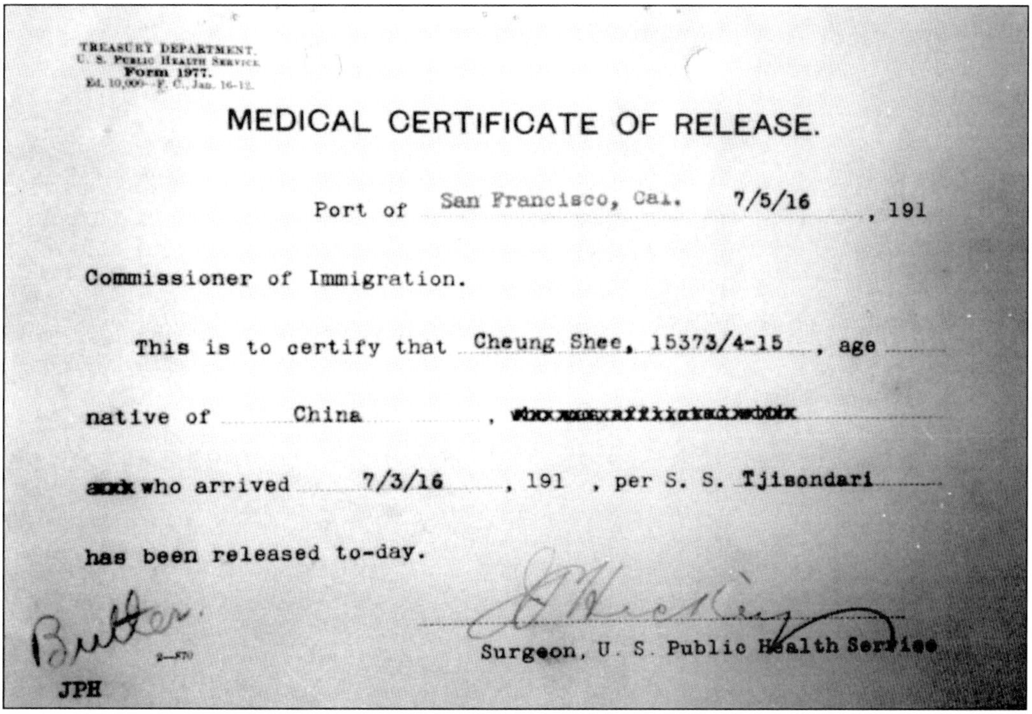

TREASURY DEPARTMENT.
U. S. PUBLIC HEALTH SERVICE.
Form 1977.
Ed. 10,000—F. C., Jan. 16-12.

MEDICAL CERTIFICATE OF RELEASE.

Port of San Francisco, Cal. 7/5/16, 191

Commissioner of Immigration.

This is to certify that Cheung Shee, 15373/4-15, age

native of China, ~~xxxxxxxxxxxxxxxxxxxx~~

~~xxx~~ who arrived 7/3/16, 191, per S. S. Tjisondari

has been released to-day.

Butler. 2—570

Surgeon, U. S. Public Health Service

JPH

Immigrants were first taken to a hospital for medical examinations. Those who were found with parasitic diseases were excluded and deported, while the rest were detained to await the hearing on their application. The medical certificate of release, seen here, indicates that its holder is free of diseases. (National Archives-Pacific Sierra Region, San Bruno, California.)

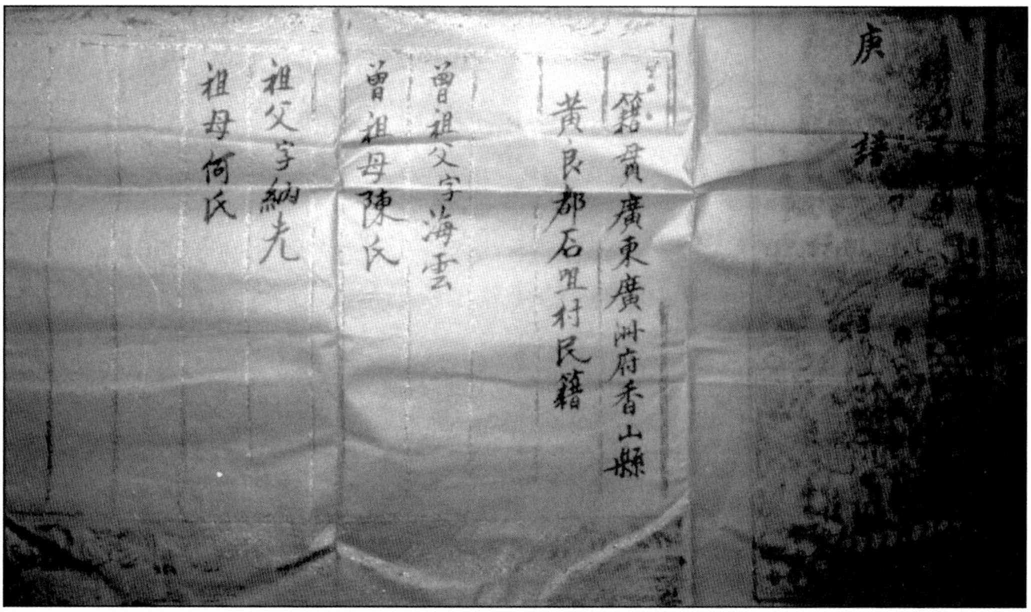

籍貫廣東廣州府香山縣
黄良都石盟村民籍
曾祖父字海雲
曾祖母陳氏
祖父字納先
祖母何氏

A family tree, served as a marriage license, was brought by a Chinese immigrant woman in 1916 to prove her marital status to a Chinese merchant. (National Archives-Pacific Sierra Region, San Bruno, California.)

Partnership list of TAI QUANG BOOK CO., San Francisco, filed in the case of 14284/4-2 & 4-3, merchant's wife and daughter.

- - - - -

Name.	Duty.	Amt. of interest.
GEE TEUNG,	MANAGER	$1000
DANG JAR HING,	Bookkeeper	1000
WONG WING FOO,	Cashier,	1000
SO HO DUCK CHUN,	Salesman,	1000
GEE WEE,	"	1000
LEE FONG,	"	1000
HOM SUN WAH,	"	1000
LOW SICK YUEN,	"	1000
GEE CHUNG LIM,	"	2000
GEE WAH,	In China,	1000
CHING GING LOY,	Silent,	1000
GEE GIN SUEY,	"	1000
WONG TAI SAI,	"	1500
WONG SICK HUNG,	"	1500
GEE BOW,	"	500
CHIN TOY,	"	1500
DONG TIN YOU,	"	1500
SO HO PANG,	"	1000
DONG JUNG,	"	1000
CHIN MUN HONG,	"	1000
YEE SING,	"	1000
YEE SECK CHING,	"	1000
GEE SIN WY,	"	1000
LOW WAH,	In China	1000
WONG DUCK,	Silent,	1000
GEE SUN,	"	1000
CHIN TEUNG,	"	1000
LEE SUNG,	"	1000
WONG JOR,	"	1000
LEE GOP,	In China	1000
	Total	$31500.

Translated by J. S. McClymont, Chinese Interpreter.

Since the 1882 Chinese Exclusion Act barred the entry of Chinese laborers, some Chinese laborers, in order to bring their families to America, changed their status from laborer to merchant by faking a partnership in a grocery store. Immigration authorities responded by assuming all Chinese immigrants were guilty of fraudulent entry until proven otherwise. A Chinese merchant had to provide documentation to prove partnership in a business. The image here is the partnership list of Tai Quang Book Company, a large Chinese company in San Francisco, in its English translation, to support the case of a Chinese merchant's wife and daughter. (National Archives-Pacific Sierra Region, San Bruno, California.)

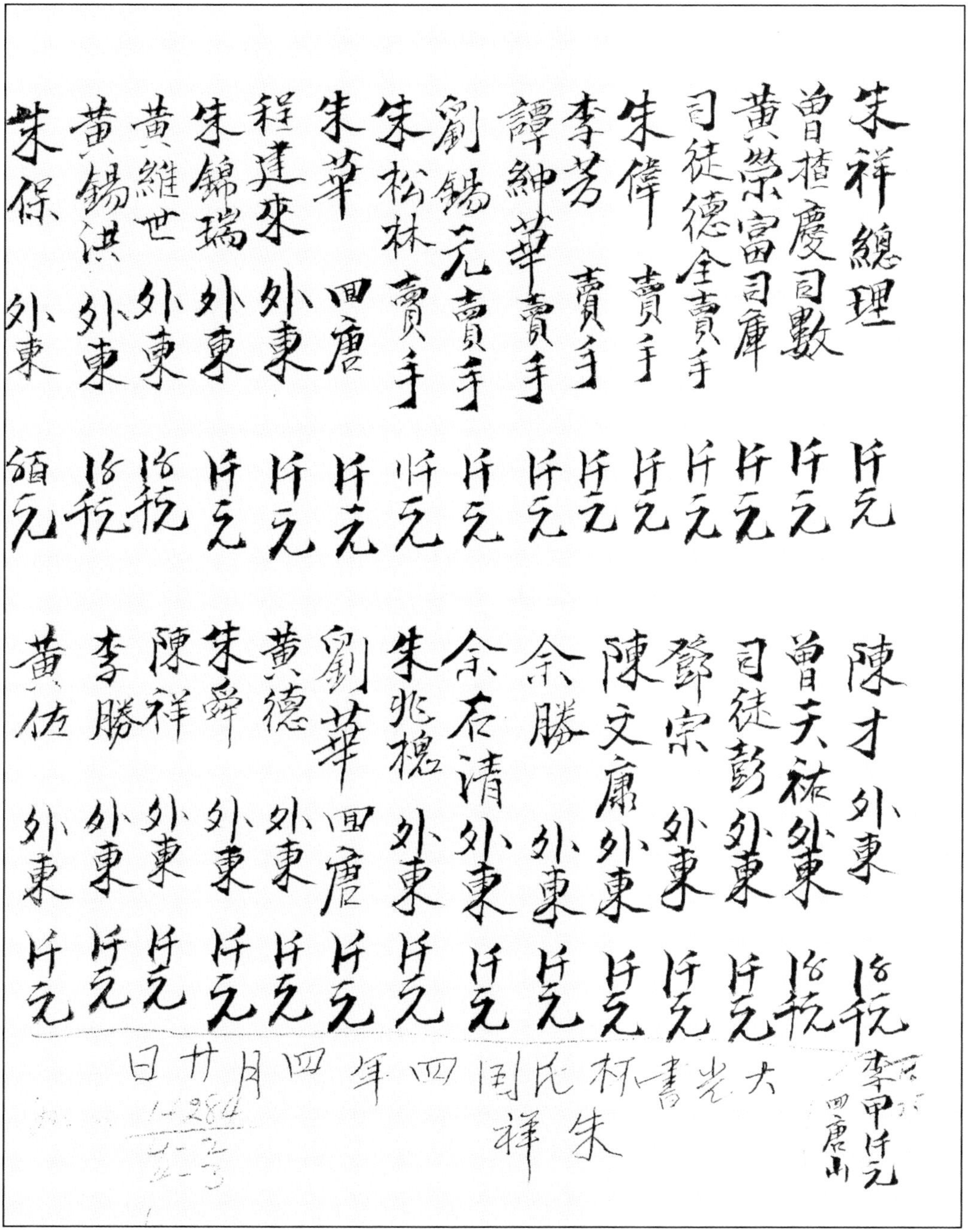

朱祥 總理 仟元
曾植慶 司數 仟元
黃榮富 司庫 仟元
司徒德全 賣手 仟元
朱偉 賣手 仟元
李芳 賣手 仟元
譚紳華 賣手 仟元
劉錫元 賣手 仟元
朱松林 賣手 仟元
朱華 四唐 仟元
程建來 外東 仟元
朱錦瑞 外東 仟元
黃維世 外東 佰元
黃錫洪 外東 佰元
朱保 外東 佰元

陳才 外東 佰元
曾天祿 外東 佰元
司徒彭 外東 仟元
鄧宗 外東 仟元
陳文康 外東 仟元
余勝 外東 仟元
余石清 外東 仟元
朱兆槐 外東 仟元
劉華 四唐 仟元
黃德 外東 仟元
朱舜 外東 仟元
陳祥 外東 仟元
李勝 外東 仟元
黃佐 外東 仟元

李甲 仟元 四唐山

大光書林 民国四年四月廿日
朱祥

The image here is the partnership list of Tai Quang Book Company, a large Chinese company in San Francisco, provided by a Chinese merchant in connection with his wife and daughter's applications for admission to the United States. (National Archives-Pacific Sierra Region, San Bruno, California.)

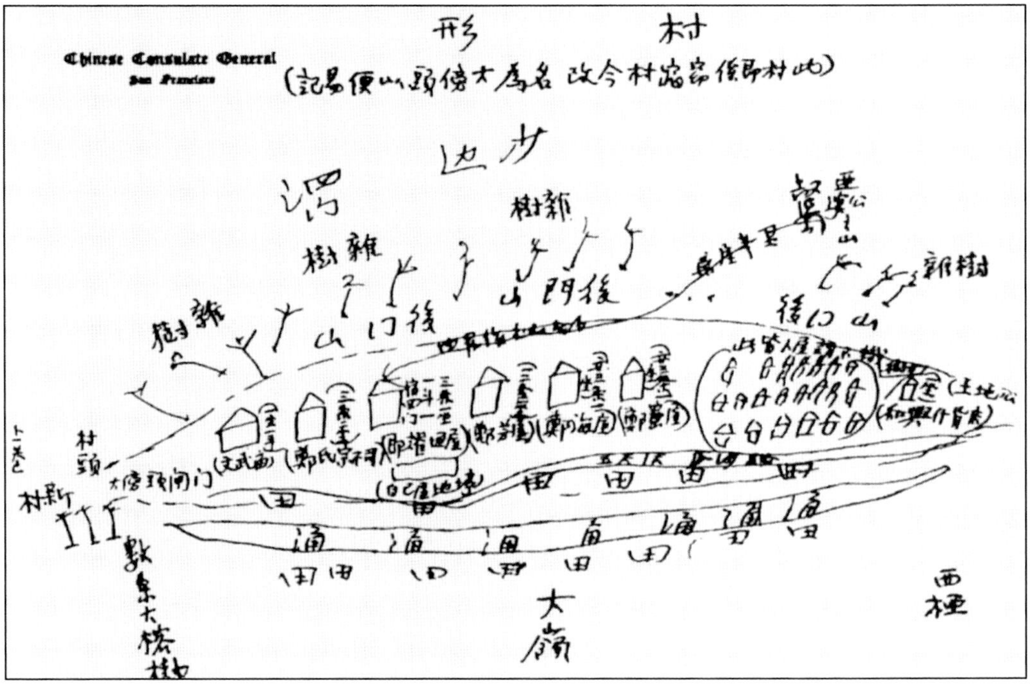

As the Chinese immigrants must go through extensive cross-interrogation on family, home life, and physical layout of their native village, and the approval of their applications primarily depended on the consistency of their testimony, they devised the coaching sheet, as shown here, to help for interrogation by American immigration officials in 1927. The image below shows the English translation of the map. (National Archives-Pacific Sierra Region, San Bruno, California.)

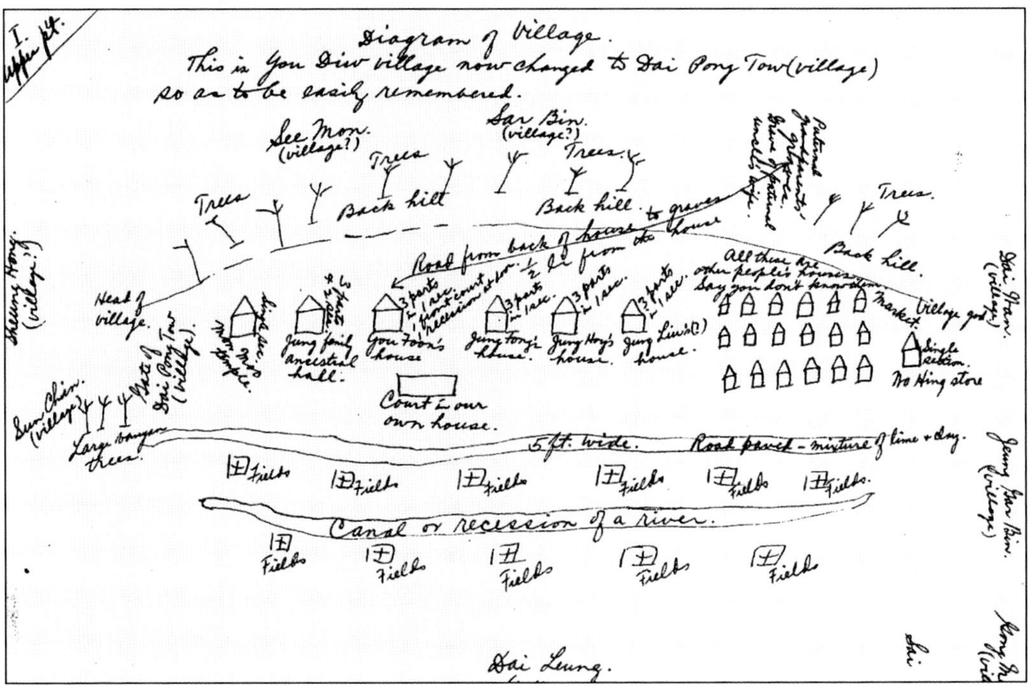

Two

Building Hop Alley

By the end of the 19th century, the Chinese community in St. Louis had grown to about 300 people. This community was physically centered in Hop Alley, a seemingly mysterious place that inspired tall tales for the old residents and is little known to the present St. Louisans. Along Seventh, Eighth, Market, and Walnut Streets, Chinese hand laundries, merchandise stores, grocery stores, restaurants, and tea shops were lined up to serve Chinese residents and the ethnically diverse larger community of St. Louis, the fourth largest city in the United States at the time. The operation of Chinese hand laundries in St. Louis resembled in many ways those in other Chinese communities across the country. The typical interior arrangement for the Chinese laundry consisted of four sections. First, the front section usually occupied one-third of the space of the house, functioning as the office-workshop of the laundryman. Here the laundryman ironed, labeled laundry, and waited on his customers. In this section, he kept the necessities for his business: the ironing board, the abacus, the laundry shelves, the lock-counter, and the secret cash drawer. Second, immediately behind the curtained doorway at the center of the house, and usually between the laundry shelves, were the living quarters. Third, the drying room, located in the center or rear part of the house, held an old-fashioned coal stove, used for drying the wet laundry. About a dozen strong wires were strung across in parallel lines to put up the wet laundry. Finally, the rear section located almost all the laundryman's machines, including washing machine, washing sink, and steam boiler. Sam Wah Laundry typified the Chinese hand laundry in St. Louis. Unlike Chinese hand laundries that primarily served non-Chinese and dispersed across the city, grocery stores catered to the Chinese community and consequently clustered around the Chinese business district, resembling the pattern in other urban Chinese communities. These stores sold merchandise imported from China, including native-made Chinese cloth with intricately embroidered parts, tea, cigars, and Chinese ingredients for cooking. They also sold locally produced fresh fruits, vegetables, and meats—necessary ingredients for Chinese cooking. Crawfish, watermelons, and fresh vegetables in bunches were delivered there daily by Chinese farmers on the other side of the river in Illinois. Some of the Chinese stores also handled the ordering and shipping of supplies to Chinese laborers in the southern and southwestern states. Community-building efforts by the Chinese in St. Louis were most evident in the formation and operation of the On Leong Merchants and Laborers Association. Although other social organizations existed before the establishment of On Leong, none possessed the power and influence of On Leong.

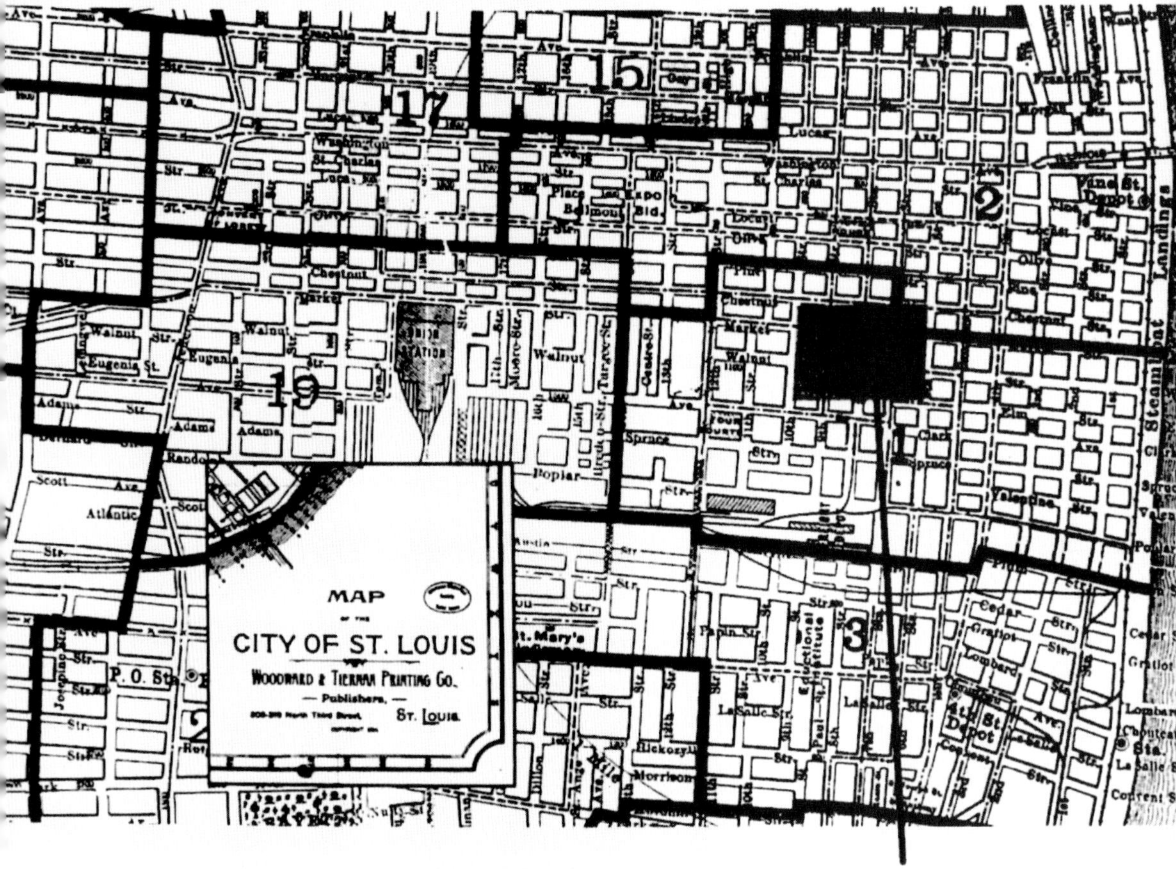

"Hop Alley"
St. Louis Chinatown
1870s-1966

Since the mid-19th century, migrants from Germany, Greece, Ireland, Italy, Poland, Russia, and the American South gathered in the booming city of St. Louis. During this time Chinese started to arrive in St. Louis, by the end of the century, the Chinese community had grown to about 300 and was physically centered in Hop Alley. Seventh, Eighth, Market, and Walnut Streets were lined with Chinese hand laundries, merchandise stores, grocery stores, restaurants, and tea shops. The St. Louis Chinatown, Hop Alley existed from the 1870s until 1966.

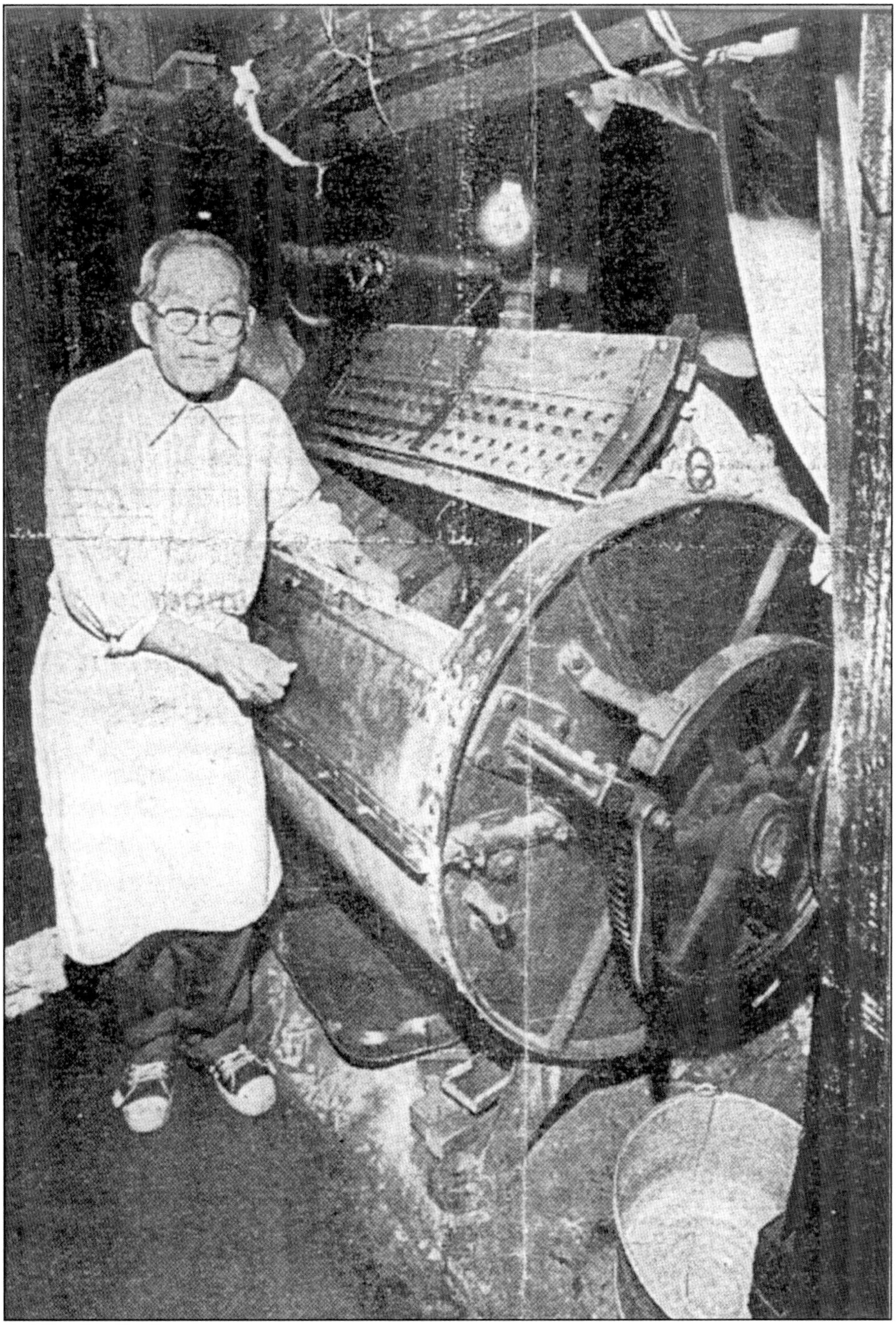

Most of the early Chinese immigrants in St. Louis were working in Chinese hand laundries in Hop Alley and the peripheral area. The Chinese laundry as a predominant trade among the Chinese in St. Louis also reflects the occupational segregation of Chinese nationwide. Sam Wah Laundry (1922–1986) at 4381 Laclede Avenue was almost a replica of the Chinese laundry that existed a century earlier. Pictured in the *St. Louis Post-Dispatch* on November 12, 1978, Sam Wah, one of the two operators, reaches in the ancient drier. (St. Louis Post-Dispatch.)

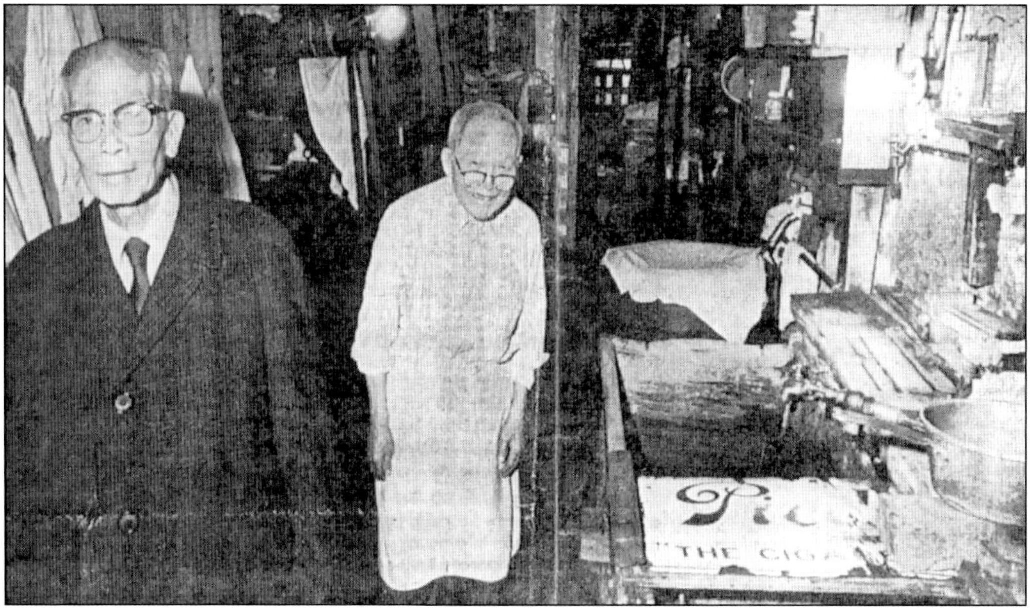

Two brothers Gee Kee One (also know as Gee Sam Wah) and Gee Hong, from Canton, China, came to St. Louis in 1922 to inherit the laundry business from their uncle. The aging Gee brothers lived and worked in Spartan quarters. They rose at dawn ironing and washing until late at night. They slept on the mats near an old stove and cooked in the back of the laundry. Pictured in the *St. Louis Post-Dispatch* on November 12, 1978, at home in the back of their laundry, are Gee Hong, 86, (in the foreground) and Gee Sam Wah, 88. (Missouri Historical Society.)

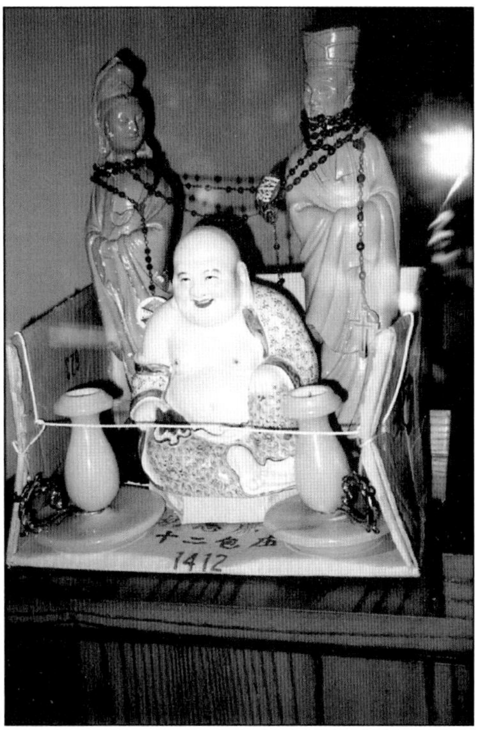

In their cluttered quarter, the Gee brothers had a homemade shrine, to which they worshiped during the Chinese New Year. After the last proprietor Gee Hong died in 1986 (Sam Wah died in 1984), the laundry was demolished right way, only giving friends of the Gee brothers enough time to save a box of old letters and this shrine. (Photograph by Huping Ling; Missouri History Museum.)

SAM WOH

Best Hand Laundry

4381 Laclede Avenue **St. Louis, Mo.,**..............................**192**...

Mr.. Mark..........................

Address..

Wanted.................................... Call.................................. $..........................

No. Pieces	Gentlemen's List	Amount	No. Pieces	Ladies' List	Amount
	Shirts...............15c			Dresses...............50c up	
	Shirts, silk...........25c up			Skirts, plain..........25c up	
	Shirts, fancy 25c			Wrappers ....15c up	
	Shirts, pleated 20c			Comb'tion suits ....15c up	
	Shirts, flannel...........20c			Night Dresses........15c up	
	Shirts, night.............15c			Chemise..........15c to 25c	
	Shirts, soft...............15c			Drawers...........8c to 20c	
	Shirts, blue 15c			Shirt Waists....20c to 50c	
	Collars, each 3c			Corset covers........10c up	
	Collars, soft................4c			Aprons ....10c up	
	Cuffs, per pair............8c			Aprons, B'galow....15c up	
	Pajama coats............10c			Stockings, pair............6c	
	Pajama drawers 10c			Handkerchiefs 2c	
	Drawers 10c			Undervests 8c	
	Undershirts 10c			Union Shirts..............15c	
	Union suits 20c			Union Suits 15c	
	B. V. D.'s.................15c			Cape collars......5c to c	
	Socks, per pair............5c			Long coats......25c to c	
	Handkerchiefs 3c			Belts 5c	
	Handkerchiefs, silk......5c			Caps ....5c up	
	Ties ....3c up			Collars ....5c up	
	Vests.............25c to 35c			**Children**	
	Coats ....20c to 35c			Dresses..........15c to c	
	Pants ....35c up			Skirts............15c to c	
	Aprons............8c to 10c			Waists............10c to 15c	
	Aprons, shop........20c up			Boys' Blouses..10c to 25c	
	Overalls ....25c up			Drawers............5c to 10c	
	Jackets...................50c up			Pants ....10c to 20c	
	Household			Night dresses....8c to 15c	
	Table cloths..........15c up			Ties.................5c to 24c	
	Sideboard cloths 10 to 15			Chemise ....5c to 25c	
	Napkins 3c			Coats 15c	
	Towels ....3c up			Wool sweater..25c to 50c	
	Bath Towels............4c up				
	Rollers ....5c up				
	Sheets...................15c up				
	Pillow Slips......5c to 15c				
	Bed Spreads ....25c up				
	Shams, each ..15c to 50c			**Household**	
	Blankets, pair..35c to 75c			Curtains ....30c to 50c	
	Lunch cloths ....5c to c			Curtains, Lace 40c to 75c	

Our work is guaranteed to be entirely satisfactory. If it does not suit you do not pay for it. We call for and deliver all goods. All kinds of family washing at the cheapest rate. We do rush work in 24 hours. Terms C. O. D.

Chinese hand laundries had a wide-spread reputation of being inexpensive and making clothing last longer, and therefore enjoyed a large number of patrons. In the 1920s, Sam Wah Laundry charged 15¢ for men's shirts, and 20¢ for women's shirt-waists as shown in the price list here. The low price of Chinese laundries was made possible by an extremely frugal way of living. To minimize the cost of living, most laundry operators dwelled in the back of laundries. (Missouri Historical Society.)

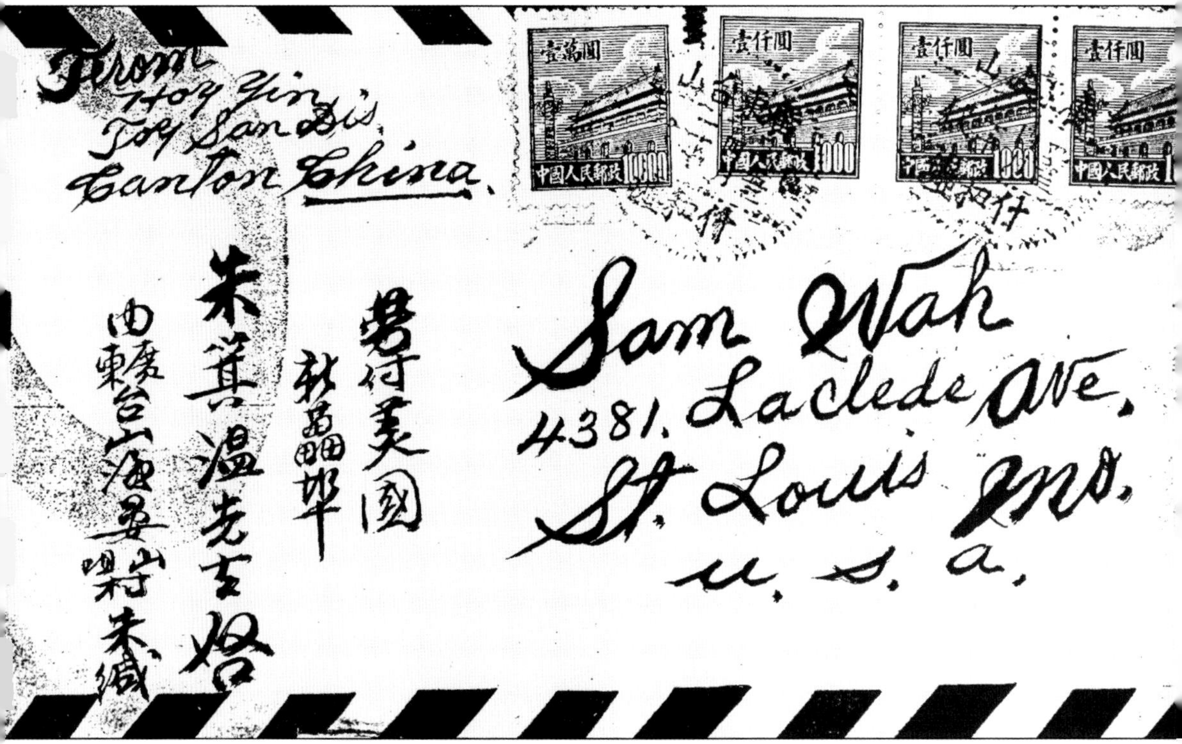

Since they came to America in 1922, the Gee brothers had never retuned home, but kept corresponding with their children and relatives in Canton. The image shows the envelope of a letter written by their nephew in Mountain Mouth Village, Toy San (Taishan), Canton, China, dated May 22, 1954. (Missouri Historical Society.)

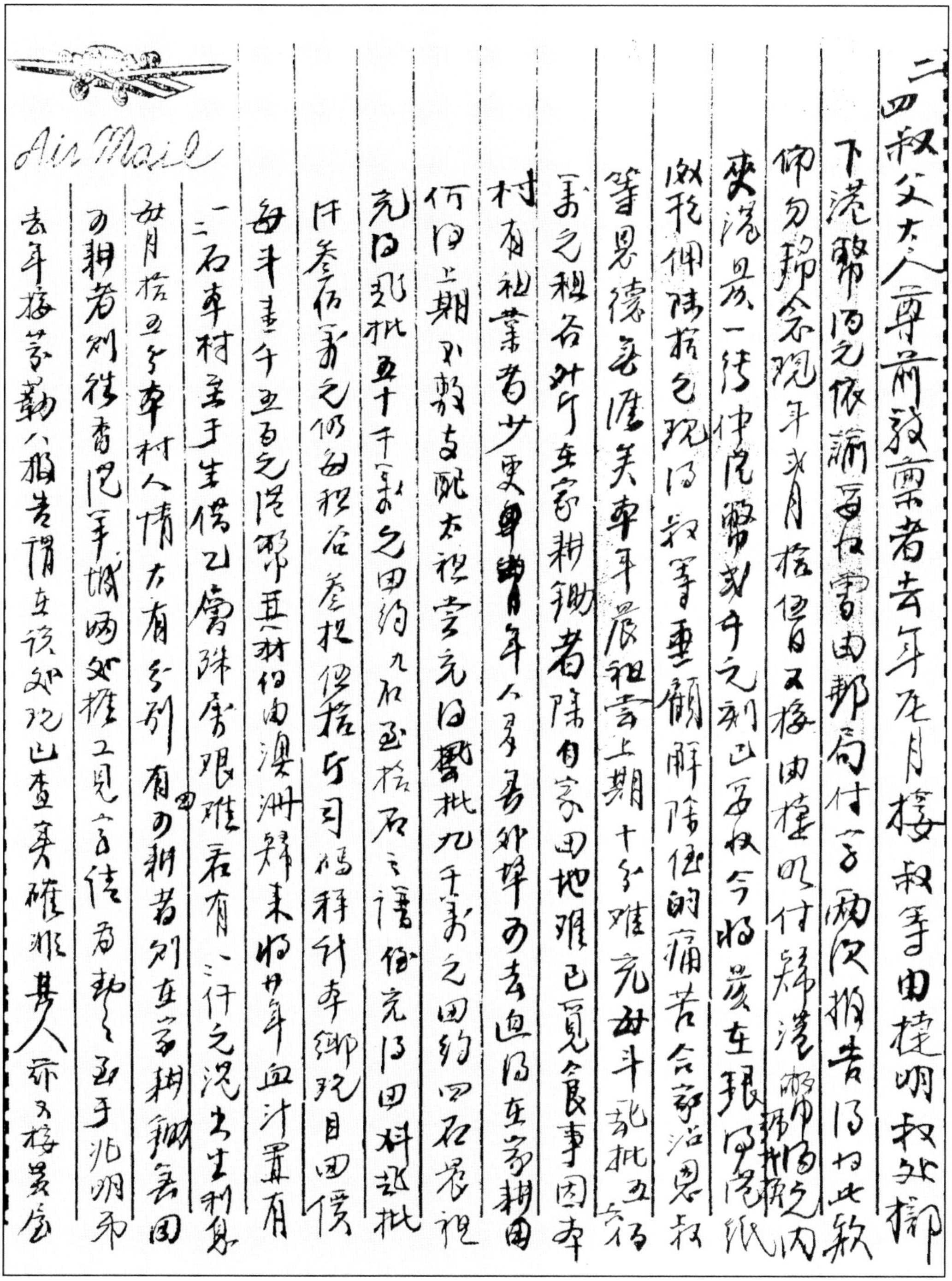

This letter to the Gee brothers from their nephew in Mountain Mouth Village, Toy San (Taishan), Canton, China, is dated May 22, 1954. Although they never visited home after their arrival in America, the Gee brothers sent their meager savings to China to help out family members and relatives, as indicated in the letter. (Missouri Historical Society.)

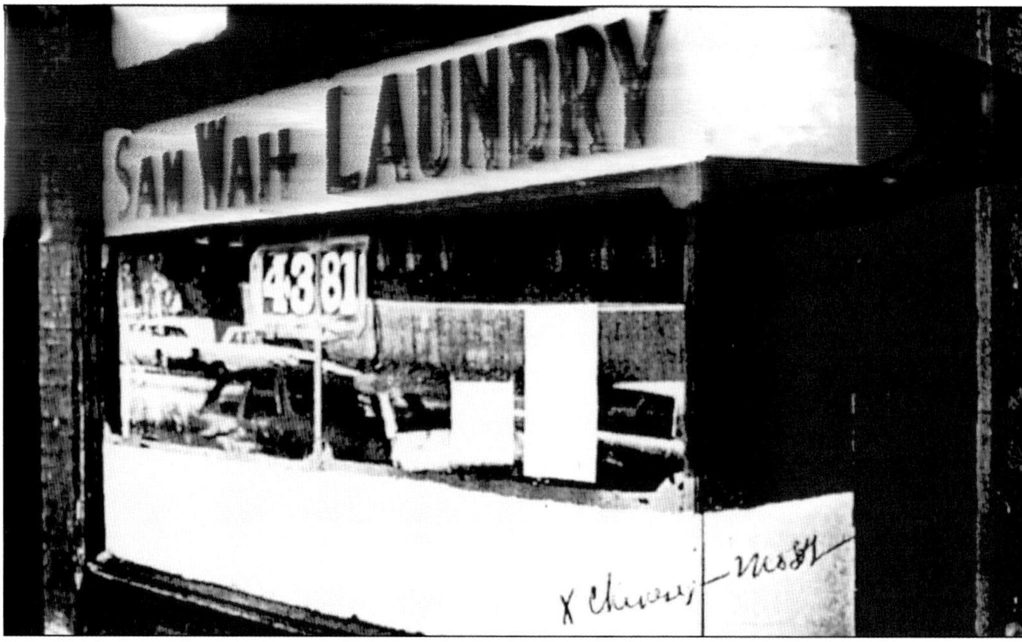

Sam Wah Laundry at 4381 Laclede Avenue, the last Chinese hand laundry in St. Louis, was pressed to close in 1978, when the owner of the property on which Sam Wah laundry was located decided to sell the property to the Washington University Medical Center Redevelopment Corporation. (Missouri Historical Society.)

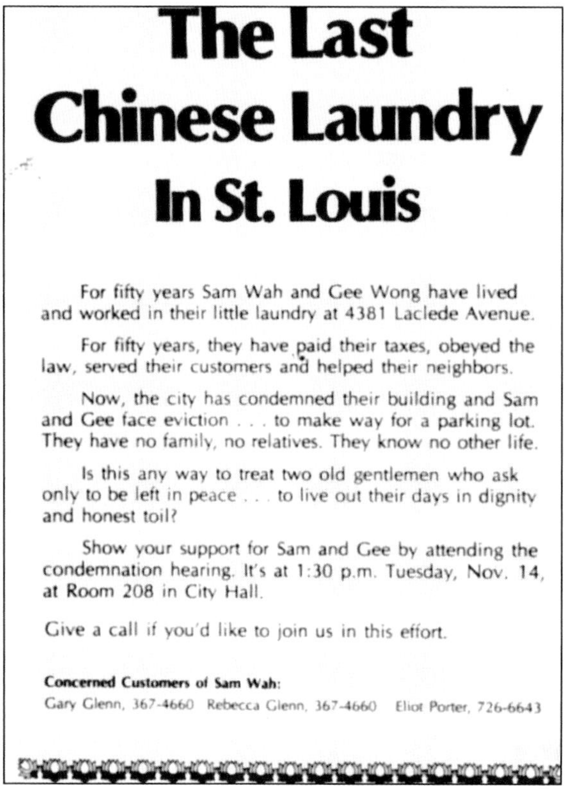

The Last Chinese Laundry In St. Louis

For fifty years Sam Wah and Gee Wong have lived and worked in their little laundry at 4381 Laclede Avenue.

For fifty years, they have paid their taxes, obeyed the law, served their customers and helped their neighbors.

Now, the city has condemned their building and Sam and Gee face eviction . . . to make way for a parking lot. They have no family, no relatives. They know no other life.

Is this any way to treat two old gentlemen who ask only to be left in peace . . . to live out their days in dignity and honest toil?

Show your support for Sam and Gee by attending the condemnation hearing. It's at 1:30 p.m. Tuesday, Nov. 14, at Room 208 in City Hall.

Give a call if you'd like to join us in this effort.

Concerned Customers of Sam Wah:
Gary Glenn, 367-4660 Rebecca Glenn, 367-4660 Eliot Porter, 726-6643

This flyer was circulated by the Friends of Sam Wah Appeal, a group consisting of mostly white customers of the laundry, in an attempt to save the last Chinese hand laundry in 1978. The campaign to save Sam Wah Laundry was able to keep the laundry surviving until 1986 when Gee Hong died. (Missouri Historical Society.)

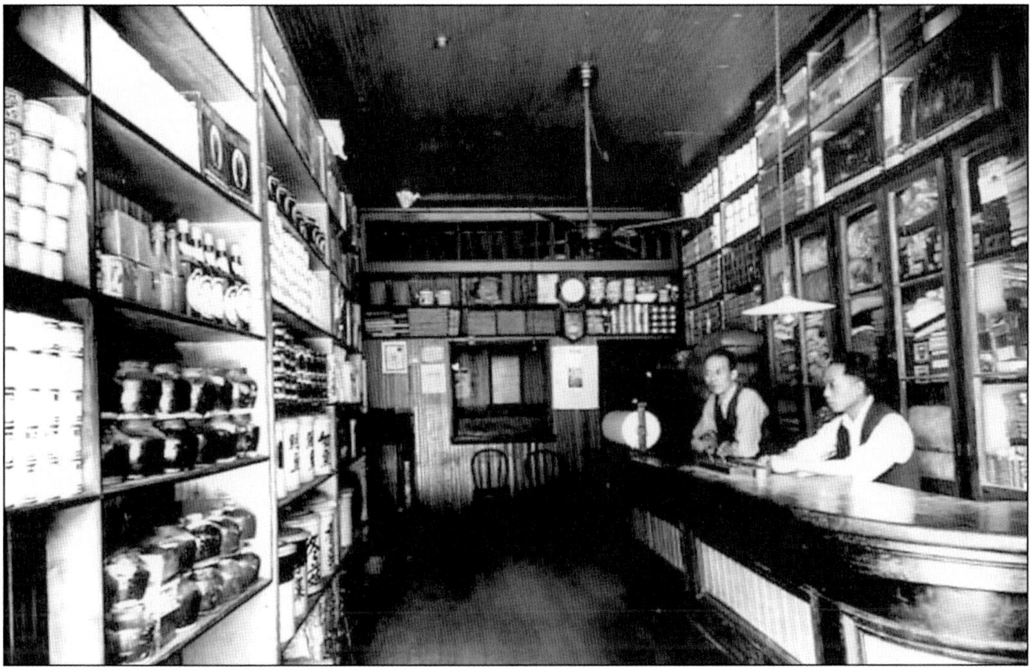

Chinese grocery stores emerged as another important Chinese business in St. Louis to provide ingredients for Chinese cooking and laundry supplies for hand laundries. On July 29, 1900, the Sunday magazine section of the *St. Louis Republic* featured an article titled "The Chinese Colony of St. Louis" written by Dick Wood, portraying a few respectable merchants running Chinese grocery stores, including Quong Hang Choung and Company at 722 Market Street, Quong On Lung at 17 South Eighth Street, and Quong Sun Wah and Company at 23 South Eighth Street. The stores would resemble the one shown in images here. (National Archives-Pacific Sierra Region, San Bruno, California.)

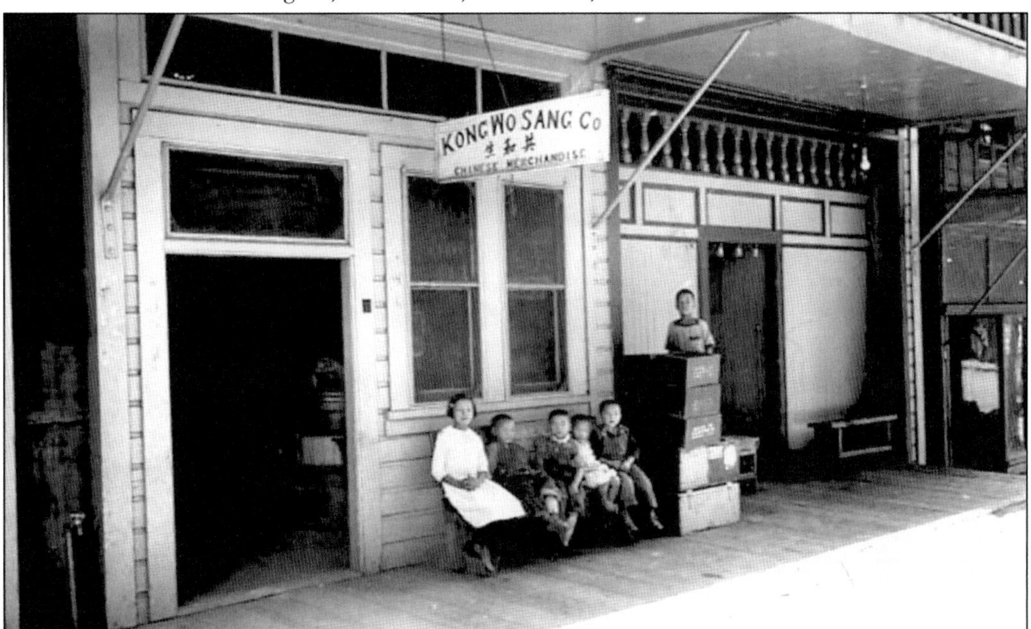

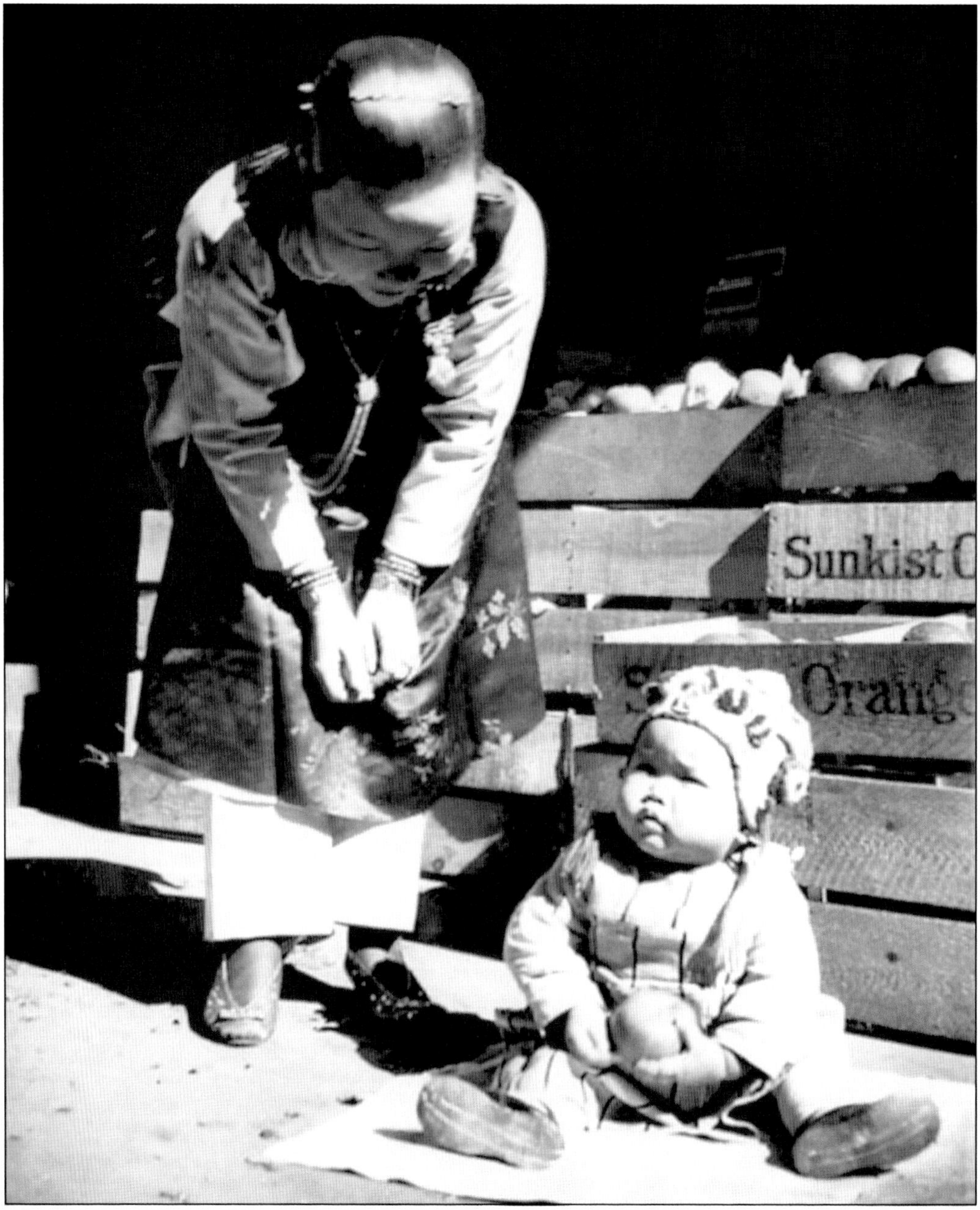

The Chinese grocery stores catered to the Chinese community, therefore they were more concentrated in the Chinese business district, similar to the pattern in other urban Chinese communities. They sold imported goods from China, including dry foods and ingredients, tea and cigars, and cloth and household items. They also sold locally-produced vegetables, fruits, and meats. Some stores handled the ordering and shipping of supplies to Chinese laborers in the smaller towns in southern and southwestern states. (National Archives-Pacific Sierra Region, San Bruno, California.)

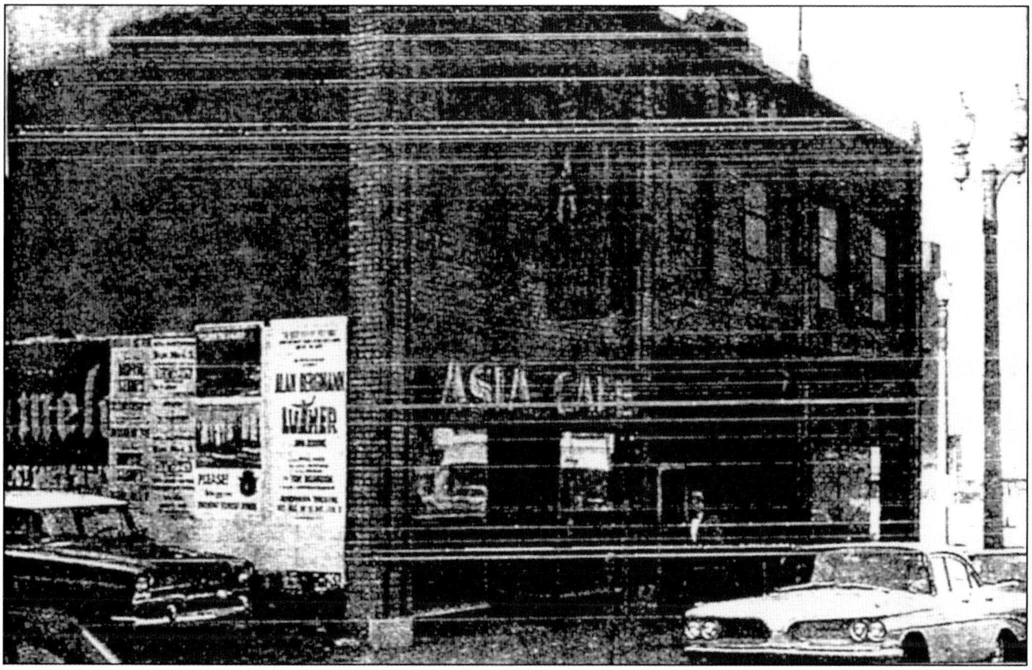

Chinese restaurants and chop suey shops were also part of the businesses in St. Louis Chinatown. Chinese restaurants were first eating places to primarily satisfy the need of Chinese bachelors who would come to eat during Sundays when they were not working. These restaurants usually served authentic Chinese dishes or delicacies that only appealed to the taste buds of Chinese tongues. Annie Leong and her two older brothers were all born and grew up in Hop Alley. During the 1920s and 1930s, the Leong family owned a Chinese restaurant downtown and a grocery store in Hop Alley. The top image shows the Leong family restaurant, Asian Café, at 720 Market Street, a year before it closed in 1965. The image below shows Annie Leong, the spokesperson of Hop Alley and owner of Chinese restaurants and grocery stores, when interviewed by the author in 1998. (Above, St. Louis Public Library; below, photograph by Huping Ling.)

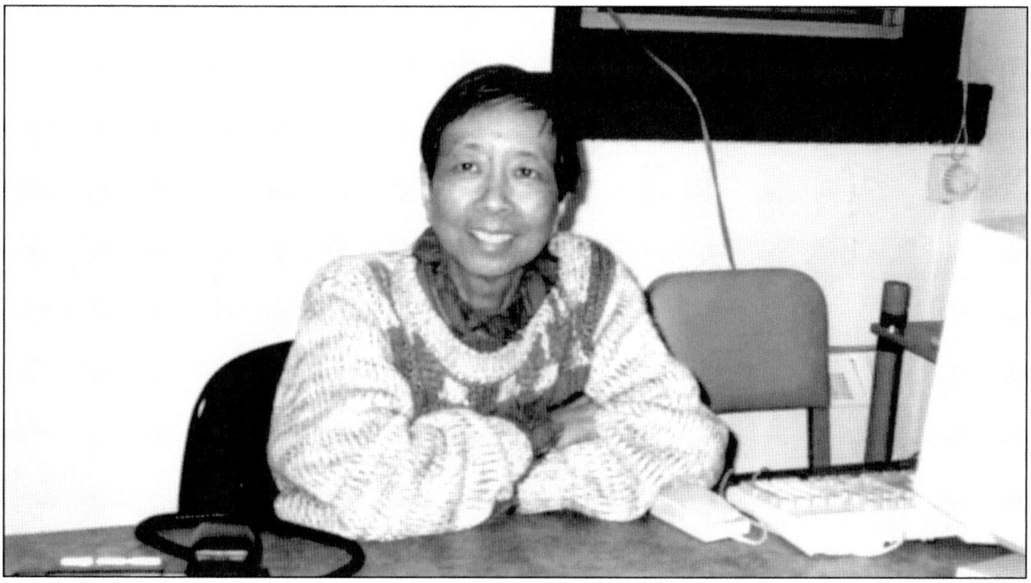

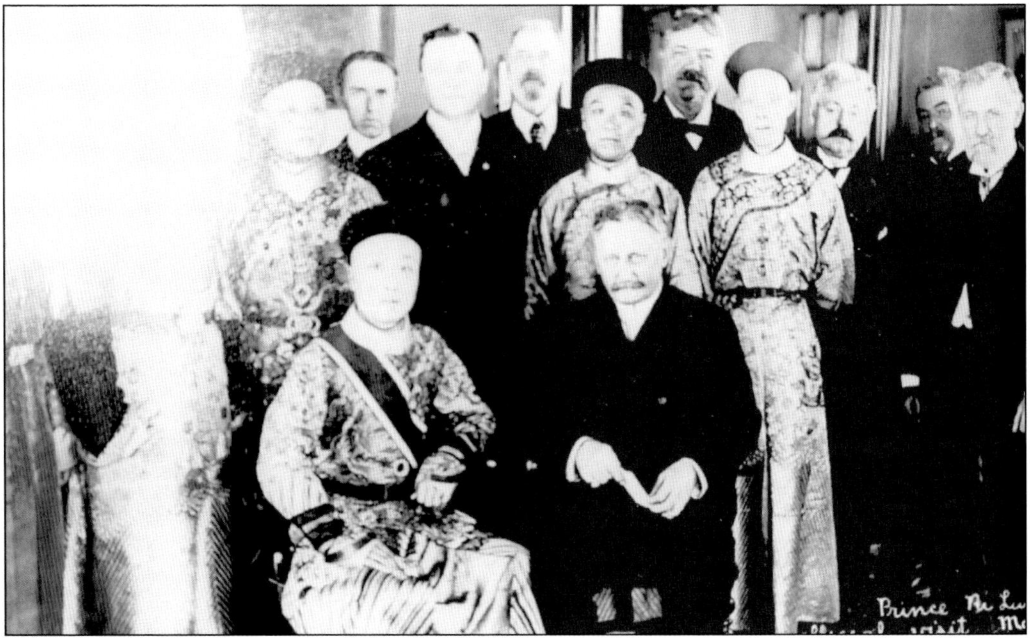

In 1904, St. Louis opened itself to the world for the grand extravaganza of the Louisiana Purchase Exposition, also known as the 1904 St. Louis World's Fair. Countries from around the globe sent their native products and artifacts proudly to show the world. The Chinese Qing government dispatched two envoys to St. Louis to supervise the preparation of the Chinese display and constructed the Chinese Pavilion, a replica of the country home of the Manchu prince Pu Lun, who had been appointed as the official head of the Chinese delegation to the fair. The image above shows Prince Pu Lun (front left) and delegation, and the image below shows embodied Chinese shoes for bound feet displayed at the fair. (Above, Missouri History Museum; below, author's collection.)

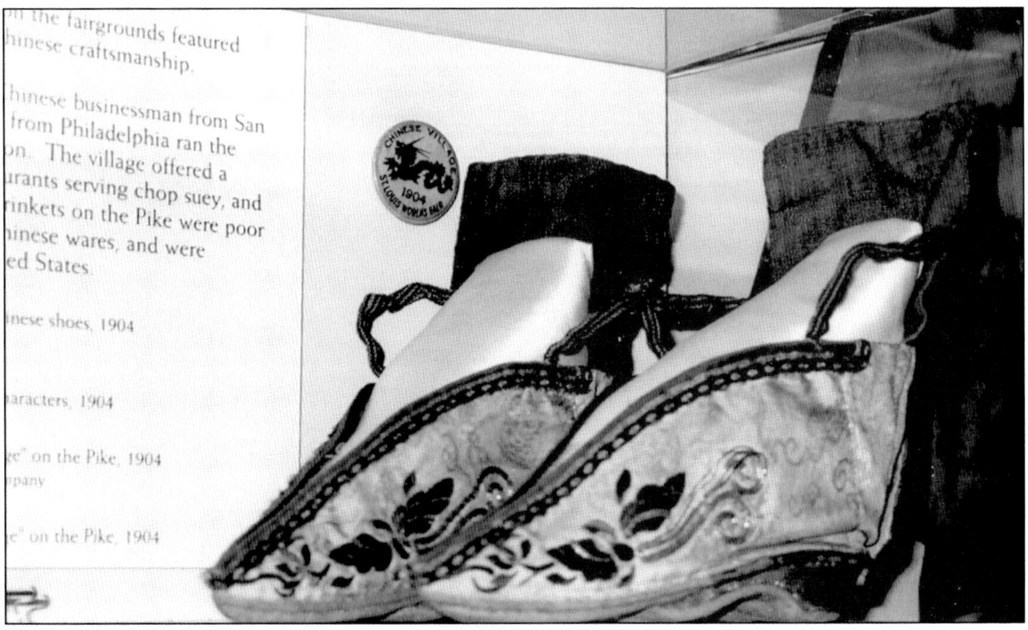

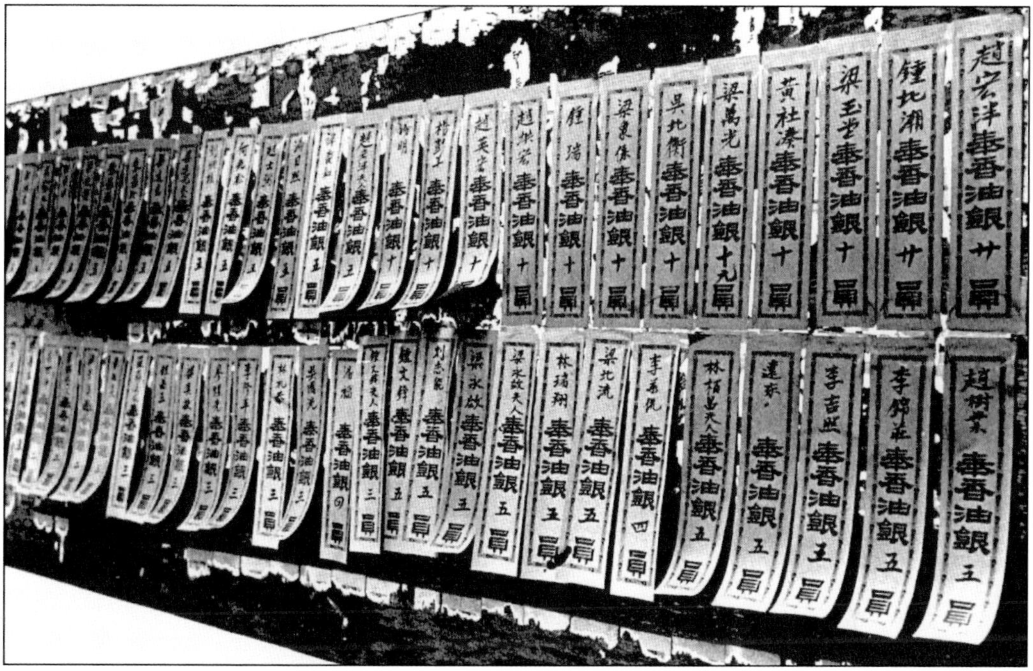

Since its founding in the beginning of the 20th century, the On Leong Chinese Merchants and Laborers Association, commonly known as On Leong, had been the dominant community organization in St. Louis Chinatown. At the On Leong Chinese Merchants and Laborers Association headquarters, at 1509 Delmar Boulevard, one could find cards with names of donors in 1972. (St. Louis Mercantile Library.)

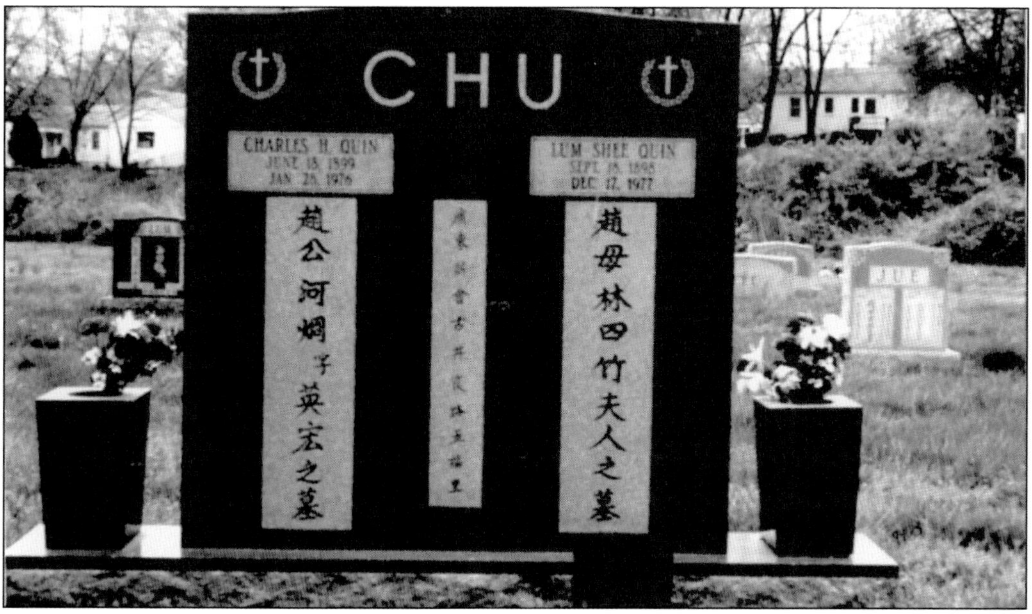

Its presidents had been referred to as "the mayors of Chinatown" by the public as the Chinese preferred resolving problems within the community. The gravestone of Charles Quin Chu (1899–1976), the last "mayor of Chinatown," sits in Valhalla Cemetery and is pictured in 1999. Note the inscription in both English and Chinese. (Photograph by Huping Ling.)

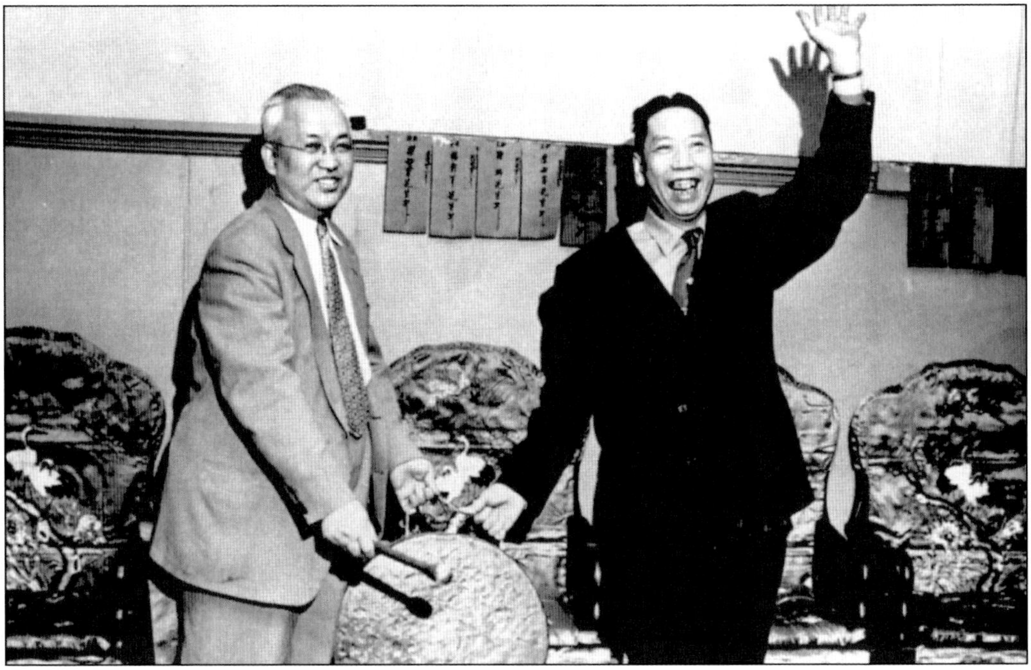

On Leong was a trade/professional organization. It sought to promote and protect Chinese businesses in the United States regardless of lineage and geographical origins of its members. On Leong also provided useful social services to its members and families. The copresidents of On Leong, Robert Chu and Hai Leong, ring the gong to start the Chinese New Year on February 5, 1959. (St. Louis Mercantile Library.)

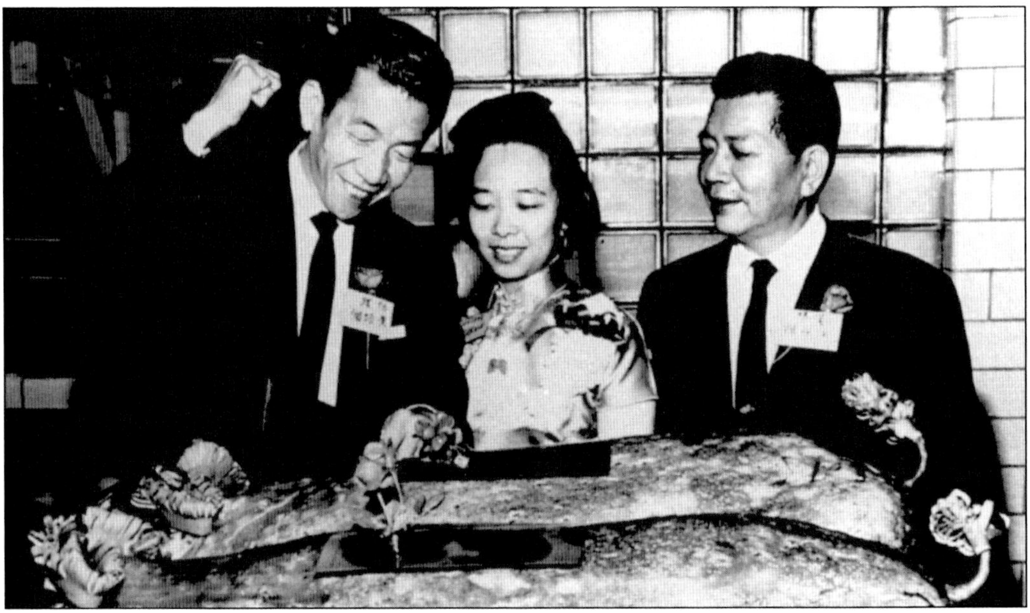

At end of the ceremonies dedicating the new On Leong headquarters at 1509 Delmar Boulevard, two huge roasted pigs were served up. Annie Leong stands between national copresidents of the association, Bob Lee (left) of Boston and Stanley Chin of New York, on February 25, 1966. (St. Louis Mercantile Library.)

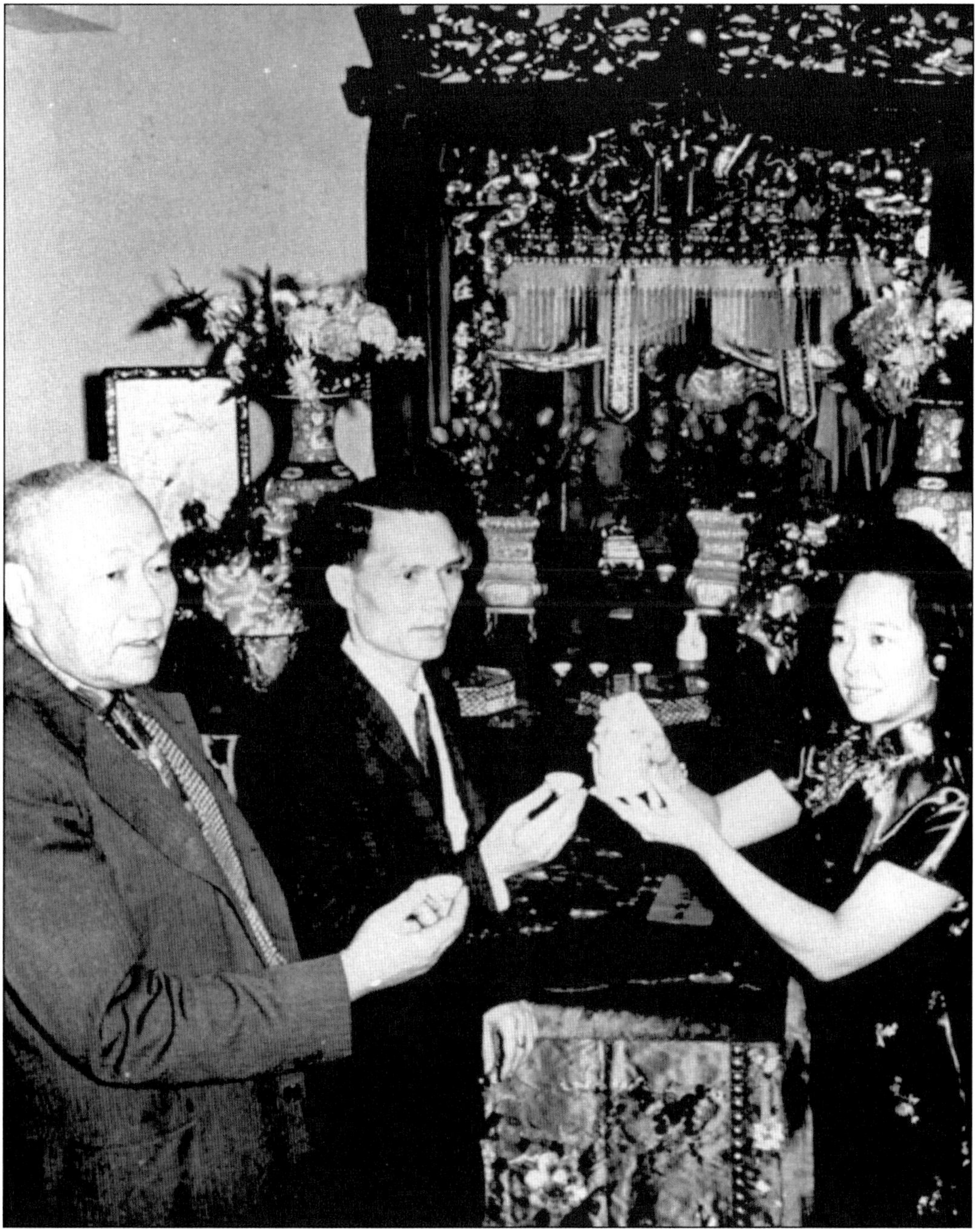

Nin Young and Jim Leong, copresidents of On Leong, and Annie Leong of the Asian Food Products Company, celebrate Year of the Sheep with the ceremonial wine on February 5, 1967. (St. Louis Mercantile Library.)

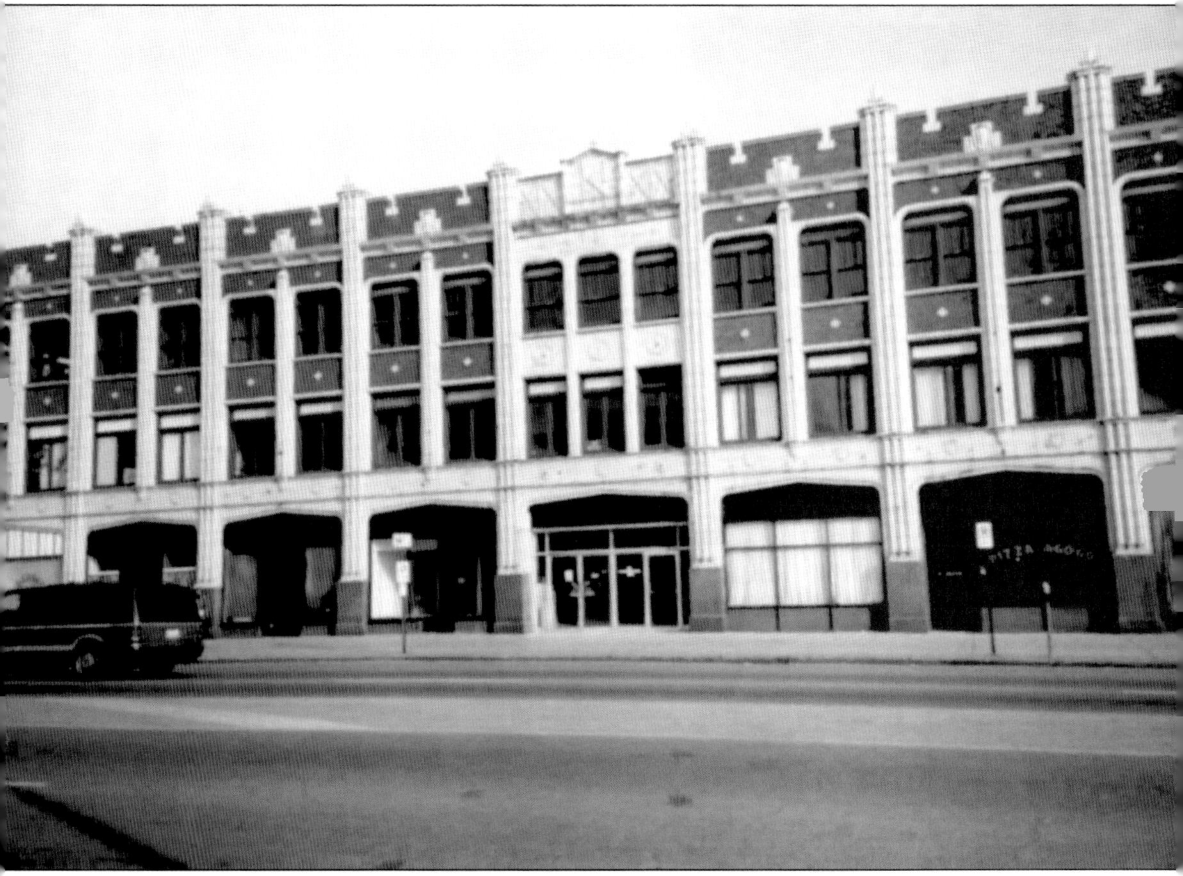

Since the 1970s, new community organizations have emerged and replaced On Leong. The last On Leong headquarters (1979–1997) is pictured at 3608 South Grand Boulevard and Gravois Avenue in 1999. (Photograph by Huping Ling.)

Three

LIVING IN HOP ALLEY

Hop Alley was not only a commercial district, but also a residential and recreational sanctuary for the Chinese in St. Louis. A few Chinese women arrived in the Mound City almost as early as their male counterparts did, running boardinghouses and helping with family businesses in addition to their domestic duties. While the affluent Chinese merchant wives enjoyed some of the leisure and comfort of American middle-class life, working-class Chinese women had to cope with the difficulties of daily survival. Meanwhile Christian institutions encouraged social interactions between the Chinese and European Americans that in some cases promoted the upward social mobility of Chinese youth. Lillie Lee Hong's family history well illustrates the daily struggle of most of the Chinese families. Hong and her mother, Gene Shee, came to the United States in 1924 to join Hong's father, owner of a restaurant named Mandarin House at 4500 Delmar Boulevard. They settled into a two-room apartment in a tenement building in Hop Alley, where Gene Shee gave birth to Hong's four sisters and two brothers. As the family was growing constantly, it had to find ways to fit the nine people into one bedroom. A large board served as the bed for all the children. Such living conditions were typical among Chinese families in Hop Alley. Back from school, Hong had to take care of her younger siblings and help her mother with the family chores of cooking, laundering, and cleaning, all being the classic second-generation responsibilities. The stories of the Chinese in Hop Alley were further told by the burials in Wesleyan and Valhalla Cemeteries where the Chinese men finally rested. While Wesleyan Cemetery served as a temporary parking place for the deceased Chinese before their remains could be shipped back to the motherland, Valhalla Cemetery has become the permanent final resting place for Chinese St. Louisans, much earlier than one might have expected.

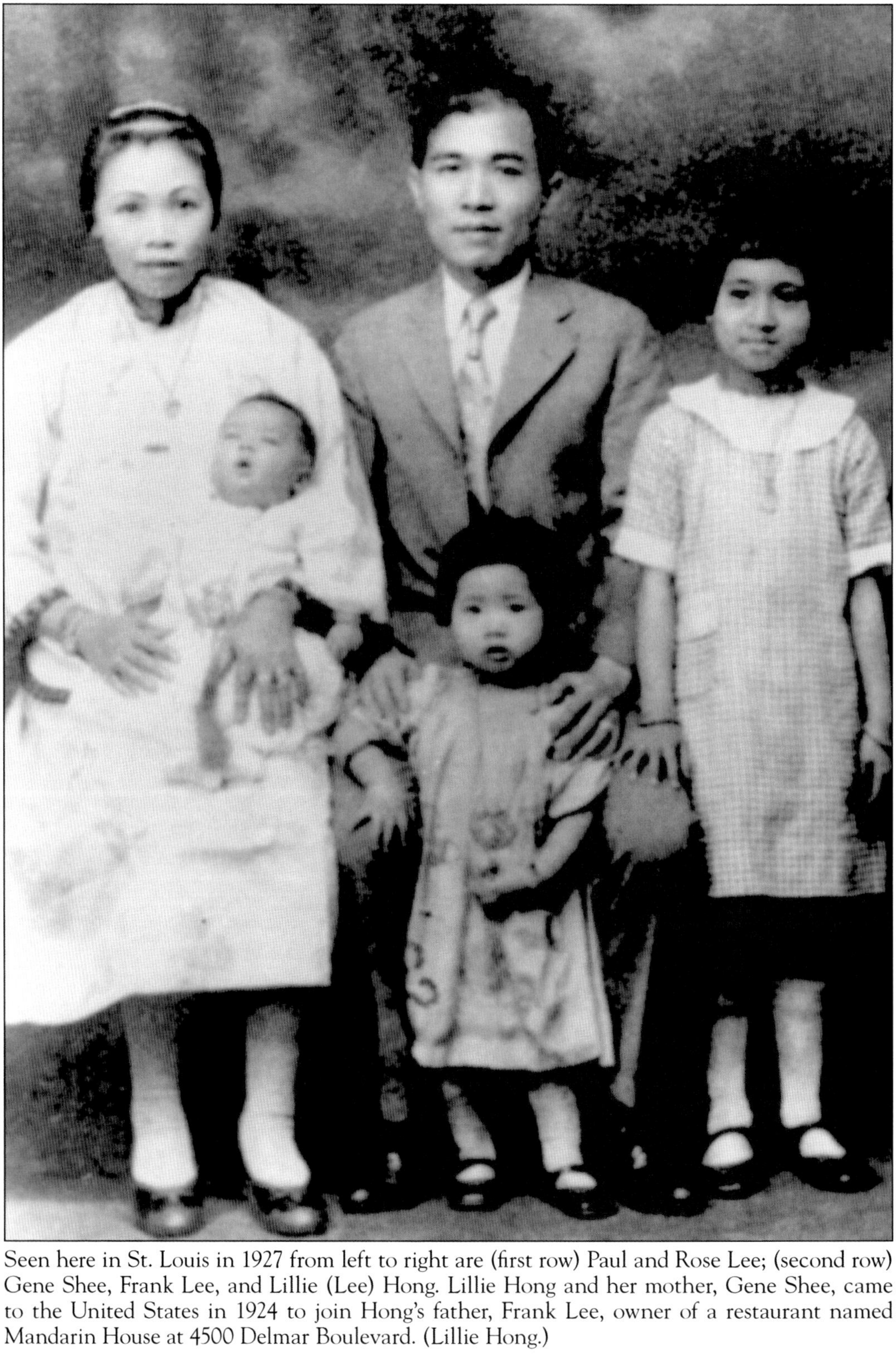

Seen here in St. Louis in 1927 from left to right are (first row) Paul and Rose Lee; (second row) Gene Shee, Frank Lee, and Lillie (Lee) Hong. Lillie Hong and her mother, Gene Shee, came to the United States in 1924 to join Hong's father, Frank Lee, owner of a restaurant named Mandarin House at 4500 Delmar Boulevard. (Lillie Hong.)

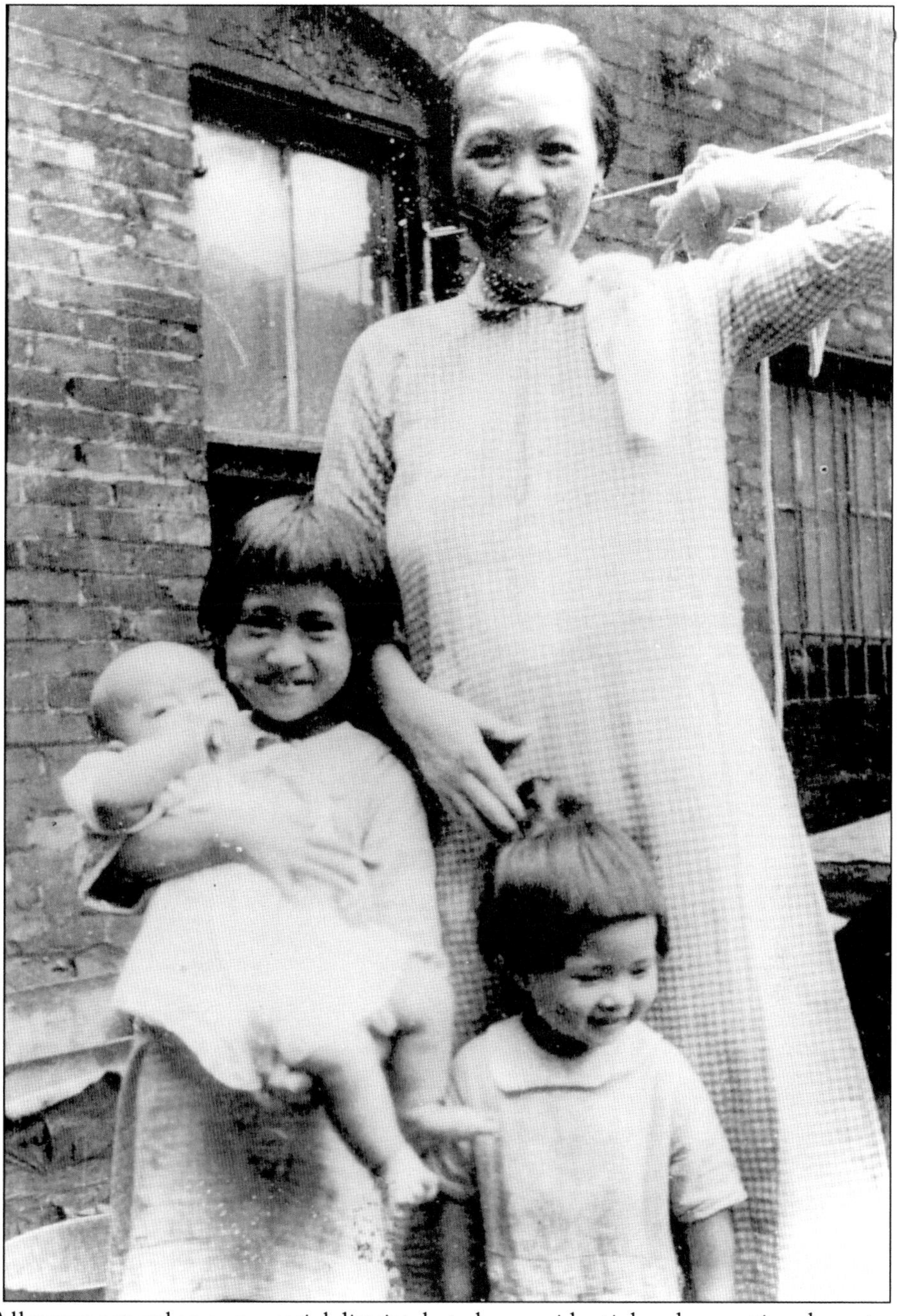

Hop Alley was not only a commercial district, but also a residential and recreational sanctuary for the Chinese in St. Louis. Wives of petty Chinese merchants and common workers struggled simply to raise their large families in Hop Alley. In the first decades of the 20th century, at least 20 Chinese families resided in Hop Alley, mostly ones of poor laundrymen and family restaurant owners. The monthly rent of a two-bedroom apartment was $12, nearly half of a laundryman's monthly earning. One room was used as a bedroom, and the other served as living room-cum-kitchen. Hong is pictured with her mother, brother Paul (in Lillie's arms), and sister Rose in the back of the family apartment in Hop Alley in 1927. (Lillie Hong.)

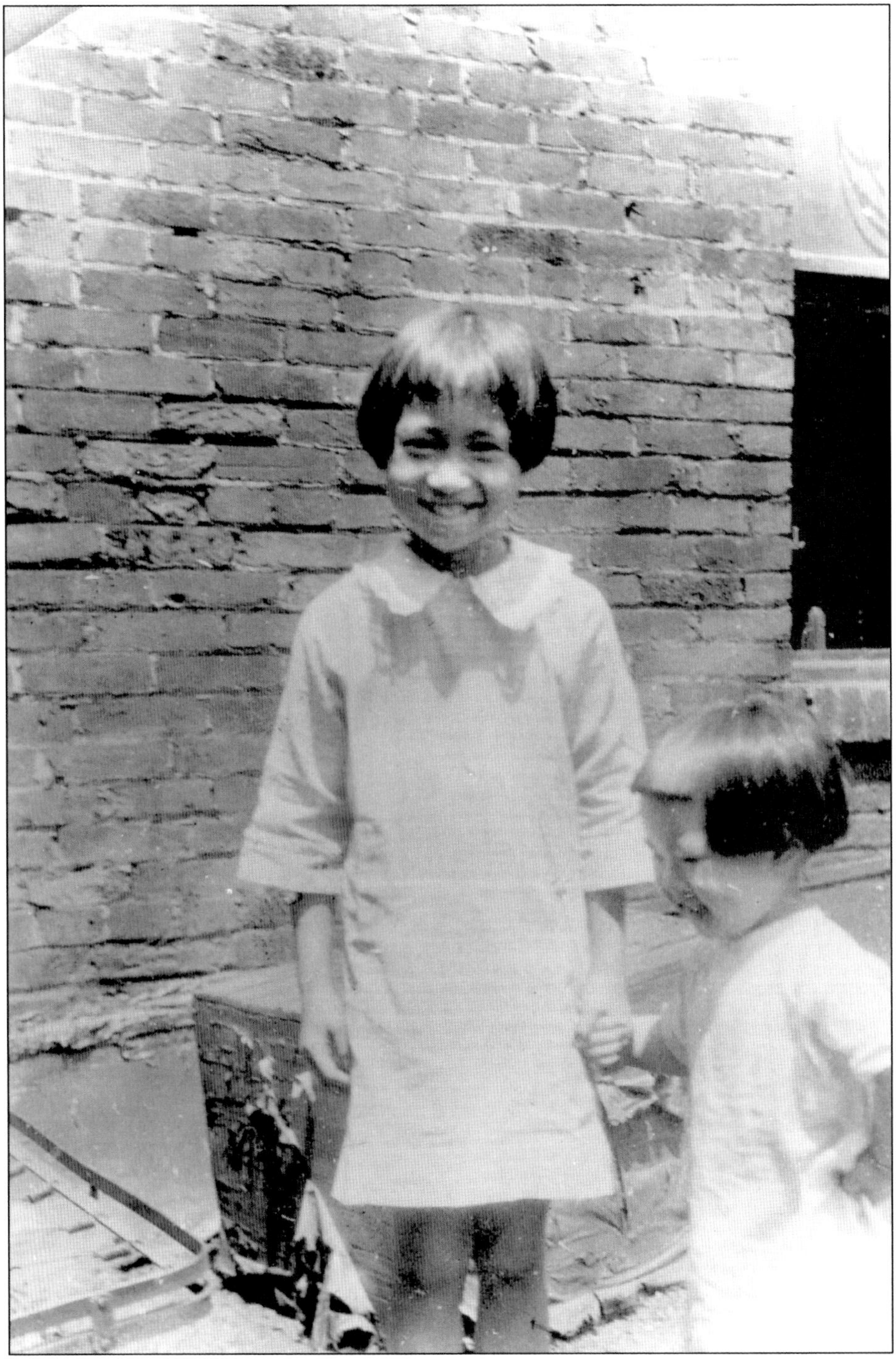

Lillie Hong and sister Rose are pictured in the back of the family apartment in Hop Alley in 1927. Without a refrigerator in the kitchen, the family had to buy 24 pounds of ice daily to fill an icebox on the porch to keep food from spoiling. After school Hong had to take care of younger siblings and help her mother with the family chores of cooking, laundering, and cleaning. (Lillie Hong.)

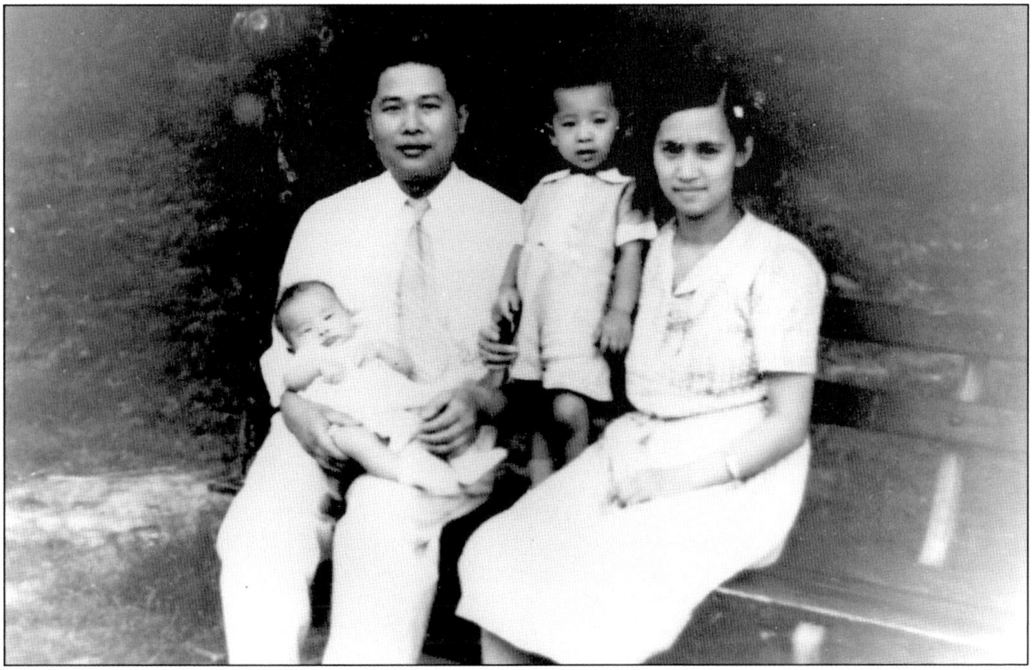

Hong's formal education continued up to eighth grade when her parents thought that she already had a good enough education and withdrew her from school. In order to collect money needed for the family's relocation in China from Hong's prospective husband, her parents married her, at the age of 17 in 1935, to Chooey Hong, a Chinese laundry owner who was 20 years her senior. (Lillie Hong.)

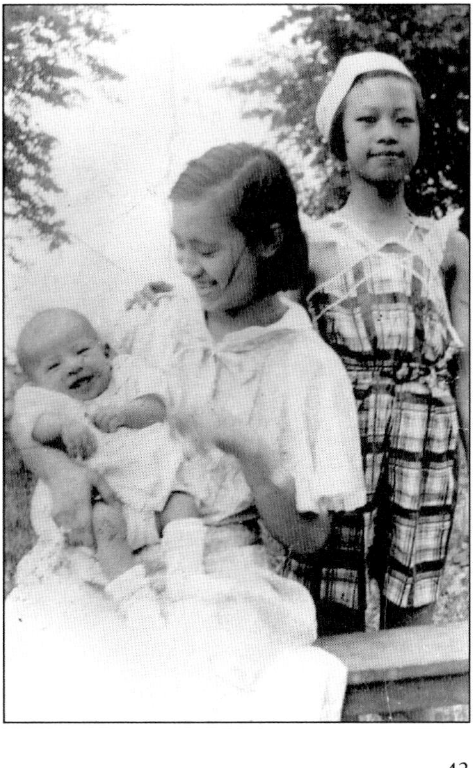

Pictured in Forest Park, a public park in St. Louis, in 1937 from left to right are Eugene David Hong (born February 19, 1937), Lillie Hong, and Rose Lee. (Lillie Hong.)

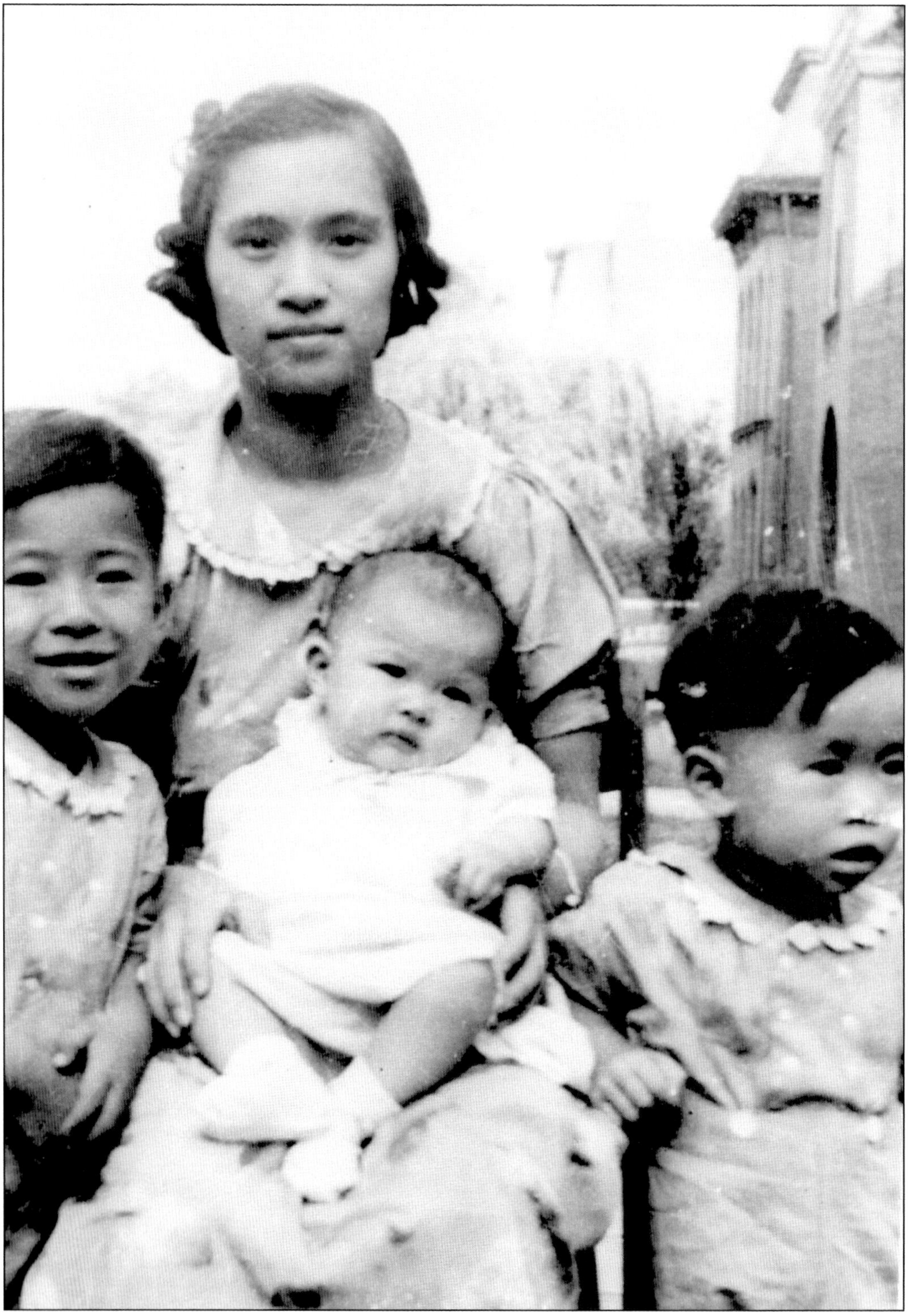

Pictured in Forest Park in 1941 from left to right are Lillie Hong's eldest son Eugene, Lillie Hong, daughter Margie, and second son Richard. (Lillie Hong.)

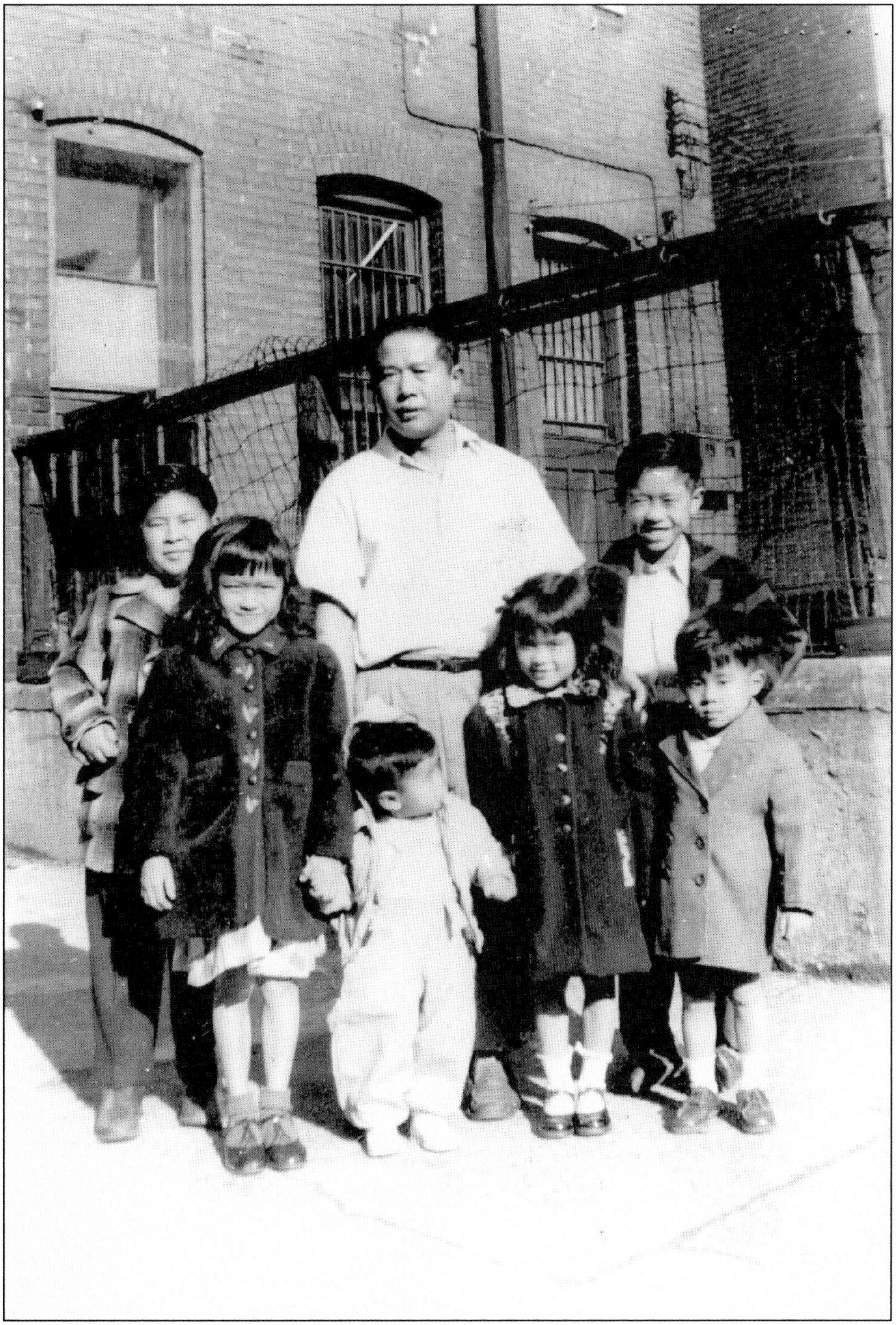

Pictured in the backyard of the family laundry J. H. Lee on Olive Boulevard and Vandeventer Avenue in St. Louis in the 1950s are, from left to right, (first row) eldest daughter Margie, fourth son Ken, second daughter Patsy, and third son William; (second row) second son Richard, father Chooey Hong, and eldest son Eugene. The building in the background is a neighbor's house. (Lillie Hong.)

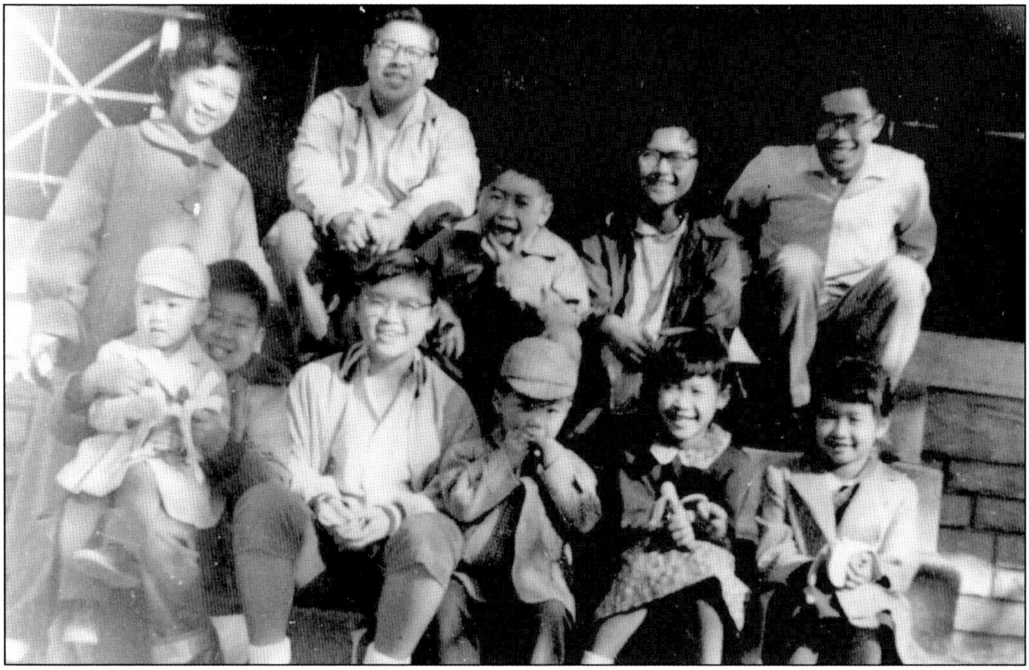

Lillie Hong single-handedly ran the family laundry and raised nine children after her husband died in 1960. She sent all her children to college and most of them are professionals. They all married Chinese. Hong and her nine children are pictured at home at 3961 Westminster Place in St. Louis around 1960 in the image above and in 1968 in the image below. Pictured below are, from left to right, (first row) Carol, Lillie, Stanley, Eugene, and Darlene; (second row) Margie, Pasty, William, Kenny, and Richard. (Lillie Hong.)

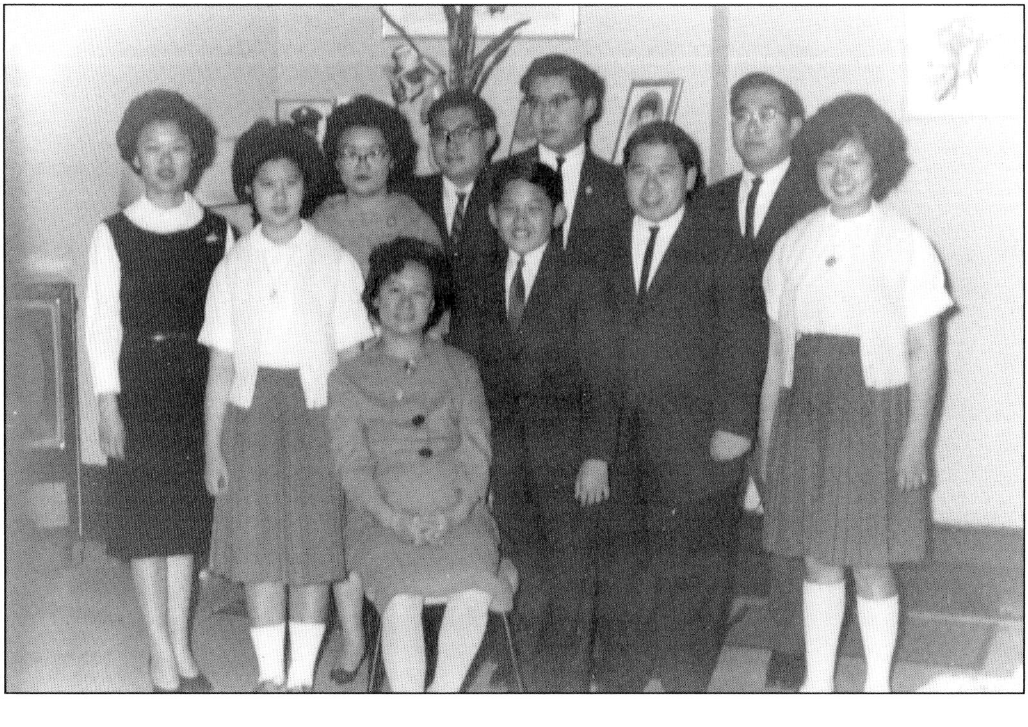

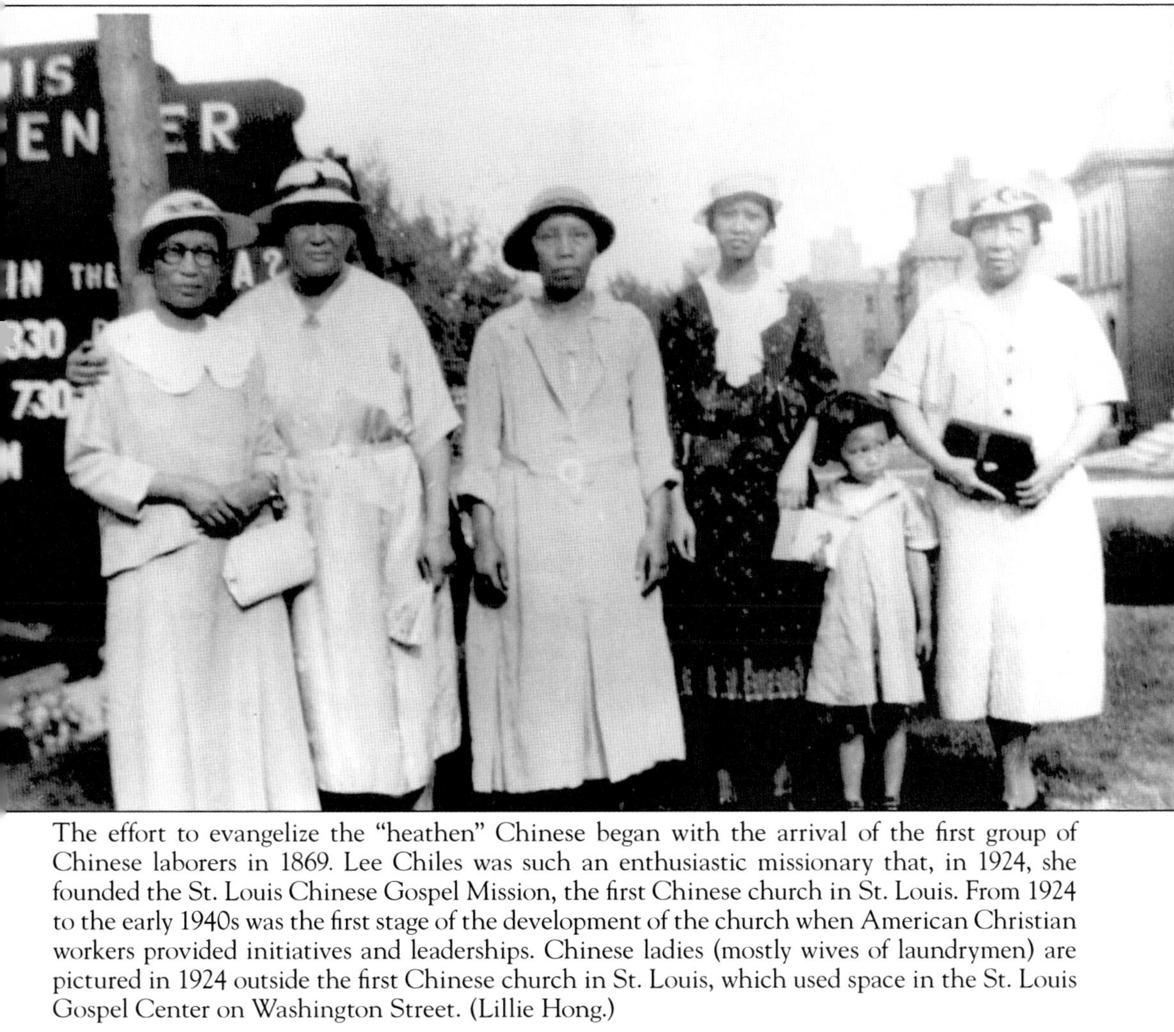

The effort to evangelize the "heathen" Chinese began with the arrival of the first group of Chinese laborers in 1869. Lee Chiles was such an enthusiastic missionary that, in 1924, she founded the St. Louis Chinese Gospel Mission, the first Chinese church in St. Louis. From 1924 to the early 1940s was the first stage of the development of the church when American Christian workers provided initiatives and leaderships. Chinese ladies (mostly wives of laundrymen) are pictured in 1924 outside the first Chinese church in St. Louis, which used space in the St. Louis Gospel Center on Washington Street. (Lillie Hong.)

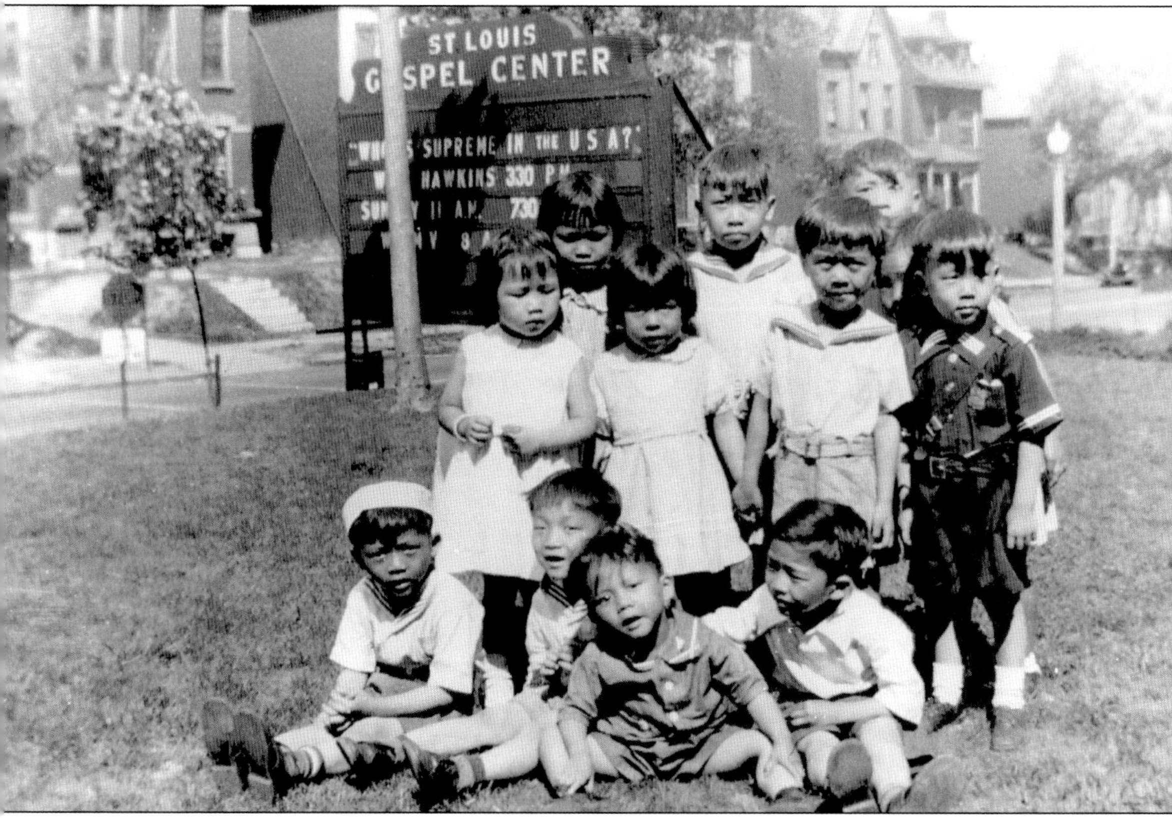

Lee Chiles was persistent and ardent in teaching the Chinese followers English, but was more successful with Chinese children than with women. After she successfully gathered a group of Chinese children, the weekly Chinese Sunday school began. Sunday school children are pictured outside the St. Louis Gospel Center in 1924. (Lillie Hong.)

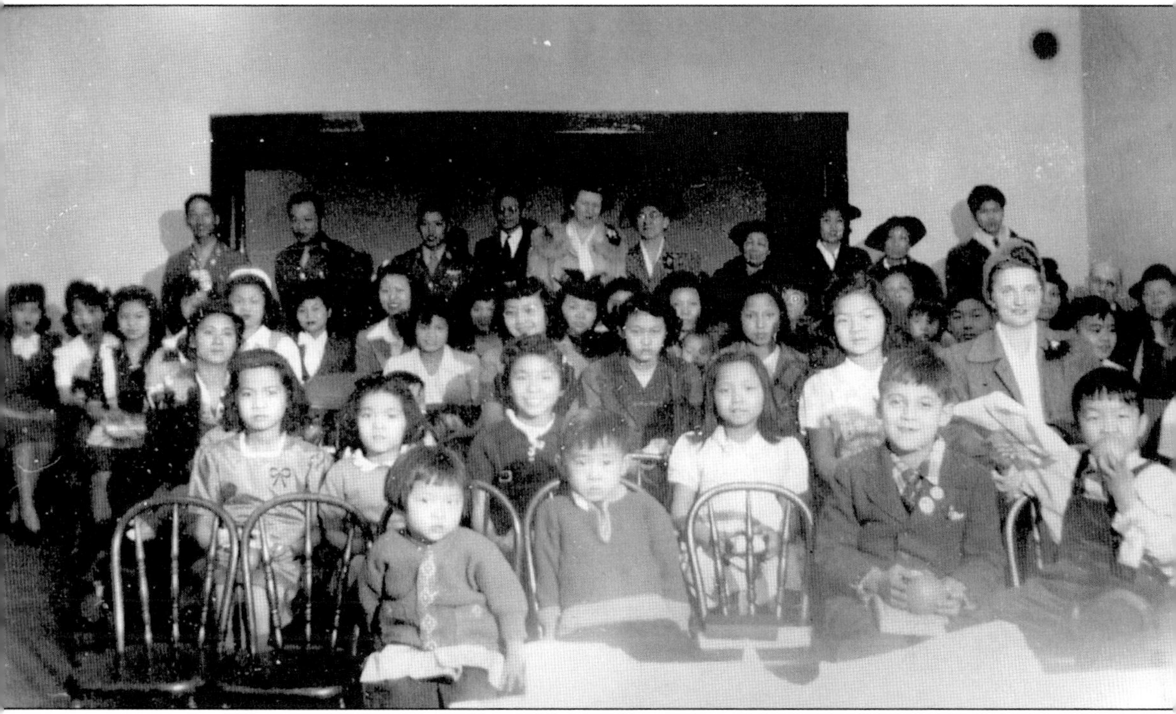

Chinese children and their parents are pictured at Sunday school in the St. Louis Gospel Center on Washington Street in the 1930s. The Chinese Sunday school initially had to borrow space from St. Louis Gospel Church on Washington Street, where the American congregation had services in the morning, and a Chinese service and Sunday school were held in the afternoon. (Lillie Hong.)

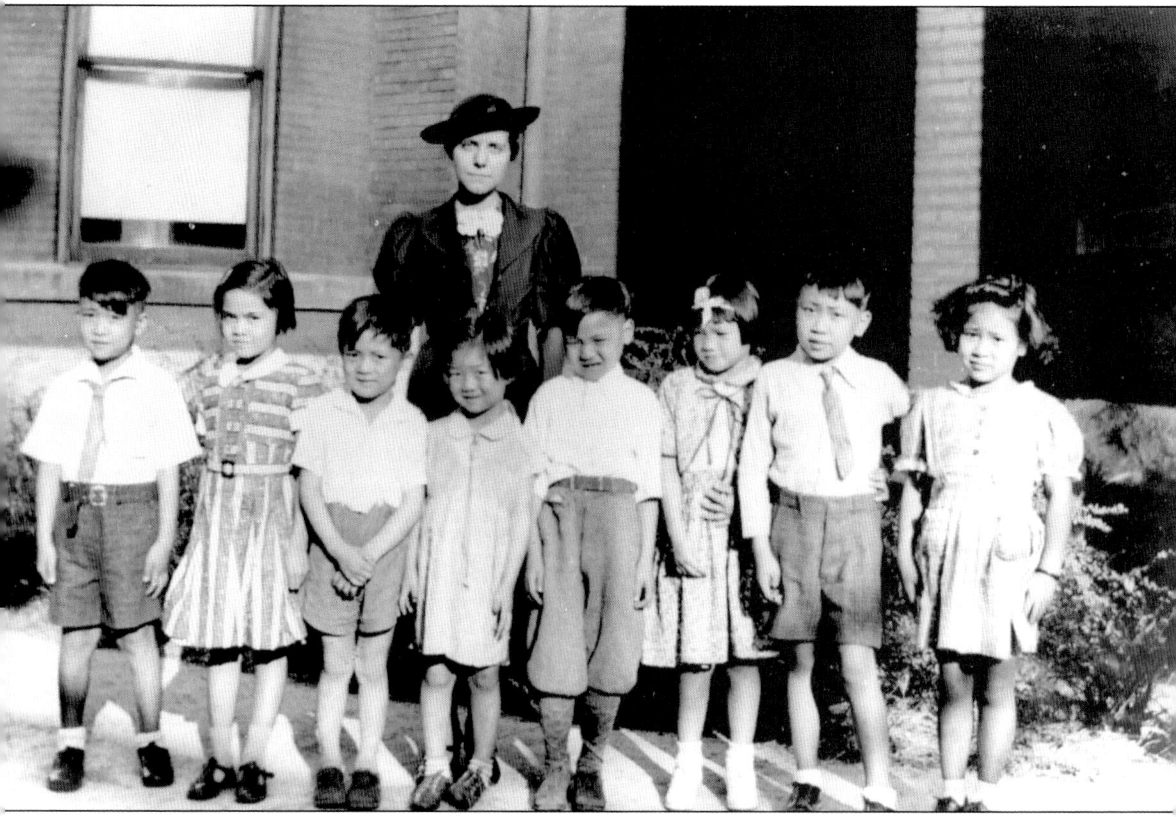

Sunday schools became vehicles of upward mobility for ambitious St. Louis Chinese youth, where they had opportunities to learn English and American ways of life. A Sunday school teacher is pictured with her class outside the St. Louis Chinese Gospel Mission at 4000 Washington Boulevard in the 1940s. (Lillie Hong.)

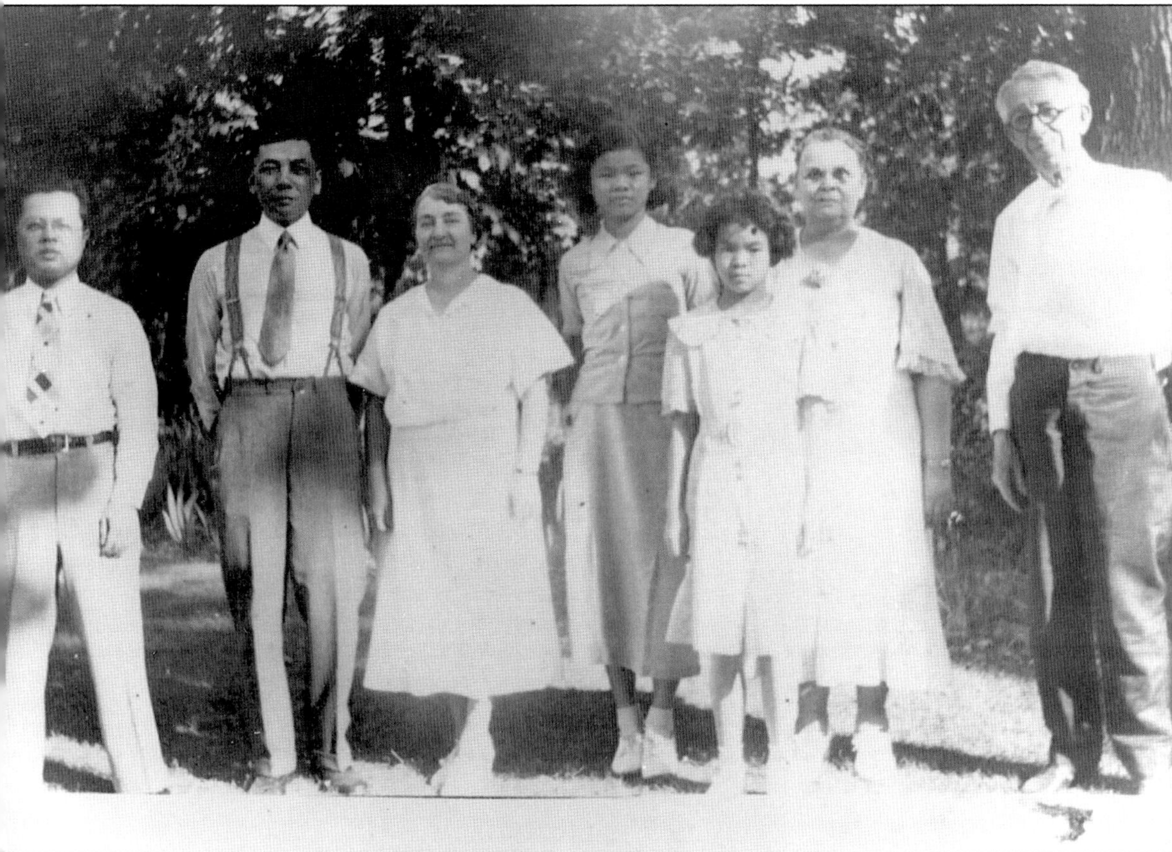

Some members of the St. Louis Chinese Gospel Church, who were small business owners and working-class people, assisted Lee Chiles. The Radfords, a devout Christian couple, would drive children and adults from Hop Alley to church for the afternoon service. The two white women in the center were Sunday school teachers in the 1930s. (Lillie Hong.)

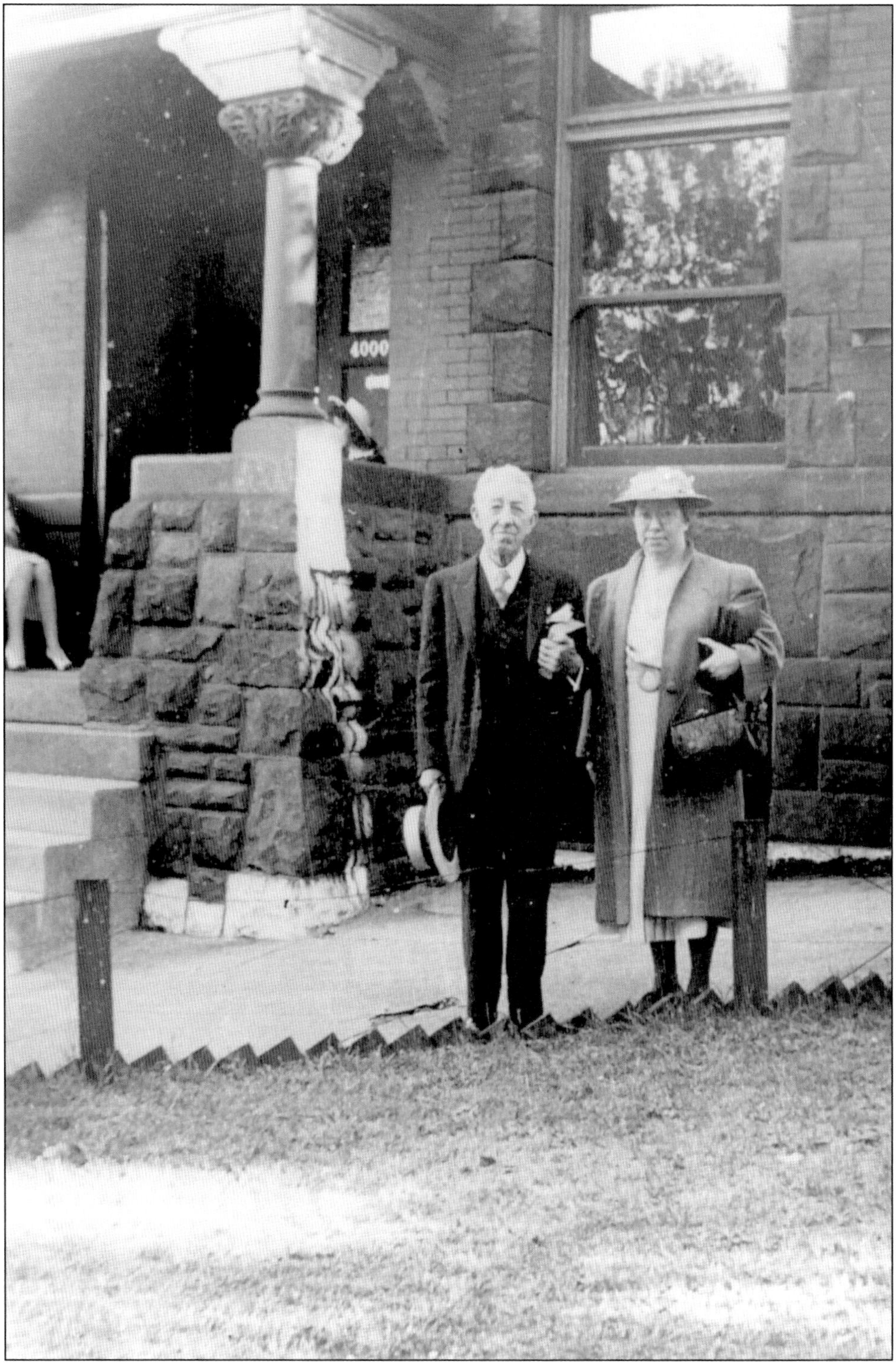

Helen Comfort taught Sunday school and visited Chinese newborns and their families. Comfort and her father are pictured outside the St. Louis Chinese Gospel Mission at 4000 Washington Boulevard in the 1940s. (Lillie Hong.)

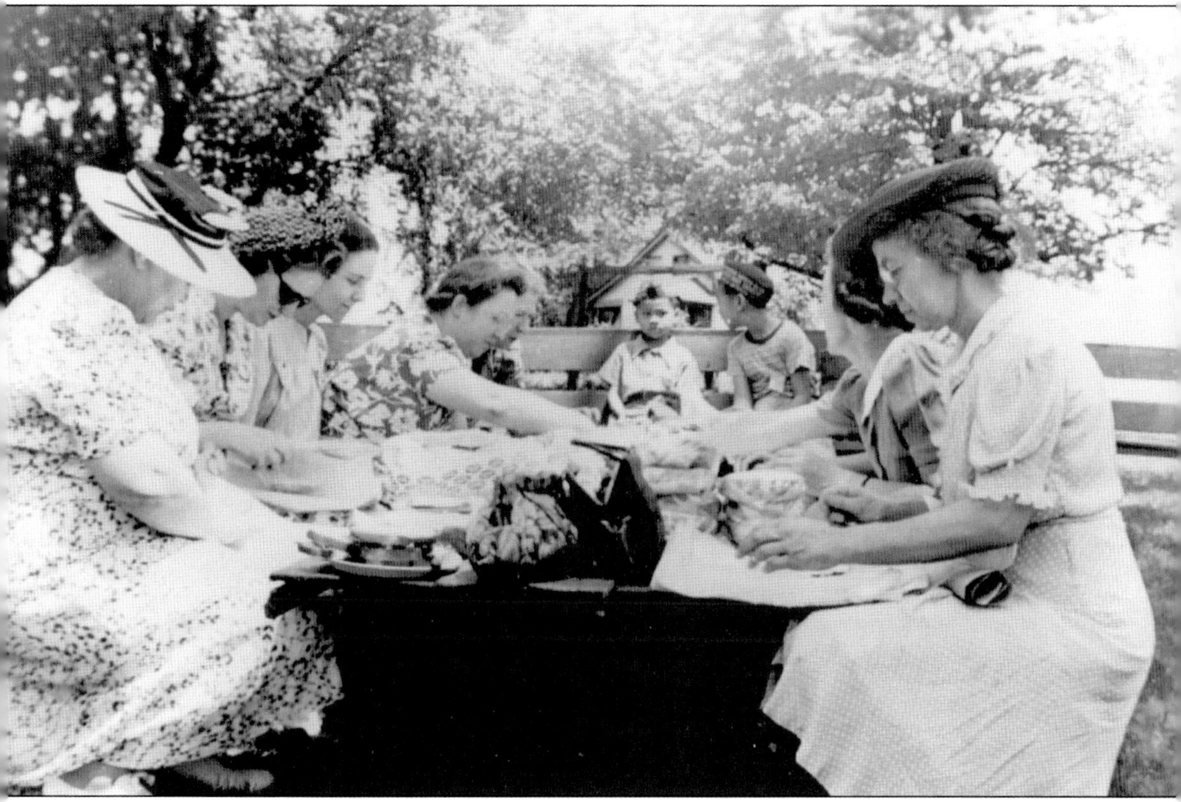

Sunday schools and church-sponsored activities eased Chinese immigrant women's transition from rural China to urban America in the initial years; they provided a window for these women to glimpse American life and culture. Annual picnics were held by the St. Louis Gospel Center on Memorial Day at Forest Park in the 1930s. (Lillie Hong.)

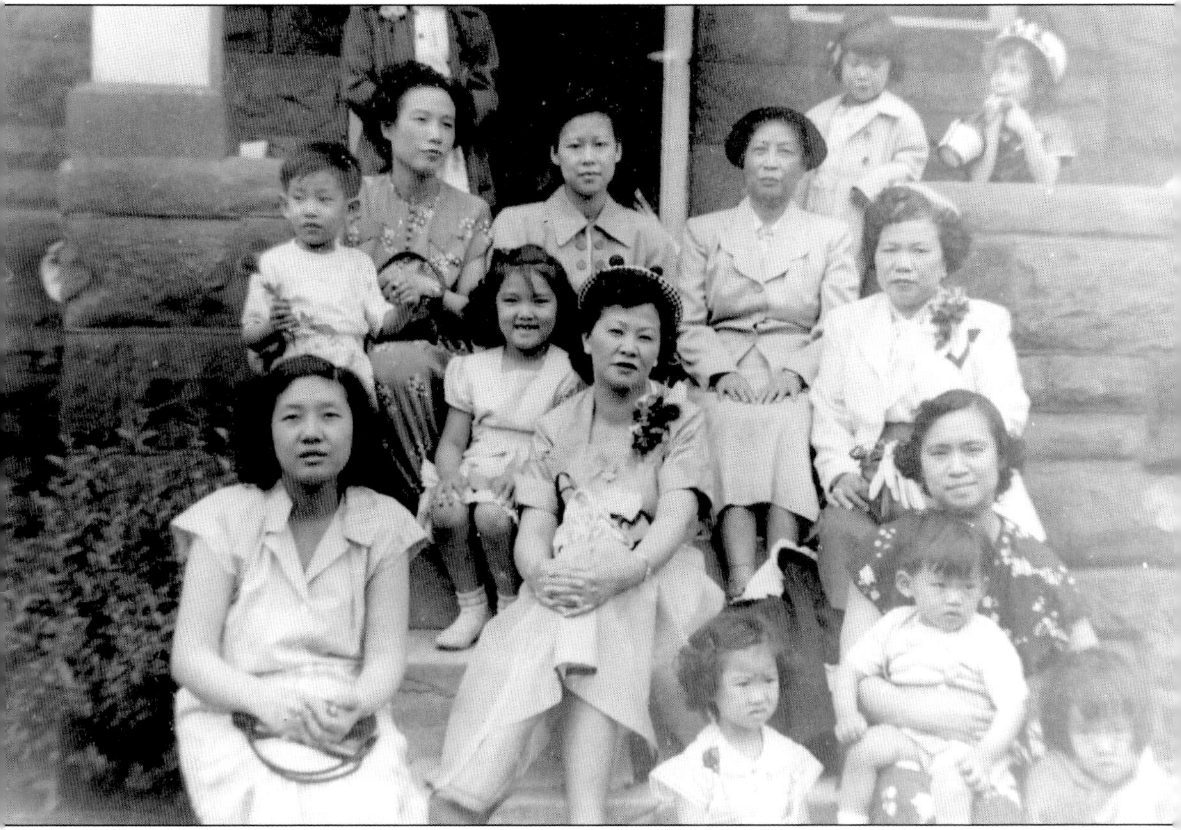

The Chinese women learned the skills of dressing, cooking, and housekeeping at sewing and cooking classes, and picnics, thus domesticity in America became less alien and intimidating. Church was also a place to exchange information, find kinship connections, and maintain friendships with other Chinese families. Lillie Hong is pictured at the bottom right with her children at the St. Louis Chinese Gospel Mission at 4000 Washington Boulevard in the 1940s. (Lillie Hong.)

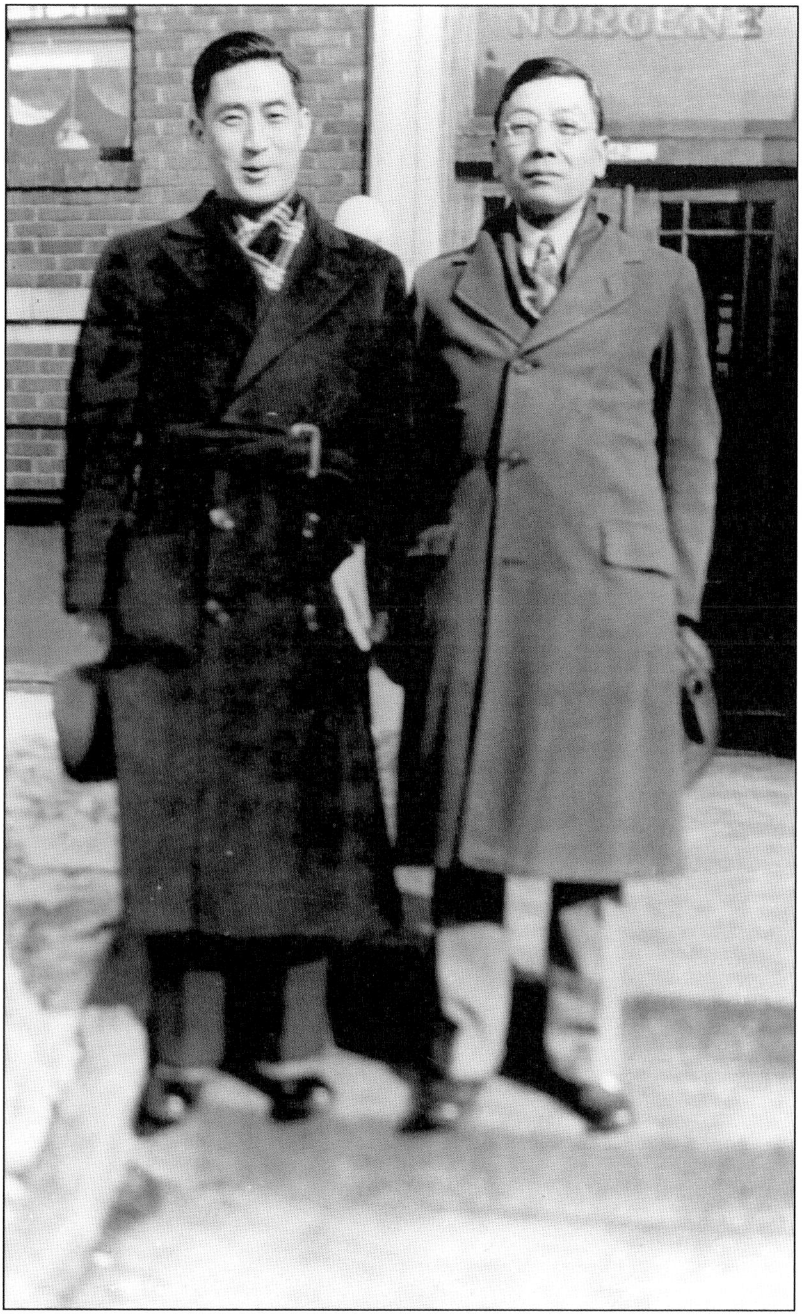

The moving of the St. Louis Chinese Gospel Mission into 4237 McPherson Avenue marked the beginning of the second stage of the church from the 1940s to 1990, when Chinese Christians emerged as leaders of the congregation. Lukin Pond, a local Chinese tailor, became the organizer of the church. Every Saturday afternoon, Pond cleaned up the building for Sunday worship. On weekdays, Pond and his wife, Beulah, visited the Chinese laundries and restaurants. Pond continued this work until his death in 1961. Seen here are Auoiew Shi (left) and Lukin Pond outside the St. Louis Chinese Gospel Mission on Washington Boulevard on January 1, 1940. Pond was interpreter of the church then. (Lillie Hong.)

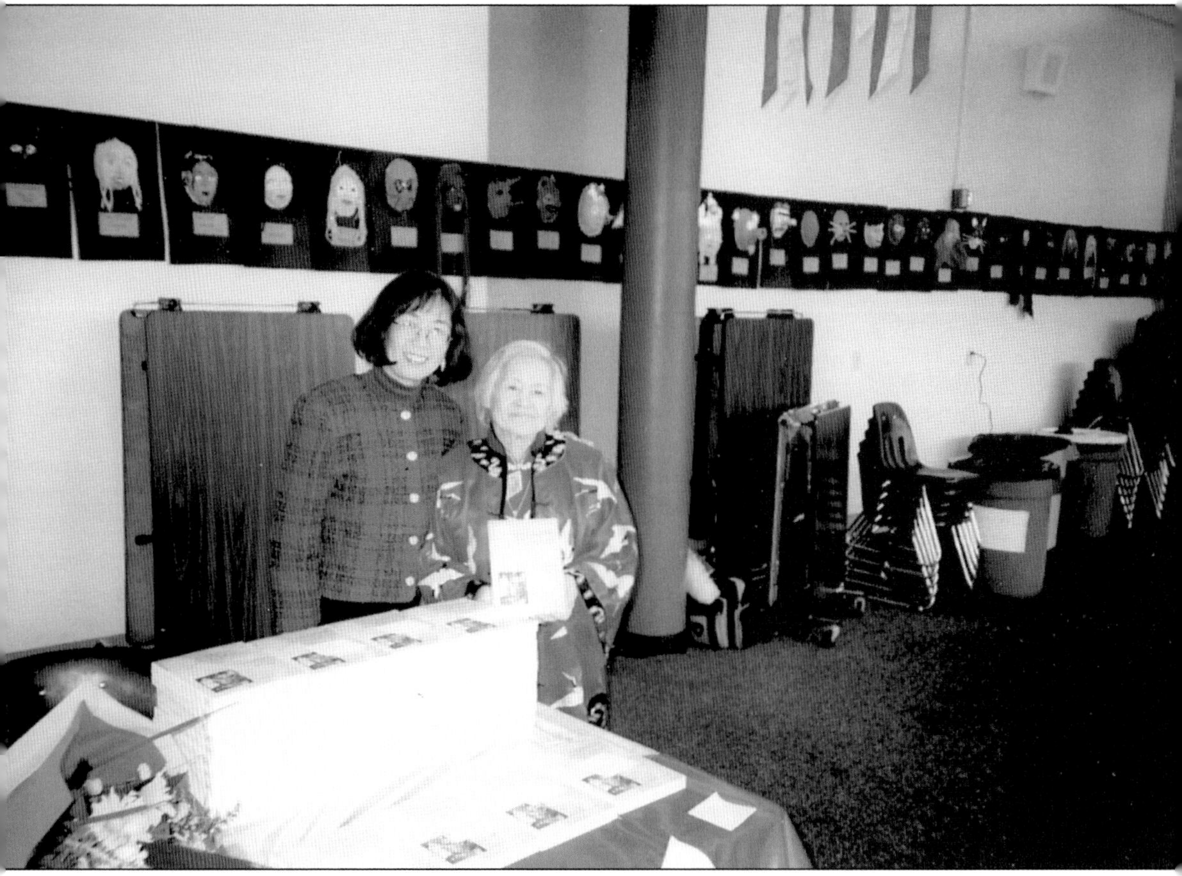

Lillie Hong, at the age of 85, is seen with the author at the presentation and book signing for *Chinese St. Louis: From Enclave to Cultural Community*, published in Philadelphia by Temple University Press in 2004, that was sponsored by St. Louis Chinese Association, St. Louis Modern Chinese School, St. Louis Chinese Culture Association, St. Louis Chinese American News, and Chinese American Forum on November 21, 2004. (Author's collection.)

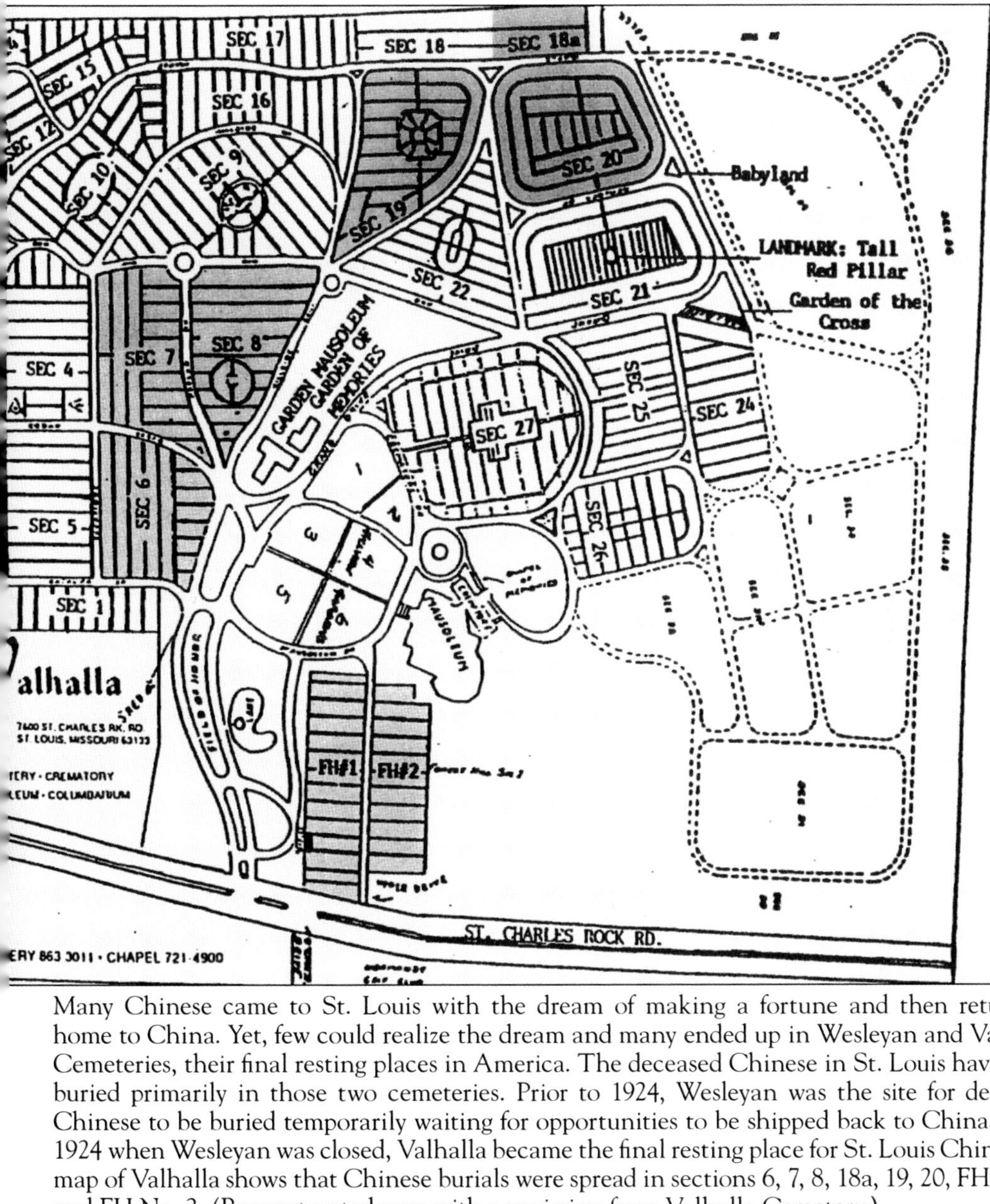

Chinese Burial Sites in Valhalla Cemetery

Many Chinese came to St. Louis with the dream of making a fortune and then returning home to China. Yet, few could realize the dream and many ended up in Wesleyan and Valhalla Cemeteries, their final resting places in America. The deceased Chinese in St. Louis have been buried primarily in those two cemeteries. Prior to 1924, Wesleyan was the site for deceased Chinese to be buried temporarily waiting for opportunities to be shipped back to China. After 1924 when Wesleyan was closed, Valhalla became the final resting place for St. Louis Chinese. A map of Valhalla shows that Chinese burials were spread in sections 6, 7, 8, 18a, 19, 20, FH No. 1, and FH No. 2. (Reconstructed map with permission from Valhalla Cemetery.)

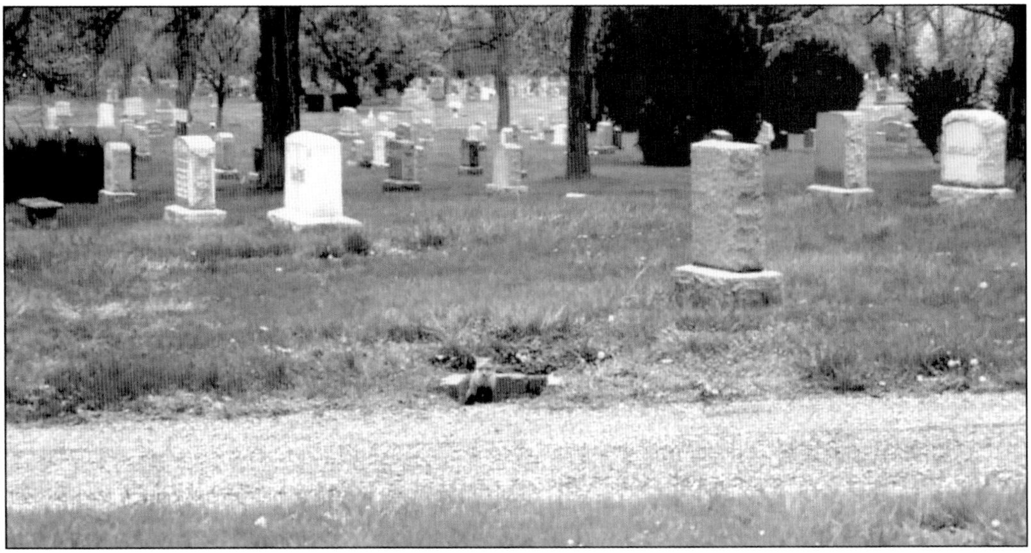

The deaths and burials of Chinese in St. Louis become significant sources revealing the lives of Chinese residents, and the study of mortuary records helped find the missing pieces of the story of Hop Alley. Section 6 in Valhalla Cemetery, one of the Chinese burial sites in St. Louis, is pictured in 1999. (Photograph by Huping Ling.)

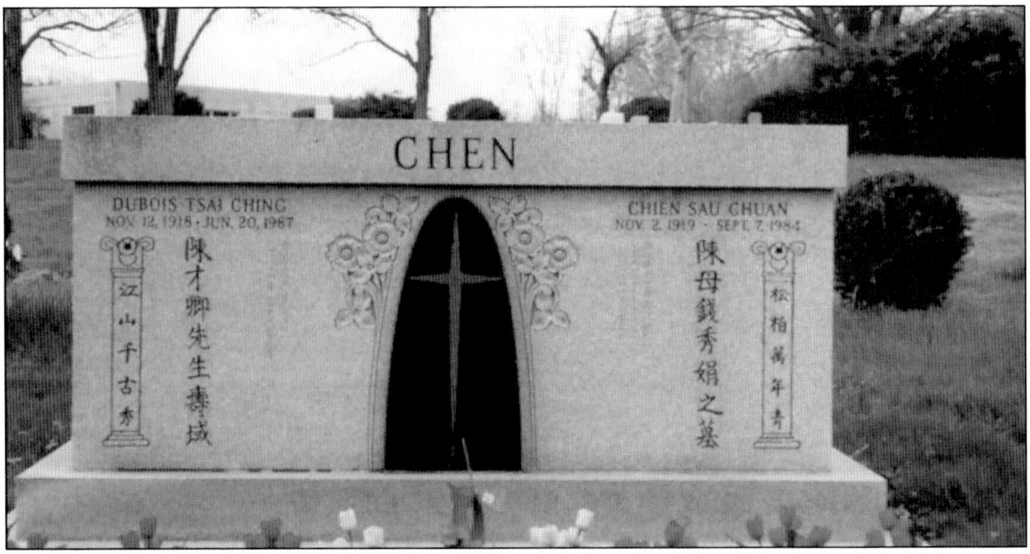

The upright gravestones along both sides of the road in section 18a, dating from the 1960s, and many other upright gravestones in sections 6, 7, 8, FH No. 1, and FH No. 2, dating from the 1970s, reflect the dramatic economic, social, and cultural transitions within the Chinese community. First, the upright gravestones display the improvement of socioeconomic conditions of Chinese since the cost for upright gravestone was higher than flat stones; second, most gravestones in these sections were inscribed with both names of the couple, indicating the community's gradual change from a bachelor society to a more family-oriented one since the 1960s; third, romanization of the Chinese surnames or full names of the deceased people was incorporated into the inscription, reflecting the Chinese efforts to integrate with the larger society. One of the more recent gravestones in Valhalla Cemetery is pictured, with inscriptions in both Chinese and English, in 1999. (Photograph by Huping Ling.)

Four

Community in Transition

While suffering from economic difficulties, Chinese St. Louisans enthusiastically participated in the country's war effort. World War II not only contributed to the final repeal of the Chinese exclusion acts, but also ushered the coming of Chinese professionals during the postwar era. The wartime economic recovery and prosperity continued in the postwar years; Americans enjoyed the greatest economic expansion in the century. The statistics indicate that the gross national product rose from $200 billion in 1945 to almost $300 billion in 1950 and to over $500 billion by 1960. Reflecting the national trend, St. Louis also witnessed economic expansion. The major businesses such as St. Louis Union Trust Company, Union Electric, Southwestern Bell, Ralston-Purina, Monsanto Chemical Company, and McDonnell Aircraft expanded rapidly. Economic expansion attracted newcomers from other parts of the country as well as from overseas. According to the U.S. censuses, the city's population jumped from 1,090,278 in 1940 to 1,262,145 in 1950 and 1,263,145 in 1960. As thousands of Americans moved to St. Louis, professionals from China also came to the city for a better economic opportunity. The early Chinese professionals were engineers, physicians, and scientists, among whom William Tao's case exemplifies the coming of the pioneer Chinese professionals. Tao was born into a well-off family in Beijing, China, in 1917. In 1947, Tao was granted a scholarship by the Mechanical Engineering Department at Washington University. Tao's first years in St. Louis were difficult. He worked hard to maintain a good academic record and served as a graduate assistant during the day and did part-time engineering design work at night. After the completion of a master's degree, Tao stayed on as an instructor. He taught during the day and designed building projects at night to prepare for his future engineering consulting business. In 1955, Tao started his private engineering practice with a partner, and later became the sole proprietor. In 1957, Tao named his practice William Tao and Associates Consulting Engineers (WTA). Within in a few years, the company grew and its reputation rose steadily. In 1963, WTA was commissioned to do all the electrical and mechanical engineering for the 17-story Pierre Laclede Building in Clayton, which marked the beginning of a distinguished career of high-rise building design throughout St. Louis, many other states, and overseas.

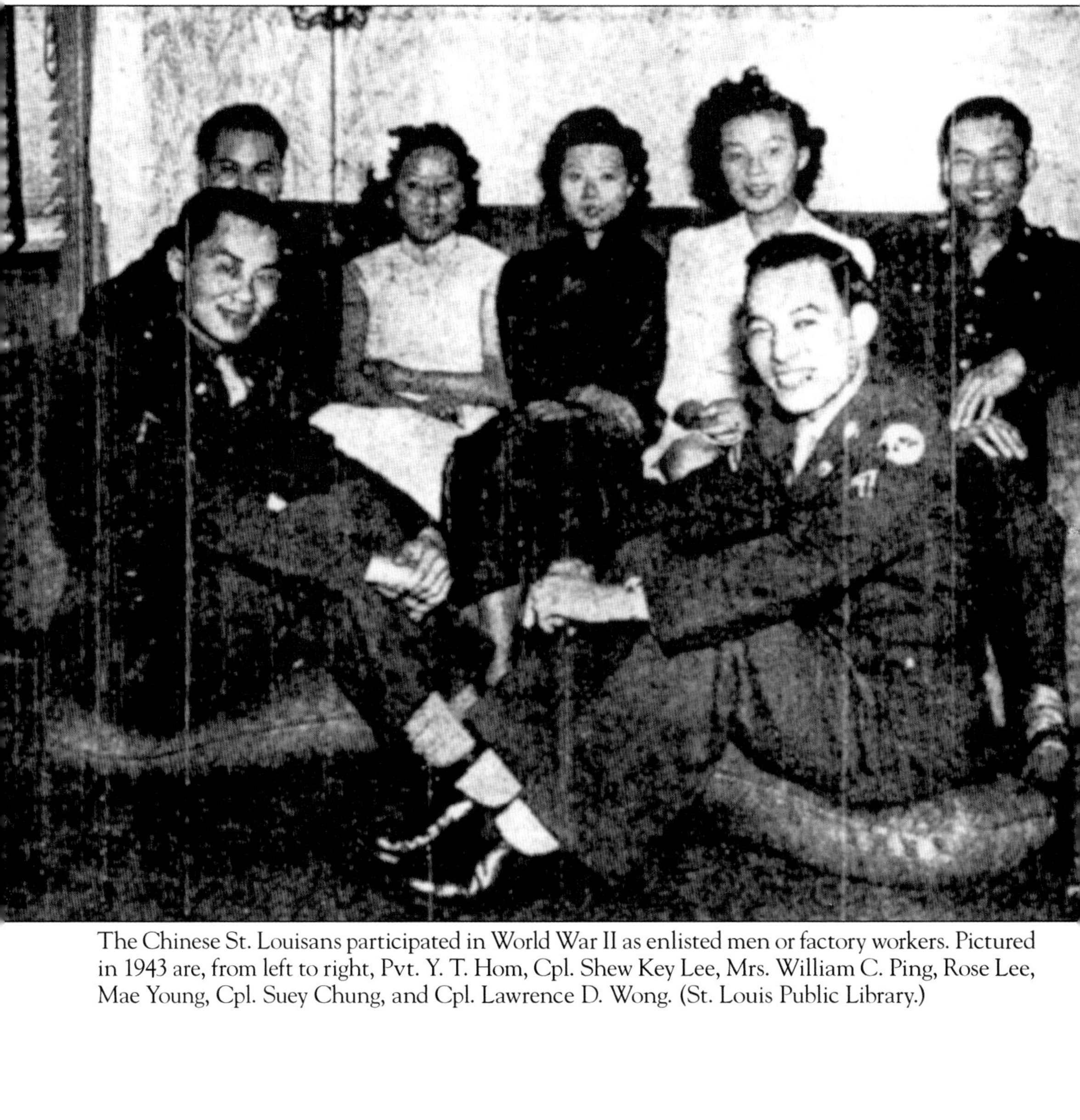

The Chinese St. Louisans participated in World War II as enlisted men or factory workers. Pictured in 1943 are, from left to right, Pvt. Y. T. Hom, Cpl. Shew Key Lee, Mrs. William C. Ping, Rose Lee, Mae Young, Cpl. Suey Chung, and Cpl. Lawrence D. Wong. (St. Louis Public Library.)

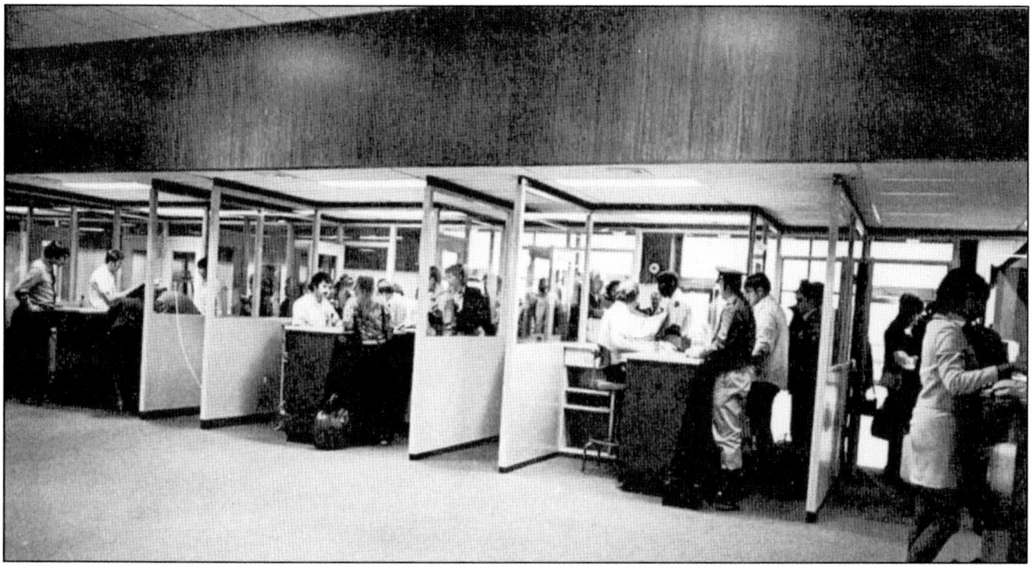

When Chinatown and On Leong were struggling for survival, the city received its new arrivals from China. The 1965 Immigration Act and the consequent influx of new Chinese immigrants contributed to the population increase. According to the U.S. censuses, by 1960, the Chinese population in St. Louis area totaled 663. Ten years later, it had more than doubled, reaching 1,451. By 1980, the Chinese population was 2,418, a fourfold increase within two decades. Passengers arriving at the new overseas terminal of Philadelphia International Airport are pictured as they are inspected by immigration inspectors. (Immigration and Naturalization Services Annual Report, 1973.)

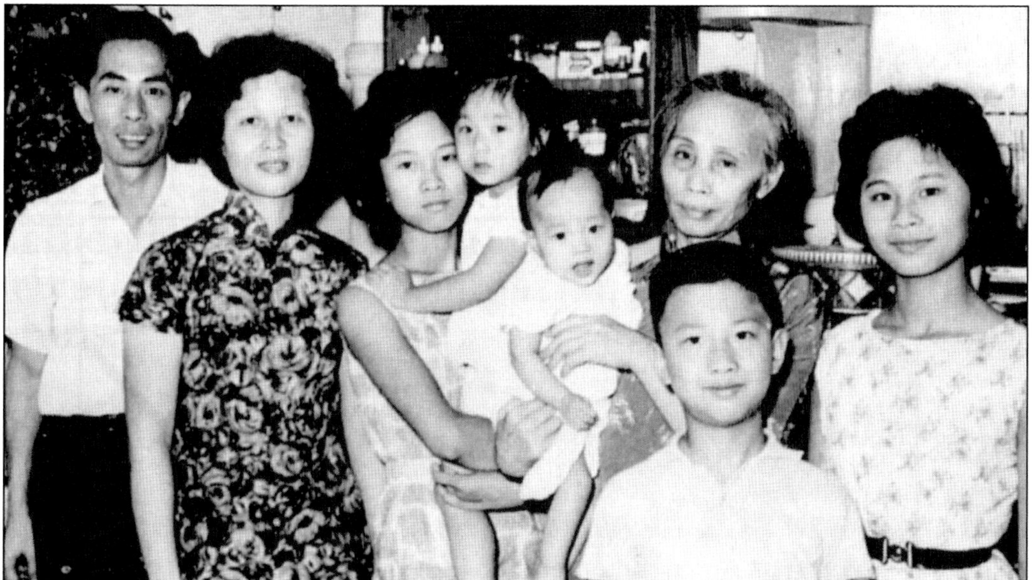

The 1965 Immigration Act abolished the 1924 quota system and set up three immigration principles of family reunification, the need for skilled workers, and the admission of refugees. A Hong Kong family is pictured in their one-room home in Kwaloon shortly before they left for the United States. (Immigration and Naturalization Services Annual Report, 1963.)

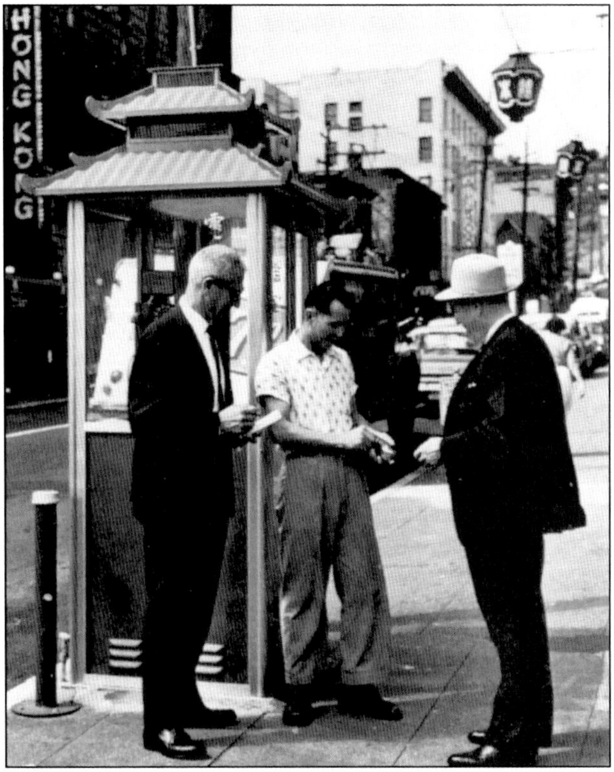

The majority of new immigrants came to America for economic reasons. Chinese refugees from Vietnam have been lured by economic opportunities in America since 1975, as have immigrants from Cuba, Jamaica, and other Caribbean islands. (Immigration and Naturalization Services Annual Report, 1963.)

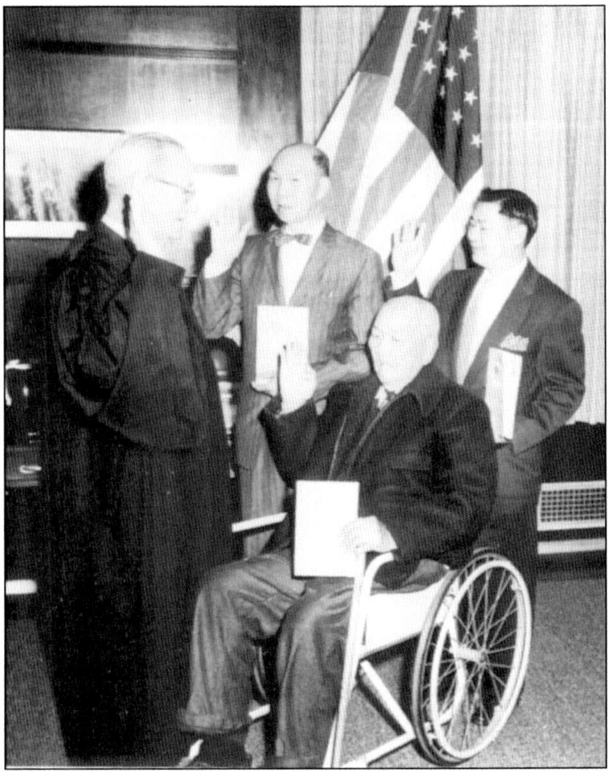

In addition to laboring immigrants, a large number of professionals, the better-educated and the wealthier from China, Taiwan, Hong Kong, and Southeast Asia, have also arrived since 1965. Seen here are three generations of a Chinese family being sworn in as U.S. citizens in the chambers of a federal district judge. (Immigration and Naturalization Services Annual Report, 1962.)

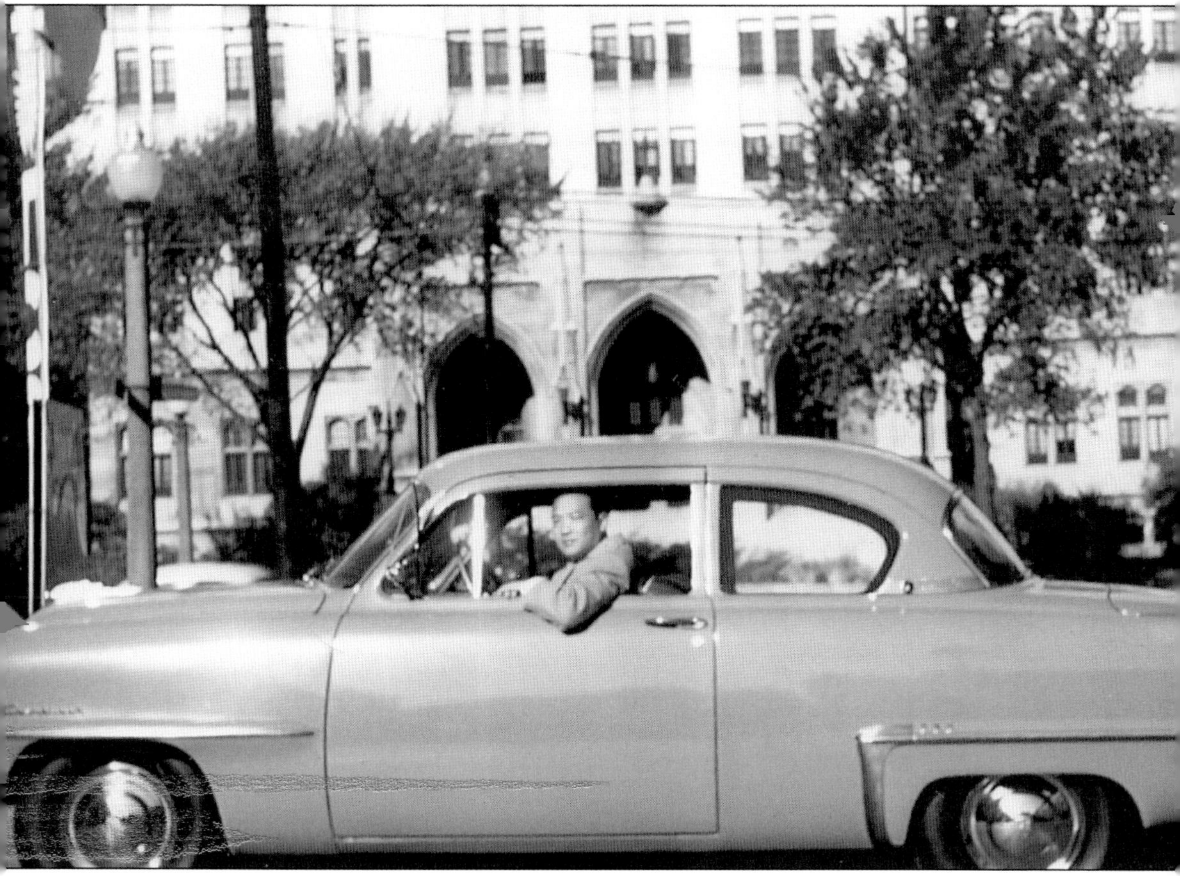

Life for the newly arrived professionals in St. Louis differed from that of their earlier counterparts. They were hired by mainstream employers as doctors and engineers. Dr. Andrew Luh is shown in a Plymouth in front of Desloge Hospital (presently St. Louis University Hospital) in 1953. (Rose Luh.)

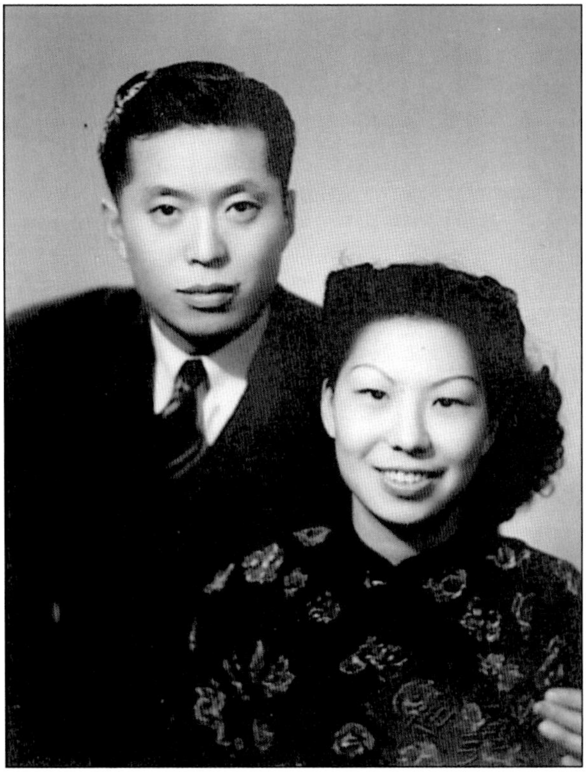

This wedding photograph was taken in Kunming where William Tao and Anne Tao were married. At that time, in 1943, William was the chief engineer at the China Transportation Company, which was responsible for the shipment of strategic material supplies from Burma to Kunming. (William Tao.)

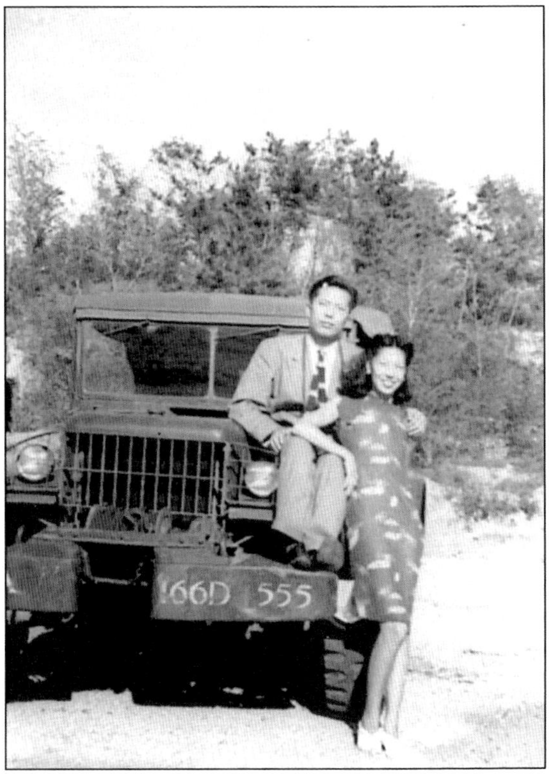

This photograph was taken with his wife, Anne, in Tsingtao in 1945 when William was assigned as chief engineer at the Tsingtao Rubber Work to take over the tire manufacturing plant from the Japanese immediately after the ending of the Second World War. (William Tao.)

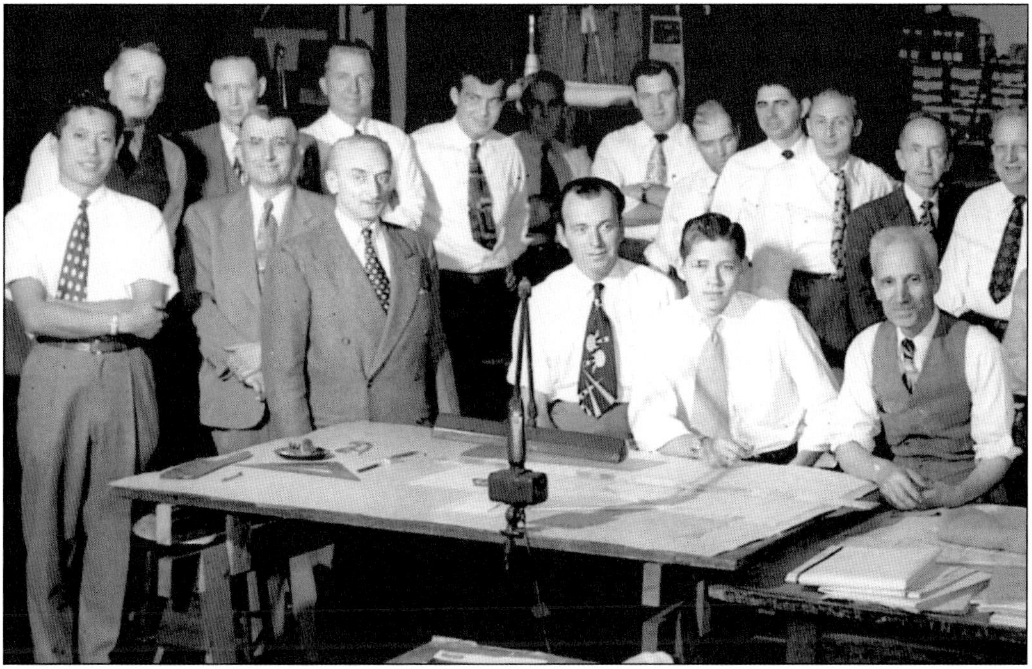

While a graduate assistant at Washington University, William found an evening job at the Board of Education of St. Louis, his first job in the United States. He was the first and only Chinese national to work in the engineering design field at this time; a fact that is reflected in the group pictured in 1948. William became a U.S. citizen in 1955.

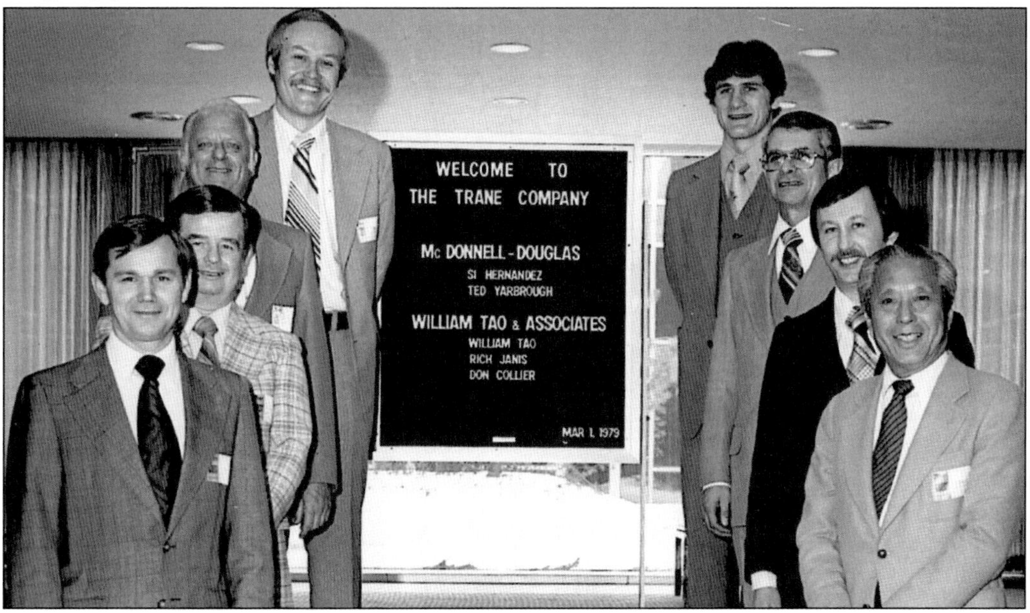

William started his private engineering design company, William Tao and Associates, in 1957. After struggling for several years, his consulting engineering company began establishing a reputation as a company with vision and creativity. The photograph shows a welcoming bulletin board for the executives of McDonnell and William Tao and Associates at a visit to the Trane Company in Wisconsin in 1979. (William Tao.)

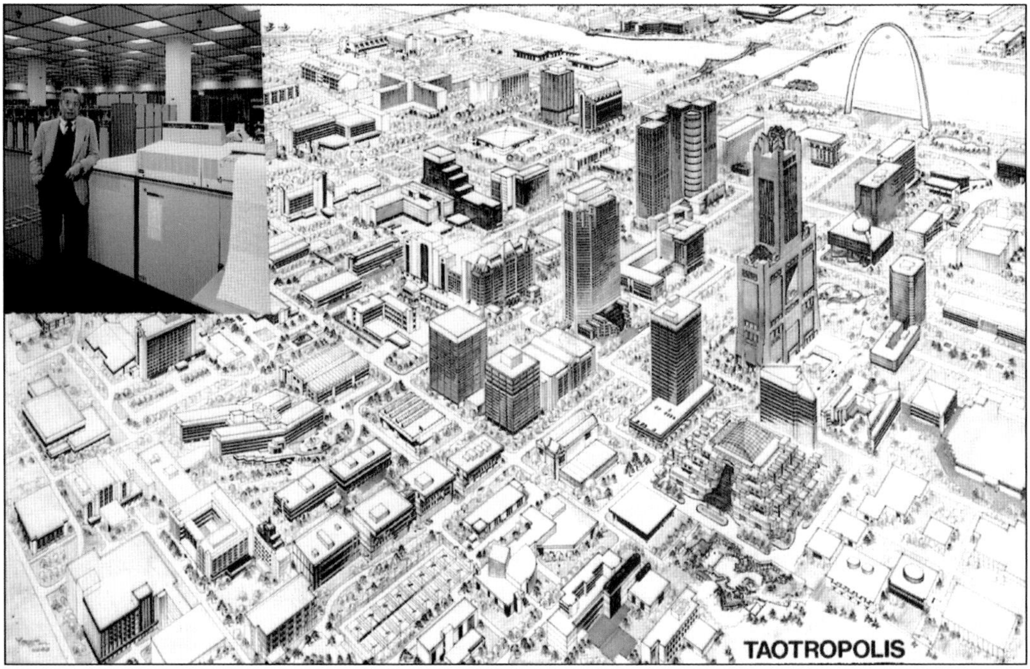

William Tao transferred his engineering company to the employees in 1989. The architectural rendering, which he named the Taotropolis, is a composite of major projects in the United States and overseas for which William Tao and Associates is responsible for the design of mechanical and electrical systems. The total project construction value is over $5 billion in terms of present value. (William Tao.)

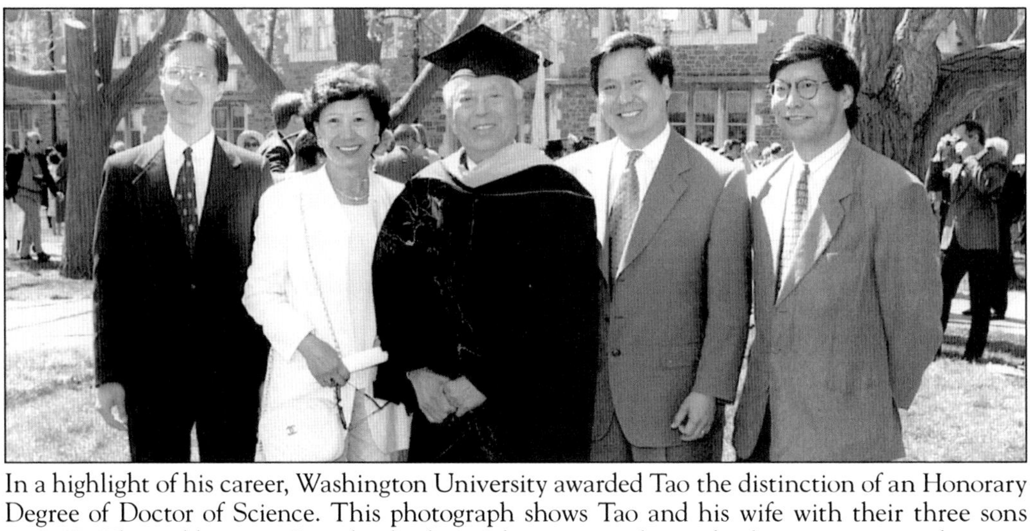

In a highlight of his career, Washington University awarded Tao the distinction of an Honorary Degree of Doctor of Science. This photograph shows Tao and his wife with their three sons in 1997. Their eldest son, David, who has a doctorate in biomedical engineering and is now director of planning at SMS Corporation in Philadelphia, is pictured on the far left. Their second son, Richard, who has a bachelor of arts degree in fine arts, is pictured second from right, and he is the president of May Design and Construction, the design subsidiary of the May department stores of United States. Their third son, Peter, who has a master of science degree in architecture, is pictured at the far right, and he is now the president of an architecture firm, Tao and Lee, started by him and his wife in St. Louis. (William Tao.)

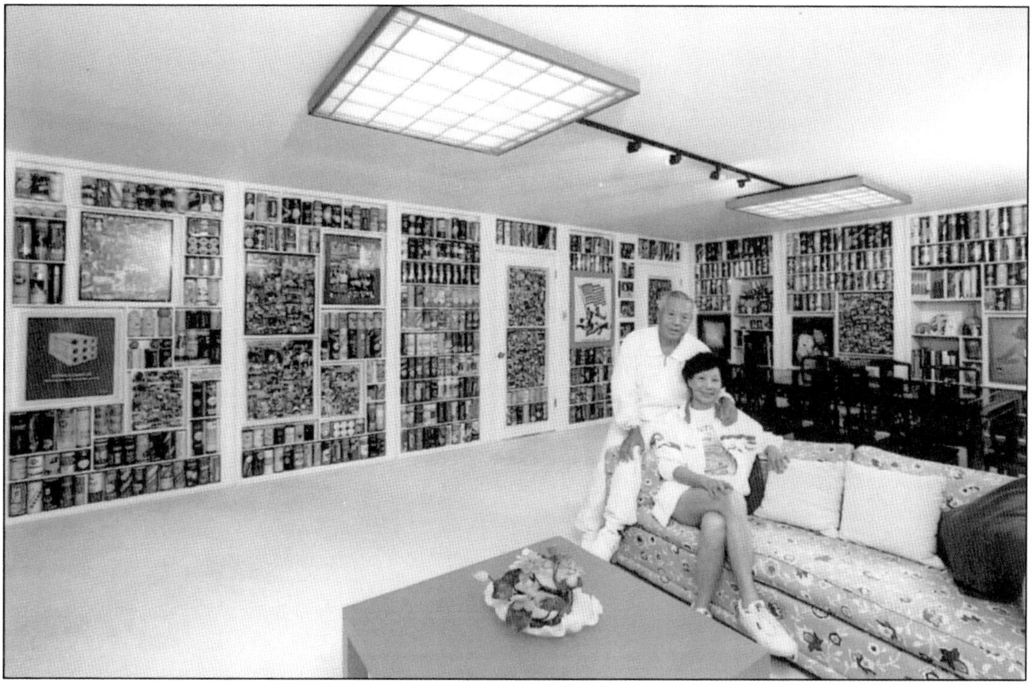

During the last three decades, William and his wife have traveled as goodwill ambassadors on the People-to-People tennis team to more than 100 cities and countries all over the world. This photograph, taken at home in St. Louis in 1995, illustrates the tennis ball collection from these overseas trips. (William Tao.)

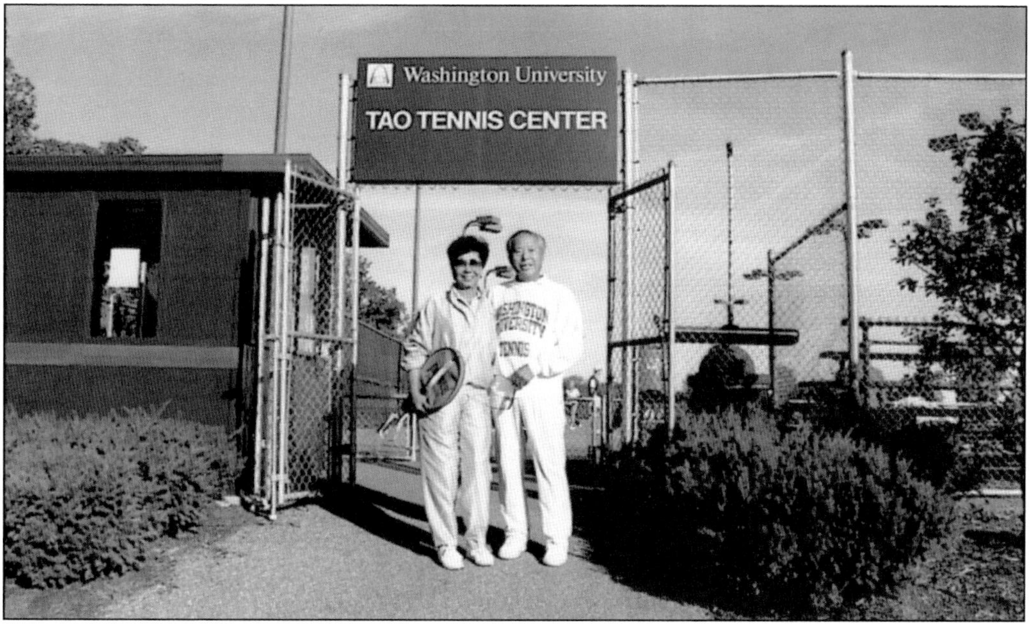

As recognition of William's volunteering effort and financial contributions, Washington University named its tennis facility the Tao Tennis Center in 1994. (William Tao.)

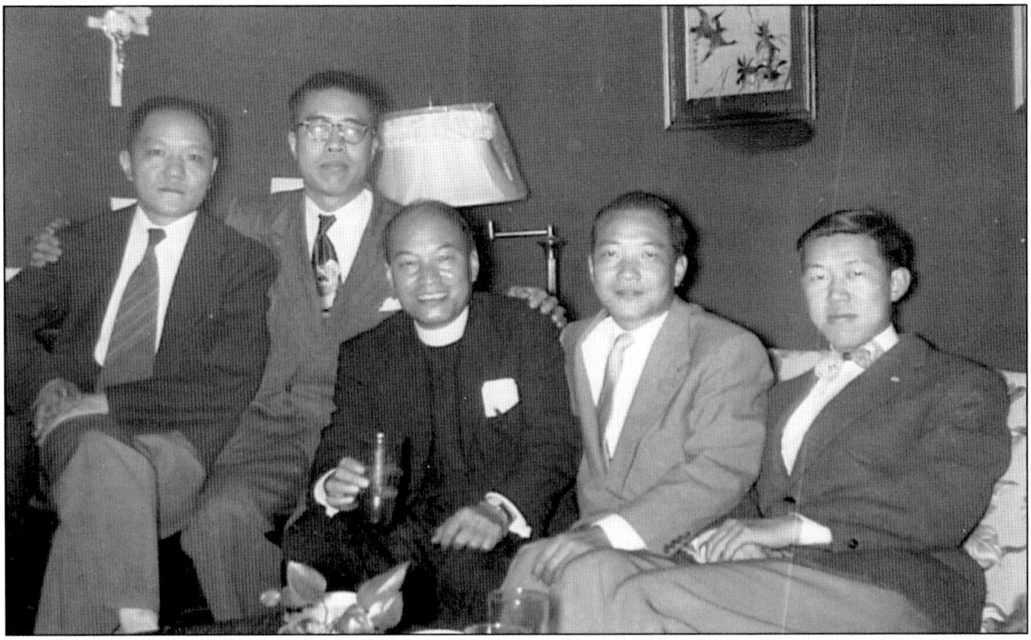

Tao was later followed by three physicians: Dr. Andrew Luh, a graduate of Zhendan University in Shanghai and an orthopedics surgeon; Dr. Louis Yuan, also a graduate of Zhendan University and an anesthetist and surgeon; and Dr. Jerome T. Y. Shen, a graduate of St. John's University in Shanghai and a pediatrician. All came to St. Louis to pursue further medical training in the medical school at St. Louis University and the local hospitals. Pictured here from left to right are Dr. Louis Yuan, Dr. Jerome Shen, Father Lee, Dr. Andrew Luh, and Yu Yong-nian. (Rose Luh.)

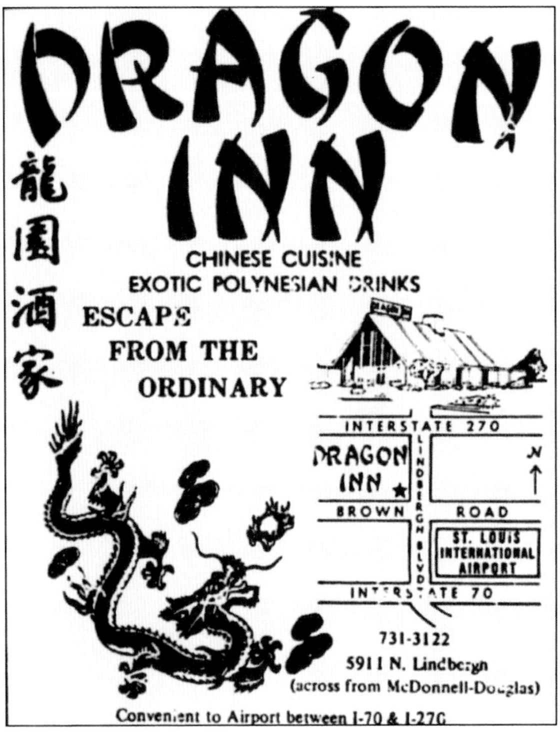

In the postwar time, the Chinese economy changed from laundry business to food service and related retailing industries. This advertisement for the Chinese restaurant Dragon Inn appeared in the magazine *St. Louis*, in August 1978. (Olin Library at Washington University.)

Five

A New Economy

While the old Chinese settlement around Hop Alley was disappearing, a new suburban Chinese American community had been quietly, yet rapidly emerging since the 1960s. In the next few decades, the ethnographic distribution changed considerably with more Chinese residing in St. Louis County, which constitutes the suburban municipalities in the south and west areas outside of St. Louis city. The U.S. censuses indicate that the number of suburban Chinese Americans increased from 106 (30 percent of the total Chinese in the St. Louis area) in 1960, to 461 (80 percent of the total) in 1970, 1,894 (78 percent of the total) in 1980, and 3,873 (83 percent of the total) in 1990. Since 1990, the Chinese population in the Greater St. Louis area has increased rapidly to 9,120 according to the U.S. census of 2000. Various unofficial estimates, however, show the figure to be between 15,000 and 20,000, with an overwhelming majority scattered in suburban communities and constituting 1 percent of the total suburban population of the St. Louis metropolitan area. The majority of the Chinese professionals have been employed at public and private institutions of higher education and in private companies as professors, engineers, computer programmers, technicians, and administrative managers. A few larger employers of the city—the Monsanto Chemical Company, Washington University, and the University of Missouri at St. Louis—have hired many of the professionals. Meanwhile, the students are largely enrolled at Washington University and St. Louis University.

While the majority of Chinese professionals were hired by larger employers and many others settled in medium- or small-sized companies, few entered business as self-employed entrepreneurs, simply because of the risks and uncertainties in running a business. Some individuals with courage and energy, however, broke the employment pattern for Chinese professionals and independently ventured into the business world. The new ethnic economy of the Chinese community has become more diversified than its earlier counterparts that centered in the traditional service industries of laundry and restaurants, it embraces not only a growing and more competitive food service industry, but also the rapidly expanding nontraditional service industries of real estate, health, insurance, construction, architecture and design, legal consultation, accounting, automobile repair, and computer services.

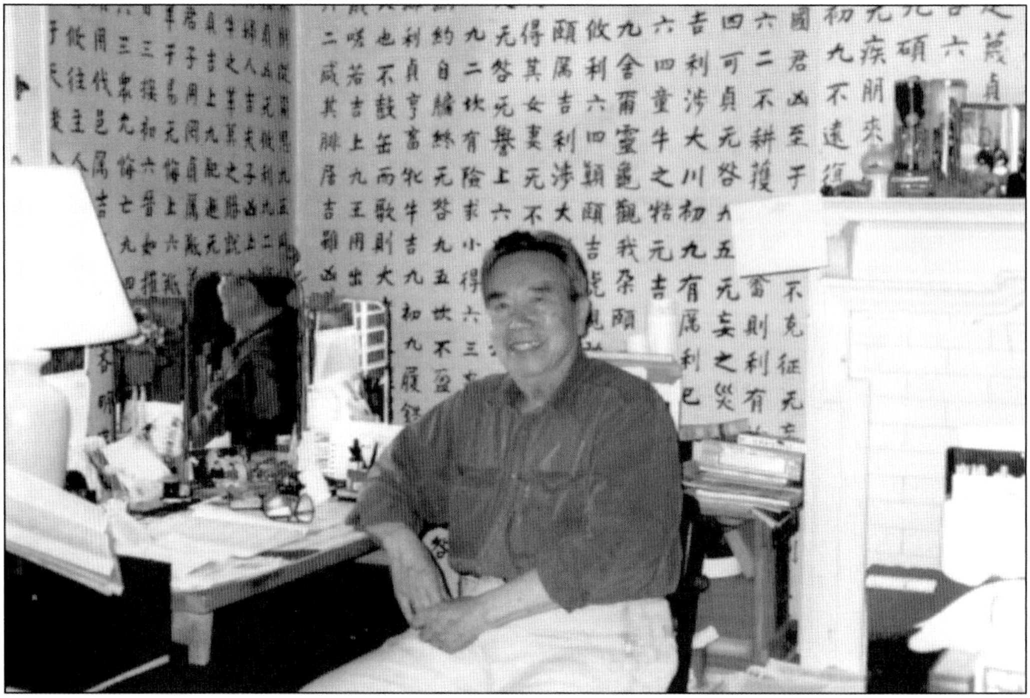

Nelson Wu (1919–2002), also known as Lu Qiao, a prominent artist, writer, and professor of art history at Washington University, is seen at home in St. Louis when interviewed by the author in 1999. In 1987, he was included in the Living Treasure program produced by the Public Broadcasting System, as one of the three most achieved artists in St. Louis—a pianist, a dancer, and a painter/calligrapher. The wallpaper in Wu's study shows Wu's calligraphy, on which he copied the Chinese classic *Yi Jing*. (Photograph by Huping Ling.)

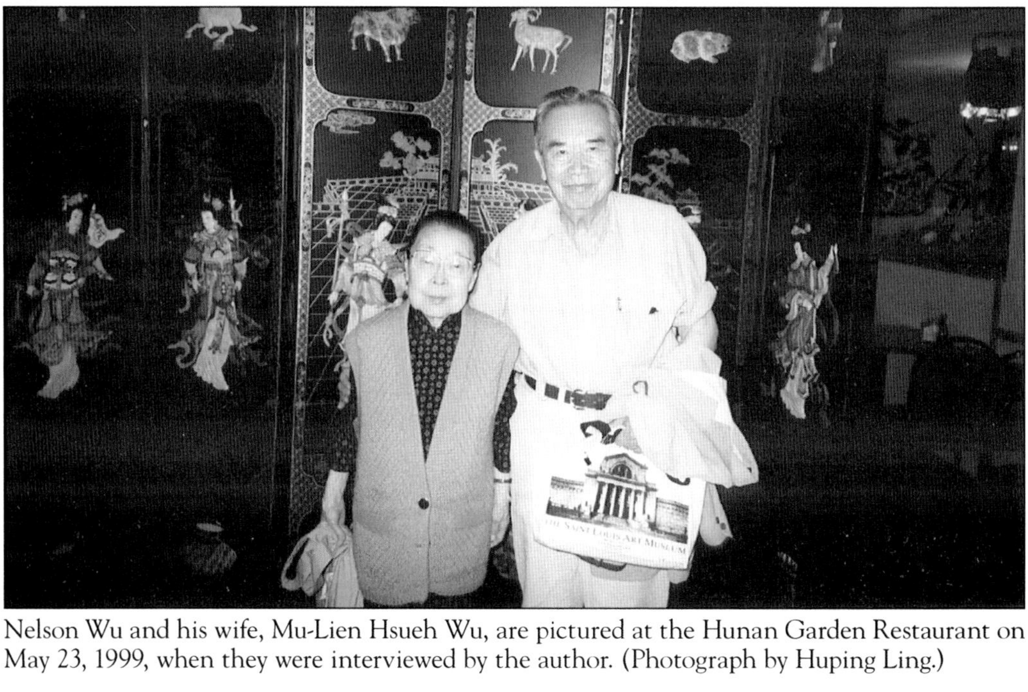

Nelson Wu and his wife, Mu-Lien Hsueh Wu, are pictured at the Hunan Garden Restaurant on May 23, 1999, when they were interviewed by the author. (Photograph by Huping Ling.)

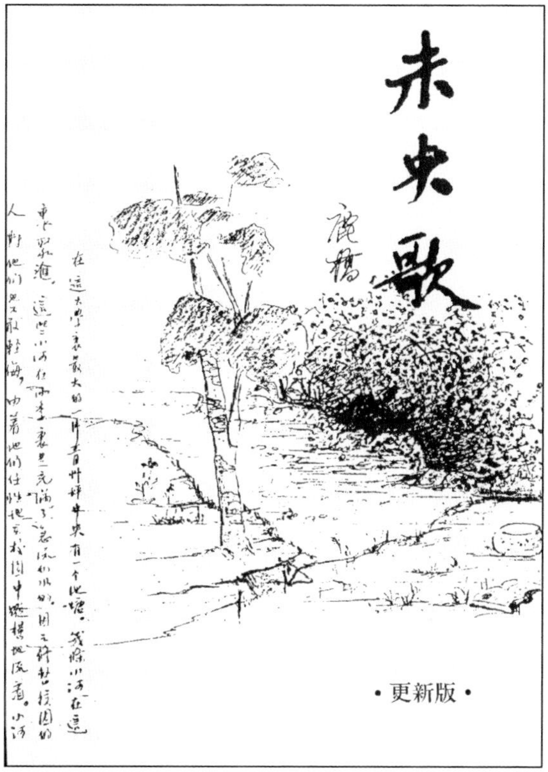

Nelson Wu entered Yale University in 1945 and earned his doctoral degree in art history in 1954. Nelson first taught at San Francisco State University, then at Yale University. In 1967, Nelson was employed by Washington University to teach art history. A prolific writer in Chinese and English, he published works in art history in English and wrote novels and prose in Chinese. Nelson's novels and collection of prose are widely circulated in Taiwan, Hong Kong, and China. (Author's collection.)

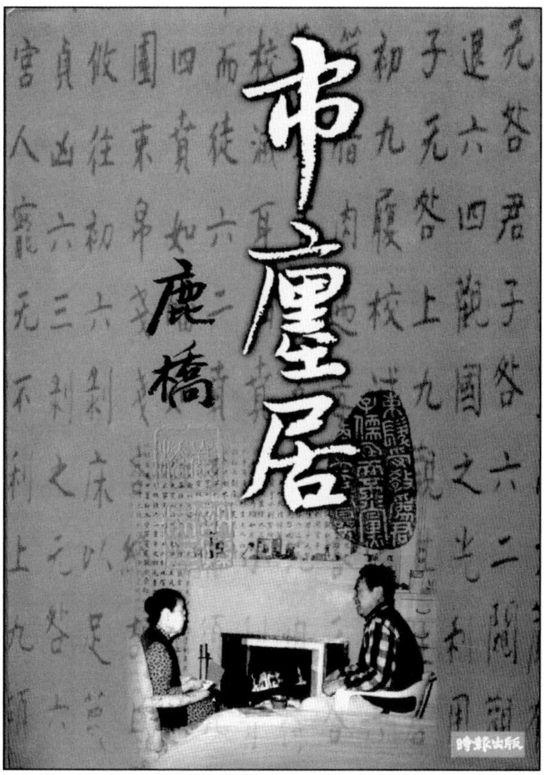

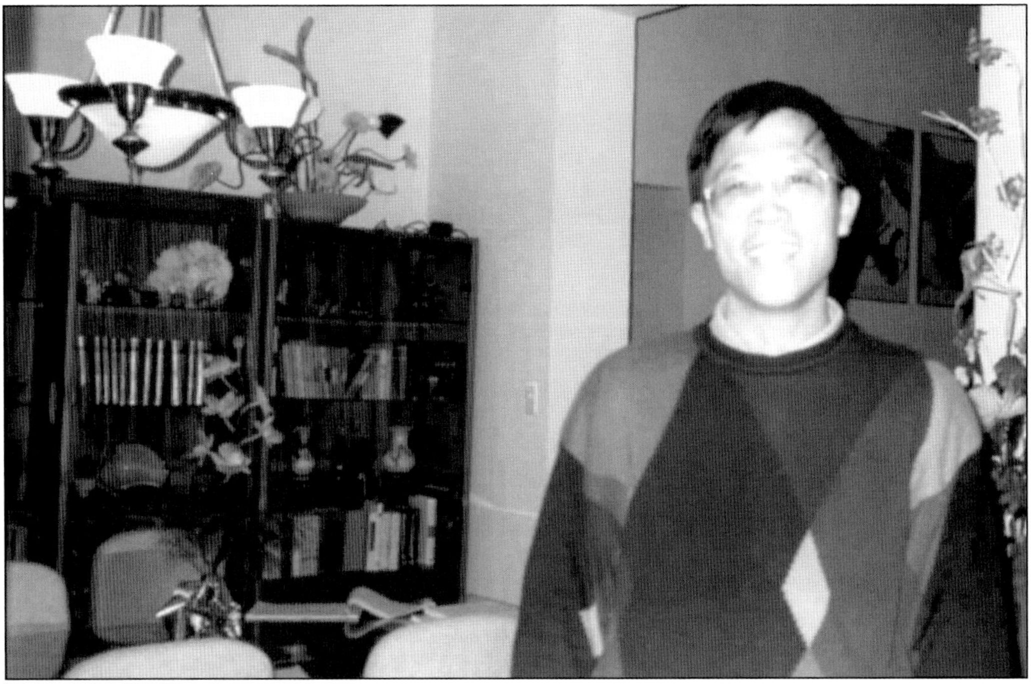

Most of the Chinese professionals were hired by the major employers of the area. Haiyan Cai, mathematics professor at the University of Missouri at St. Louis, is seen at home when interviewed by the author in 1999. (Photograph by Huping Ling.)

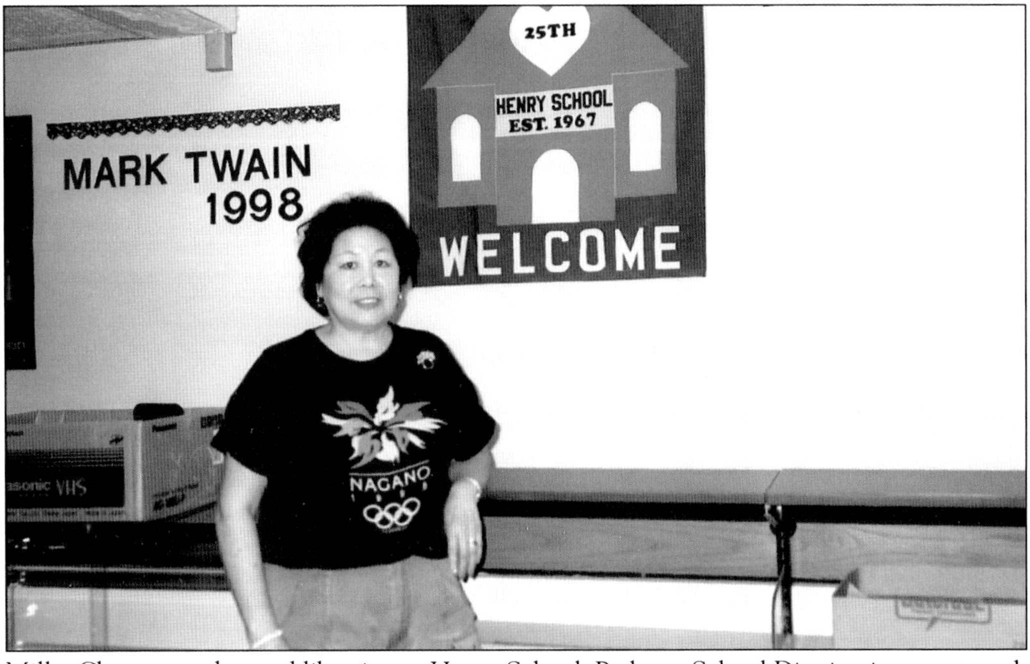

Miller Chow, a teacher and librarian at Henry School, Parkway School District, is seen at work when interviewed by the author on June 2, 1999. In 1937, after they had lived in St. Louis for six years working in a hand laundry, Chow's parents went to Earle, Arkansas, where they owned two grocery stores. (Photograph by Huping Ling.)

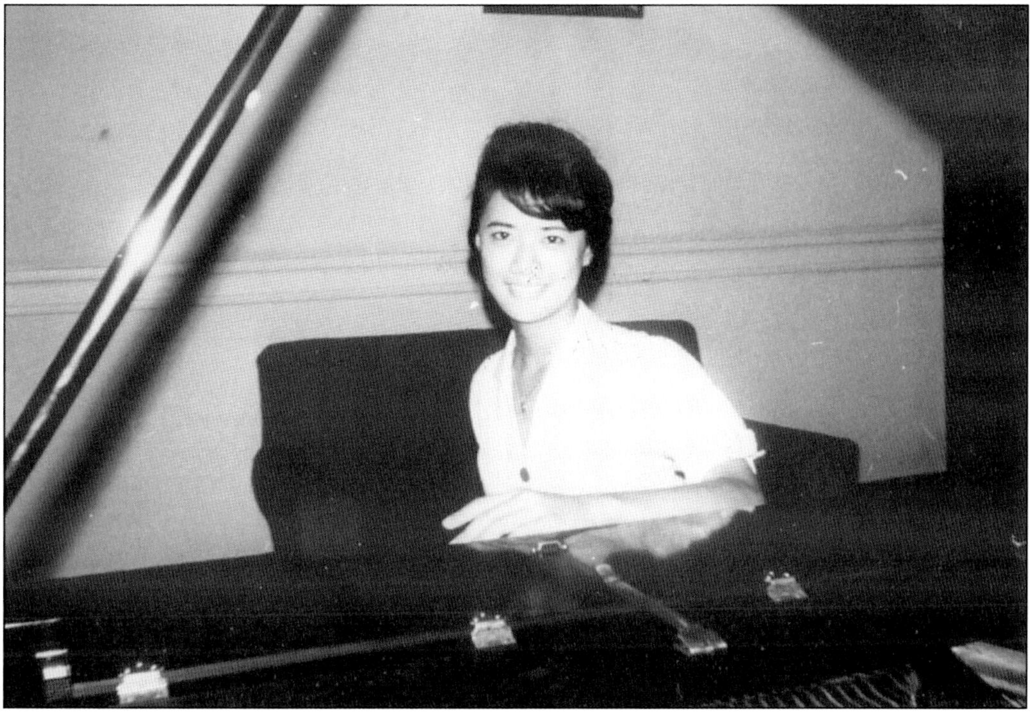

Grace Chen Yin was born in Taiwan and trained in the United States as a pianist. She taught at Peabody Observatory in Baltimore, Maryland, and has lived in St. Louis since 1998 when her husband, Frank Yin, was hired as the founding chair of the Biomedical Engineering Department at Washington University. In the image above, Grace is pictured at the New England Conservatory of Music in Boston in 1965. In the image below, Grace is pictured at home when interviewed by the author on September 8, 1998. (Above, Grace Yin; below, photograph by Huping Ling.)

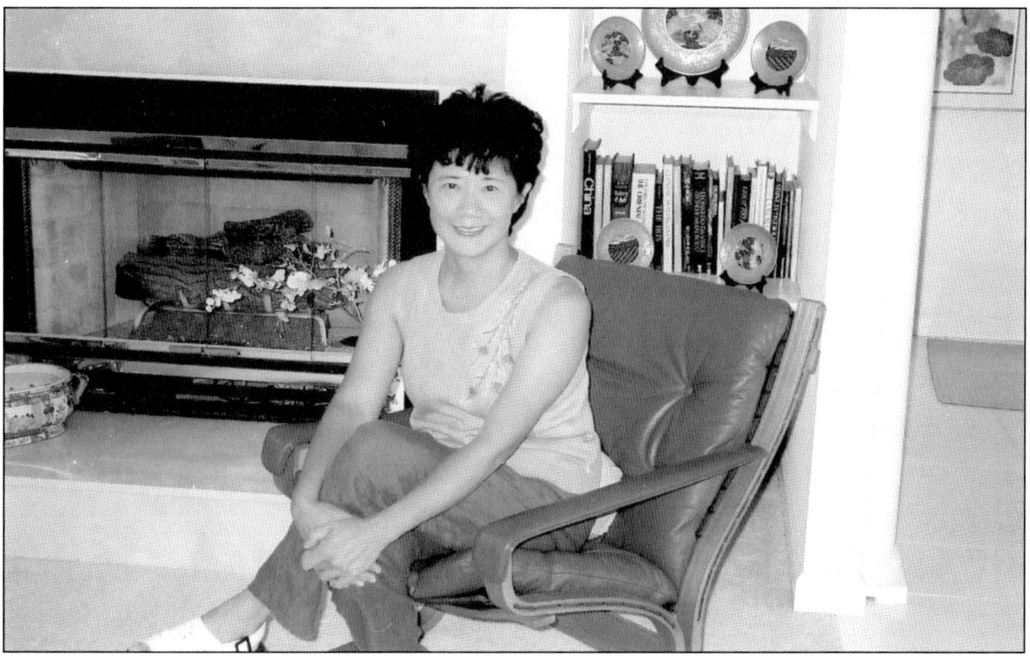

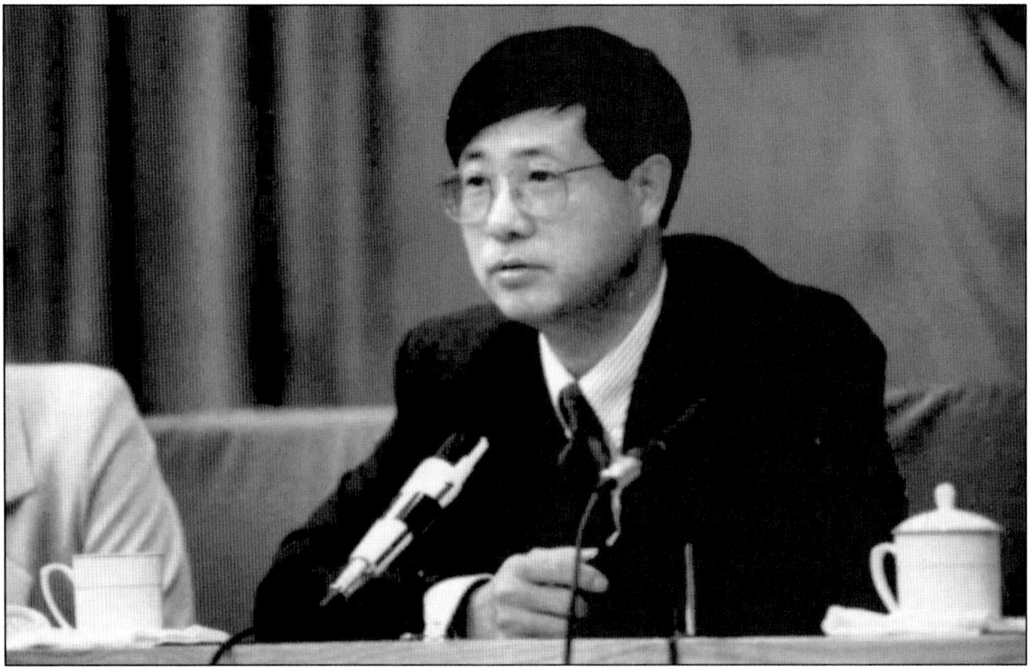

Chinese professionals not only entered into academia, but also the legal profession. Zhihai Liang received advanced training in English in China but he chose to attend St. Louis University Law School in 1987 and started his own law firm in 1992. Liang, an attorney, is pictured speaking at an international conference in Beijing in 1990. (Zhihai Liang.)

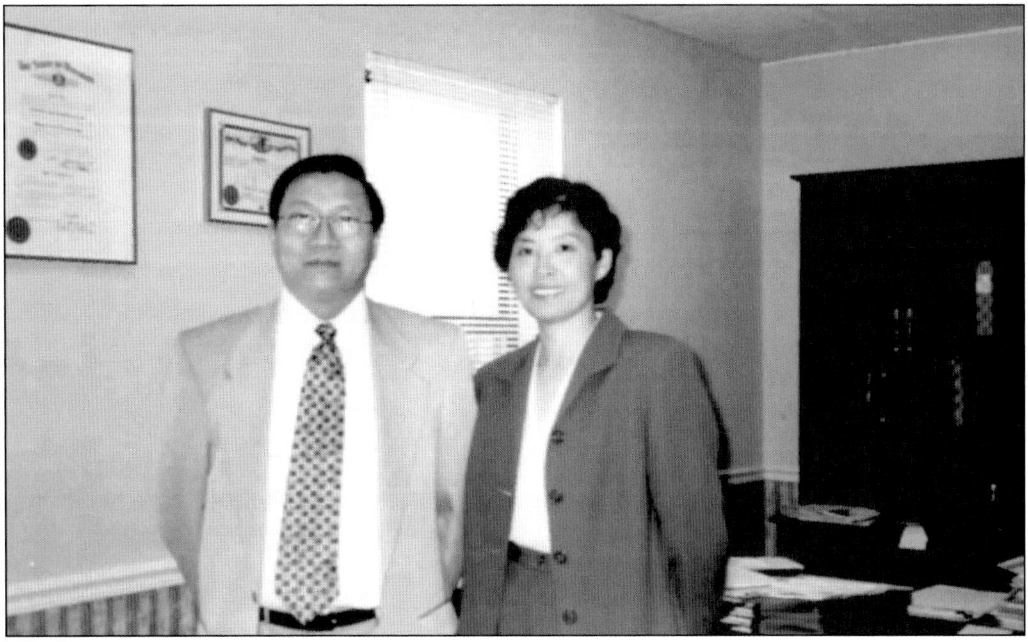

Tony Gao is another example of a successful Chinese lawyer. Gao came to the United States in 1988 to study law at the St. Louis University Law School and graduated in 1991. He started his own legal practice in 1994. Gao is pictured with his wife, Wubing Zong, in his law firm at 8011 Clayton Road in 1999. (Photograph by Huping Ling.)

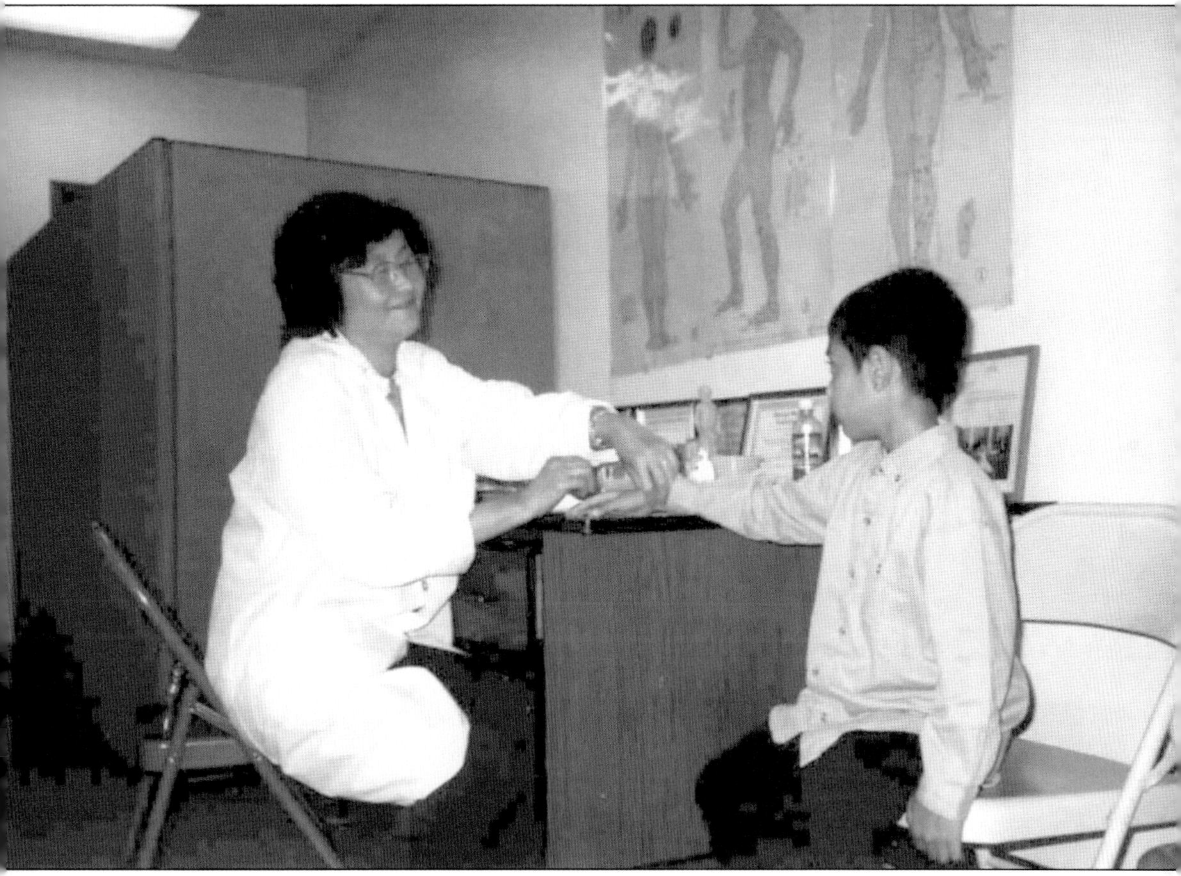

Xinsheng Jiang graduated from Beijing Medical University in 1970 and was a physician in the department of neurology at the Hospital of Beijing Medical University for 14 years. In 1988, she came to the United States as a postdoctoral fellow. In 1997, Jiang started an acupuncture practice in the back of the Oriental Ginseng and Gift Shop at 8146 Olive Boulevard. Jiang is photographed here in 2000, when interviewed by the author. (Photograph by Huping Ling.)

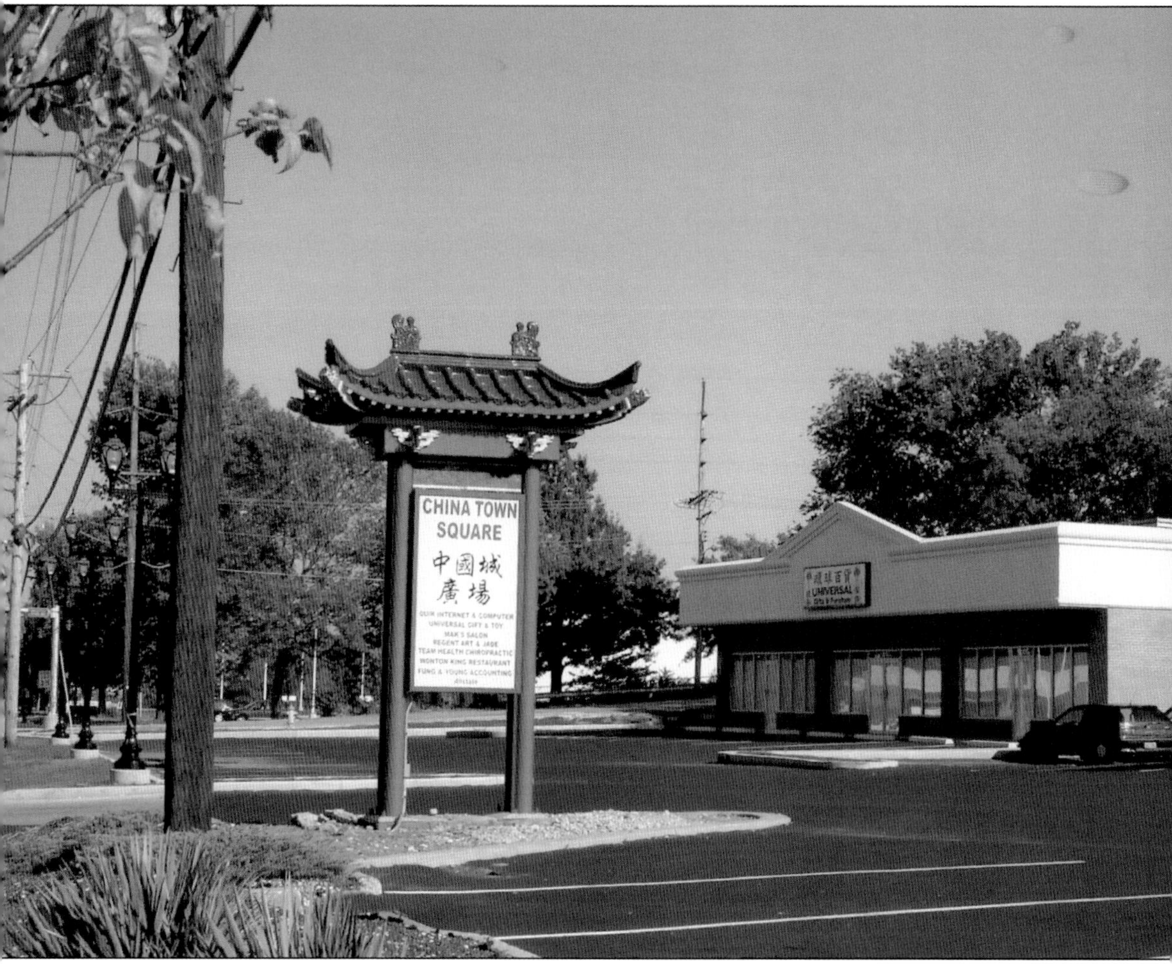

The economy of the St. Louis Chinese since the 1990s has been more diversified. While the food service industry has rapidly grown and continued to remain the primary sector of the Chinese American economy, other nontraditional Chinese service businesses have also joined and further expanded the ethnic economy. Chinatown Square, at Olive Boulevard and Eighty-second Street, is pictured on September 16, 2006. (Photograph by Huping Ling.)

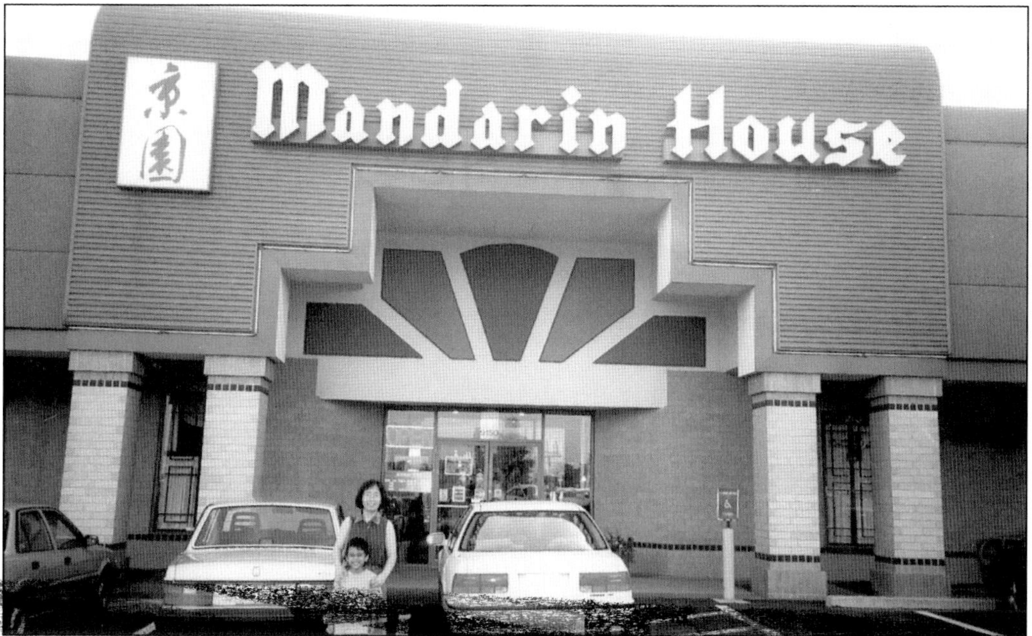

The Mandarin House restaurant at 9150 Overland Plaza is pictured in 1999. One of the large Chinese restaurants in St. Louis, it serves primarily northern Chinese cuisine as well as popular Chinese American dishes. It has 11,000 square feet and can serve 350 guests at one time. Many individual families order wedding banquets in the restaurant and community organizations also hold large celebrations of Chinese holidays here. (Photograph by Huping Ling.)

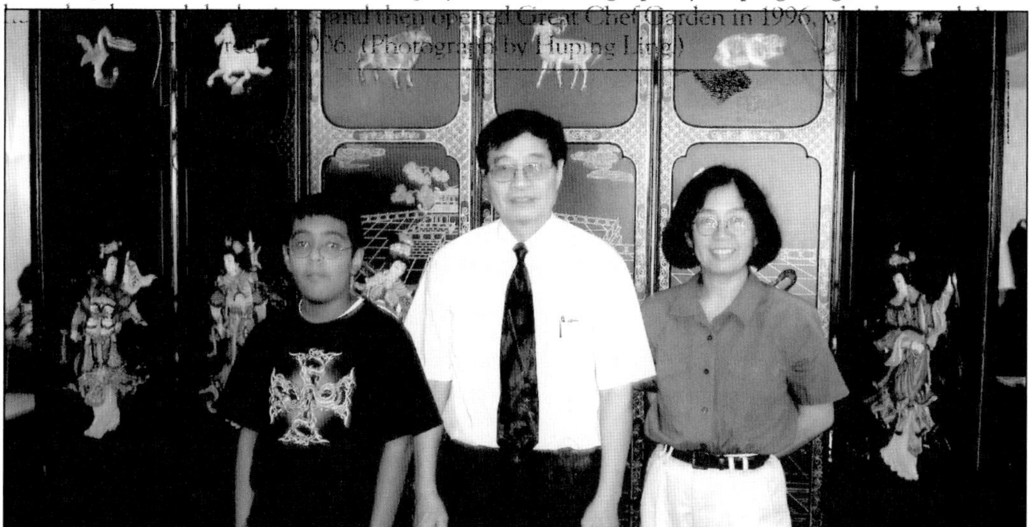

The Hunan Garden restaurant, located at 11532 Page Service Road, was another popular Chinese restaurant frequented by the locals. Owner Yee M. Kwong studied engineering in China and went to Hong Kong in 1965 where he worked as an engineer for four years. In 1969, Kwong and his wife came to St. Louis to join his father-in-law, a Chinese restaurant owner. He worked in Chinese restaurants throughout his years in St. Louis, first as a restaurant worker, later as an owner of his father-in-law's restaurant. Kwong is pictured at his restaurant with the author in 2005. (Author's collection.)

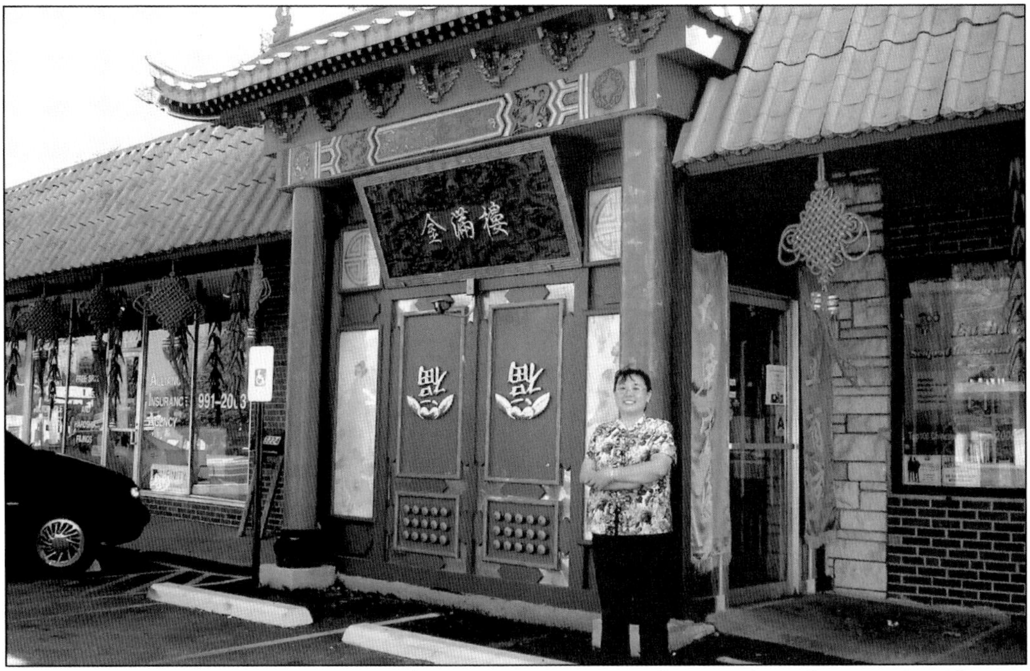

Jenny Lu is the owner of Lulu Seafood Restaurant at 8224 Olive Boulevard, a popular Chinese restaurant with national recognition. Lu came to St. Louis to join her husband in 1991. Although with a degree in economics from Tongji University, she could only find a job in a Chinese restaurant. Lu and her husband first bought a Chinese restaurant in downtown St. Louis in 1994 where they learned the business and then opened Great Chef Garden in 1996, which served dim sum buffet. Lu is pictured in 2006. (Photograph by Huping Ling.)

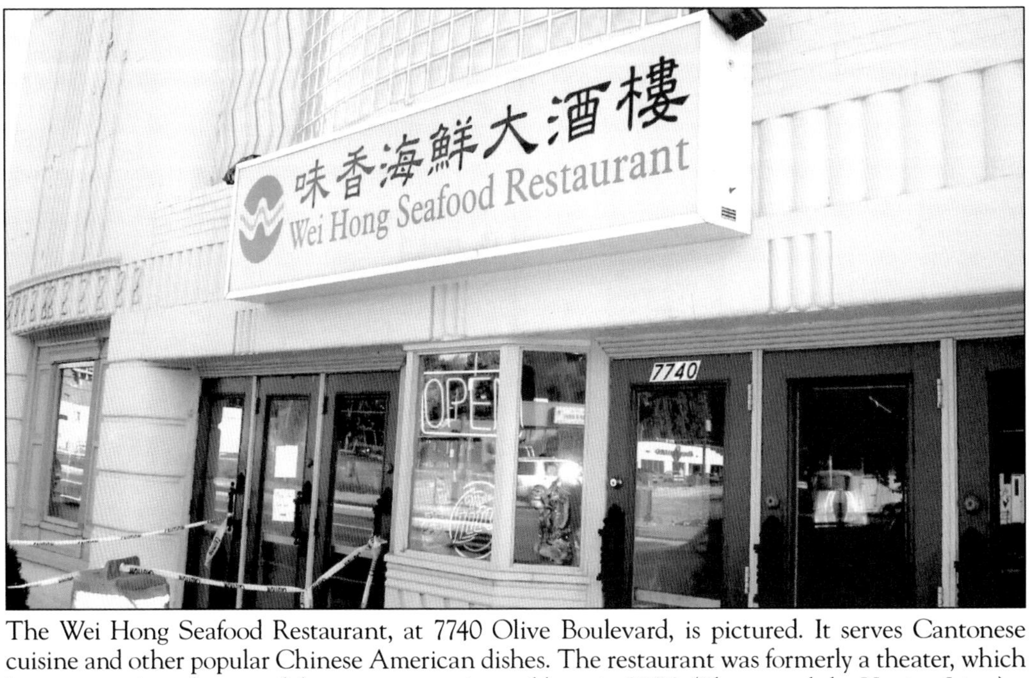

The Wei Hong Seafood Restaurant, at 7740 Olive Boulevard, is pictured. It serves Cantonese cuisine and other popular Chinese American dishes. The restaurant was formerly a theater, which became a unique feature of the restaurant, pictured here in 2006. (Photograph by Huping Ling.)

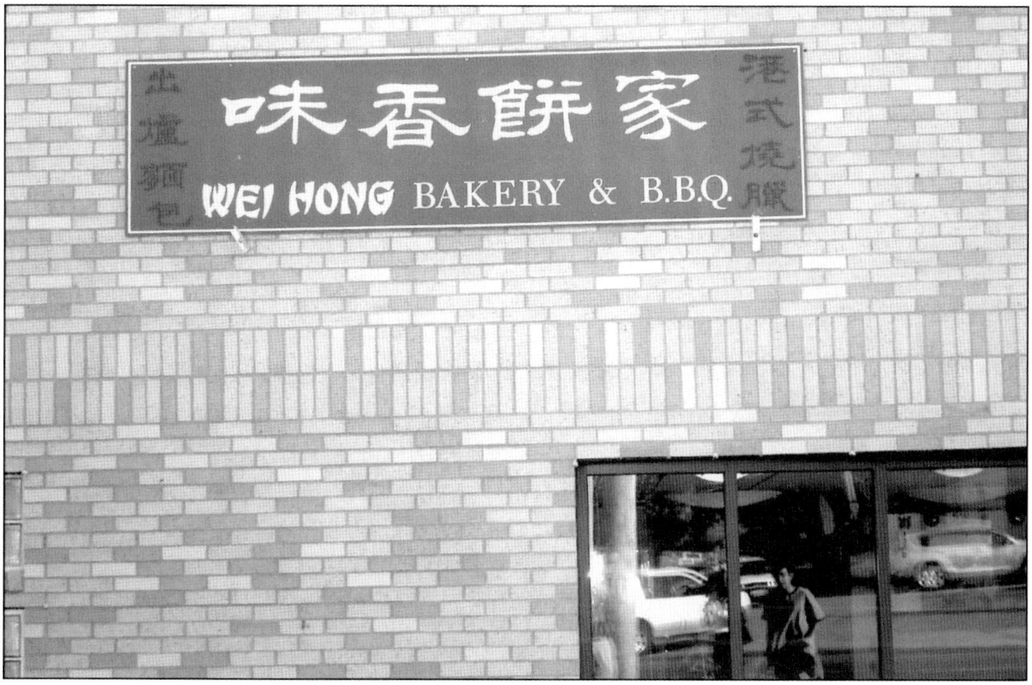

The Wei Hong Bakery and B.B.Q., at 7740 Olive Boulevard, is pictured in 2006. Owned by the owner of Wei Hong Seafood Restaurant, it is a popular bakery for the locals. (Photograph by Huping Ling.)

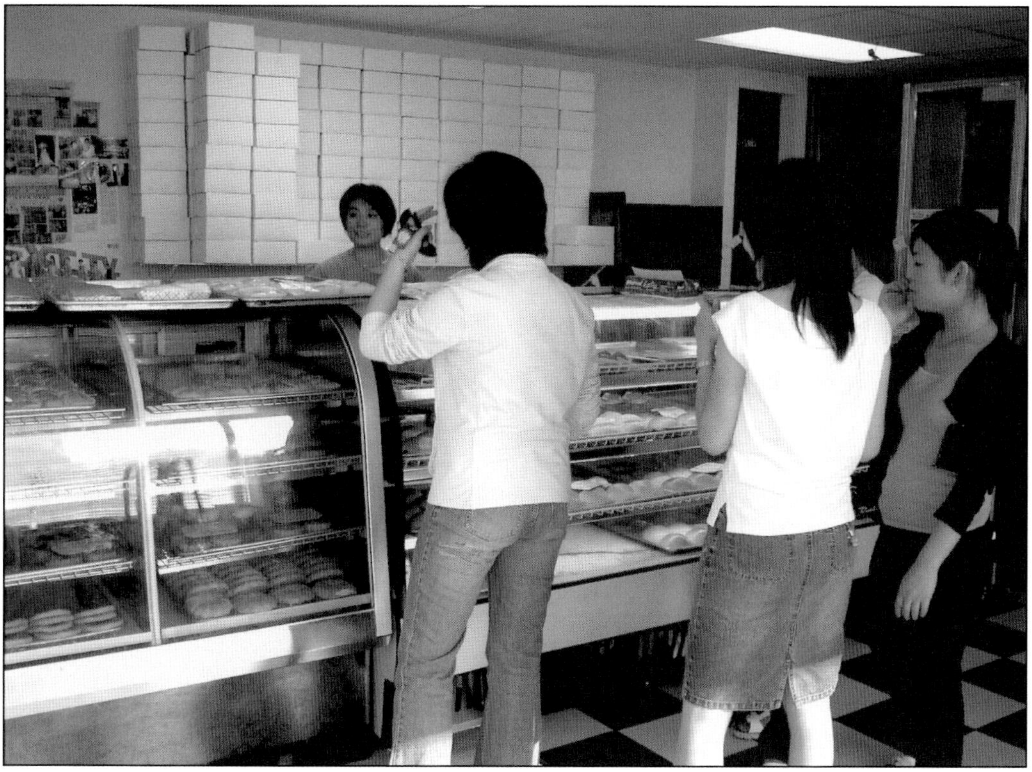

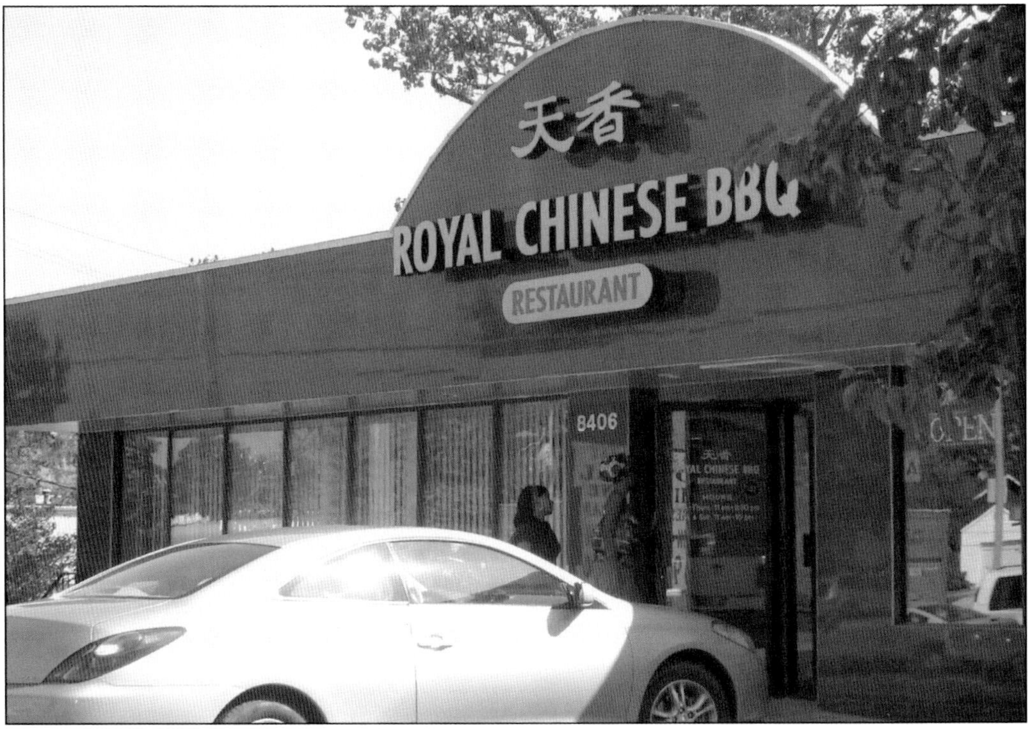

The Royal Chinese BBQ at 8406 Olive Boulevard is pictured in 2006. This popular Chinese restaurant has been frequented by both Chinese and non-Chinese St. Louisans. (Photograph by Huping Ling.)

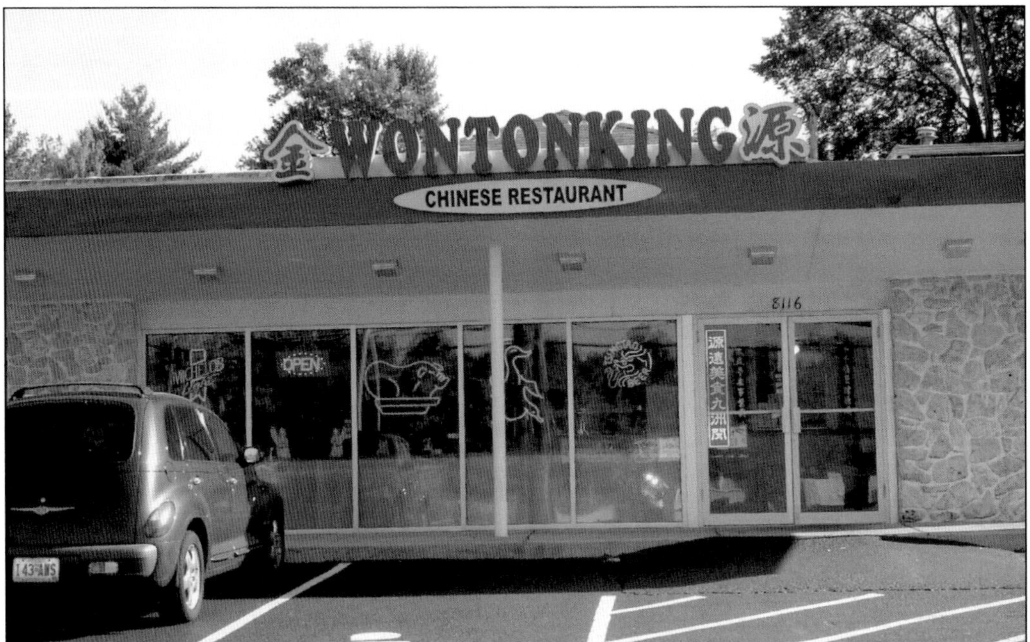

The Wonton King Chinese restaurant, at 8116 Olive Boulevard, is pictured in 2006. (Photograph by Huping Ling.)

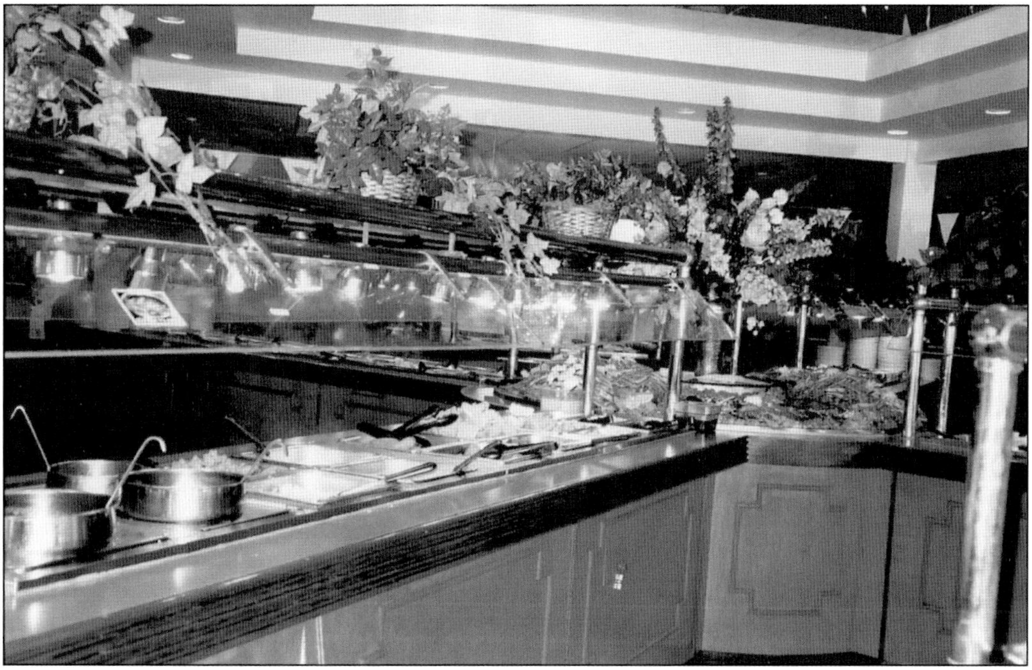

The management of Chinese restaurants can generally be divided into three categories: formal restaurants, buffet restaurants, and carryout or fast-food restaurants. The buffet restaurants range from large- to medium-sized and are usually located along major commercial roads, catering both to Chinese and non-Chinese diners. The image above shows the buffet line at Lee's Family Buffet, at 12277 Natural Bridge Road, in 1998. The image below shows the buffet counter at Great Chef Garden restaurant at 17 Nationalway Shopping Center in Manchester in 1999. (Photograph by Huping Ling.)

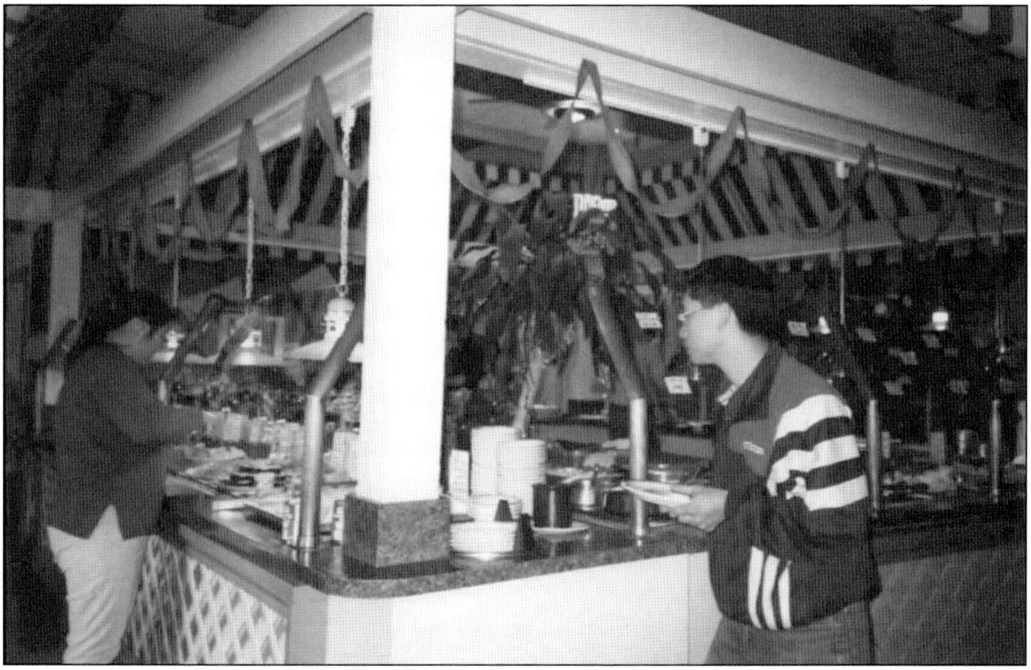

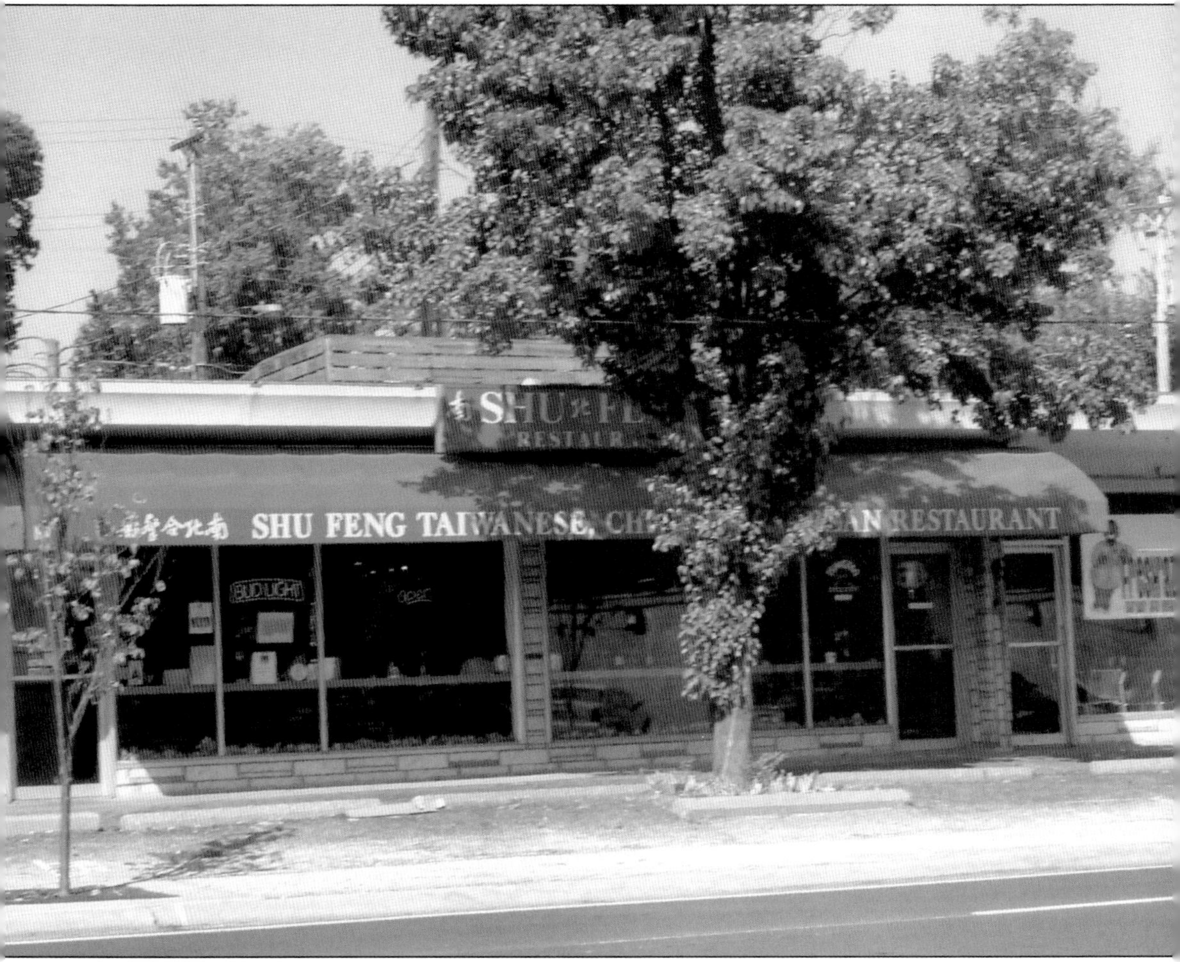

Shu Feng Taiwanese Chinese and Korean restaurant at 8435 Olive Boulevard, pictured in 2006, reflects the diverse background of the contemporary Chinese Americans in St. Louis, both in name and cuisines. (Photograph by Huping Ling.)

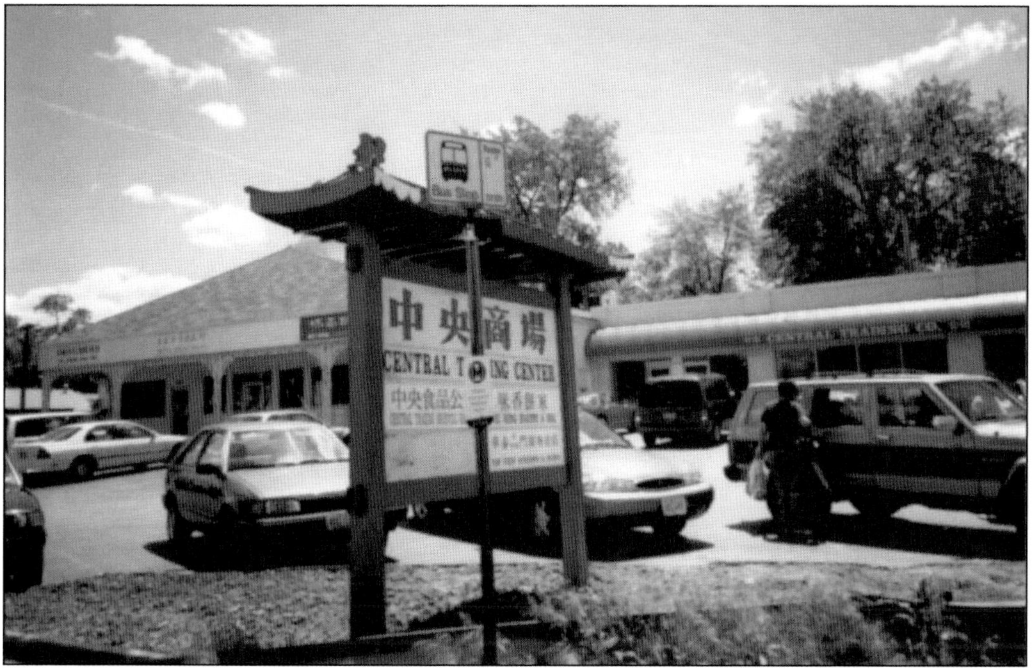

The grocer-wholesale business has trailed after restaurants as the second major traditional Chinese business. In 2003, there were 21 Chinese grocer-wholesalers in St. Louis. Unlike the Chinese restaurant business, the grocer-wholesale business has always displayed a tendency toward geographical concentration. Five Chinese grocer-wholesalers are operating businesses on Olive Boulevard. Central Trading Center, a shopping center with a number of Chinese businesses located at the 8200 block of Olive Boulevard, is pictured in 1999. (Photograph by Huping Ling.)

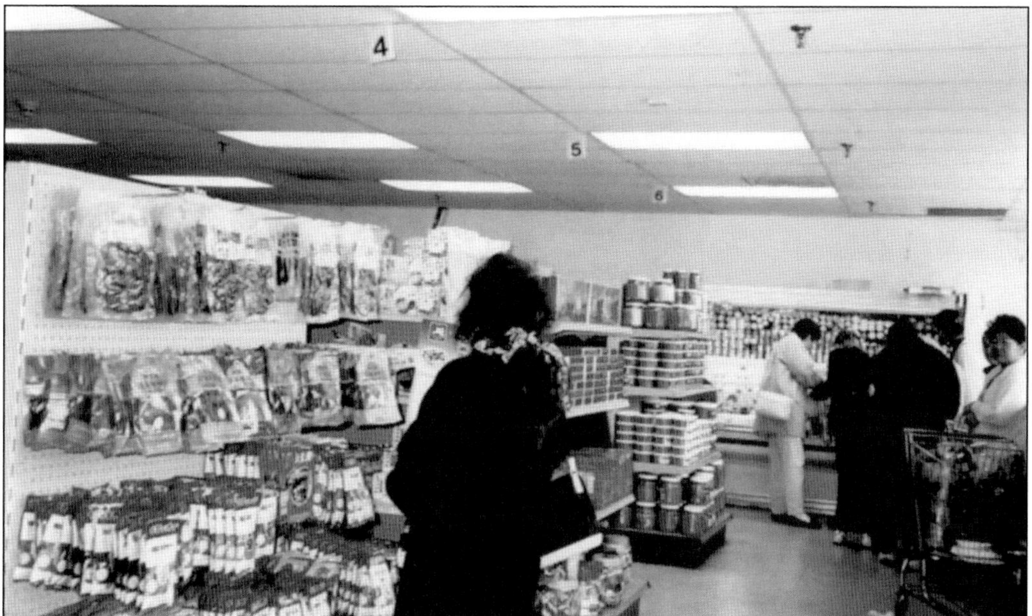

Central Trading Company, one of the busiest Chinese grocery stores, located at 8150 Olive Boulevard, is pictured in 2001. (Photograph by Huping Ling.)

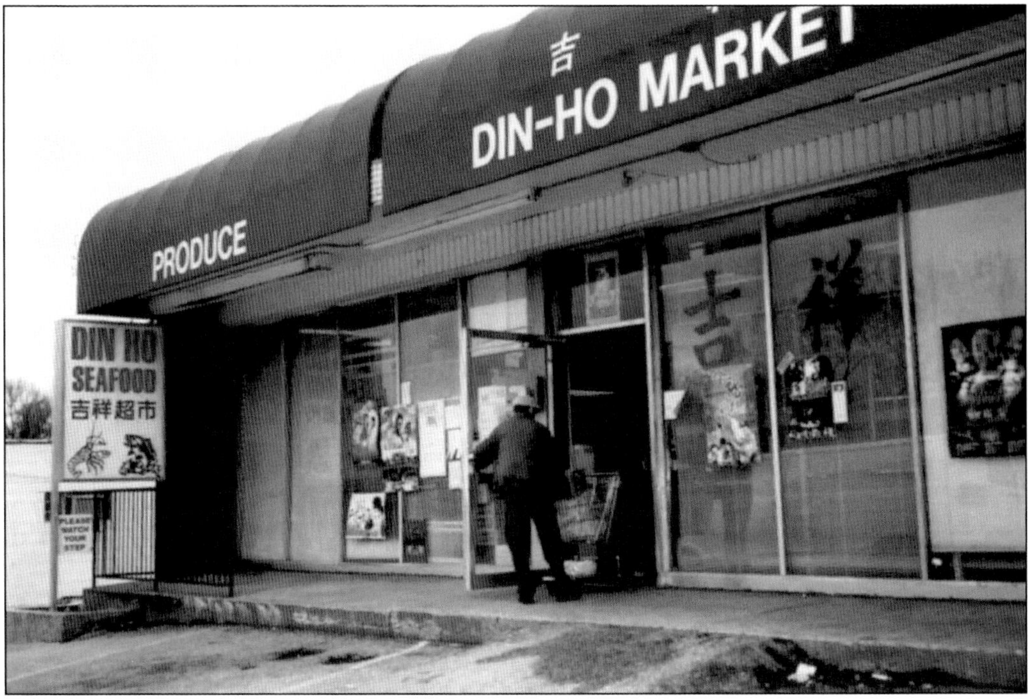

Ding-Ho Market, a Chinese grocery store located at 8324 Olive Boulevard, is pictured in 2001. (Photograph by Huping Ling.)

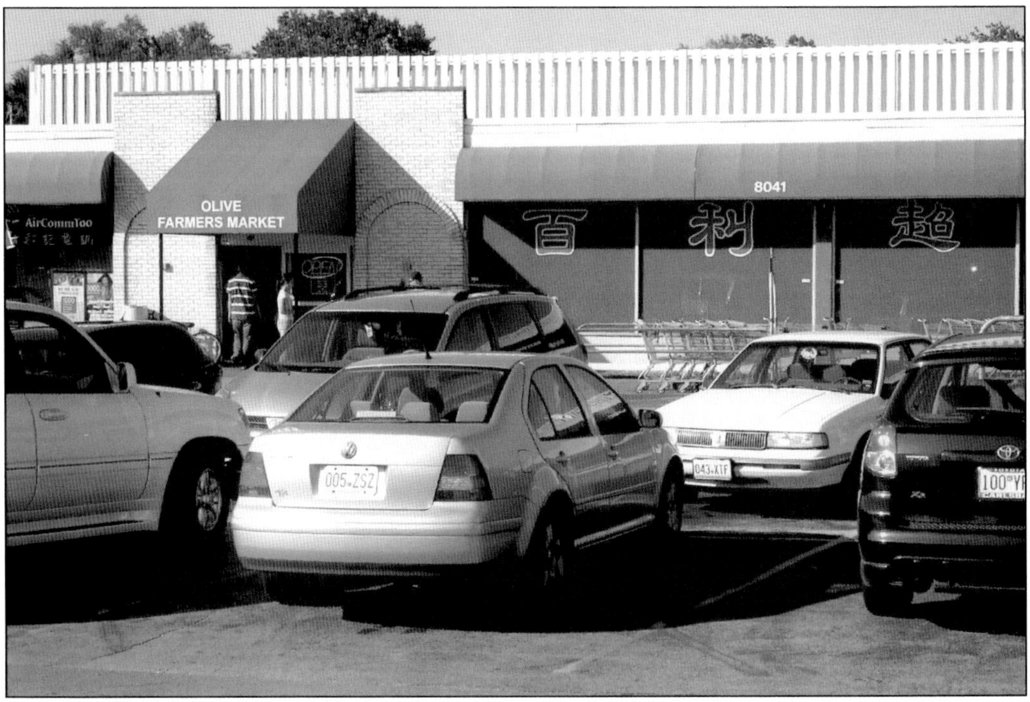

The Olive Farmers Market, located at 8041 Olive Boulevard, is a Chinese supermarket. Photographed in 2006, it attracts more customers than the traditional Chinese grocery stores. (Photograph by Huping Ling.)

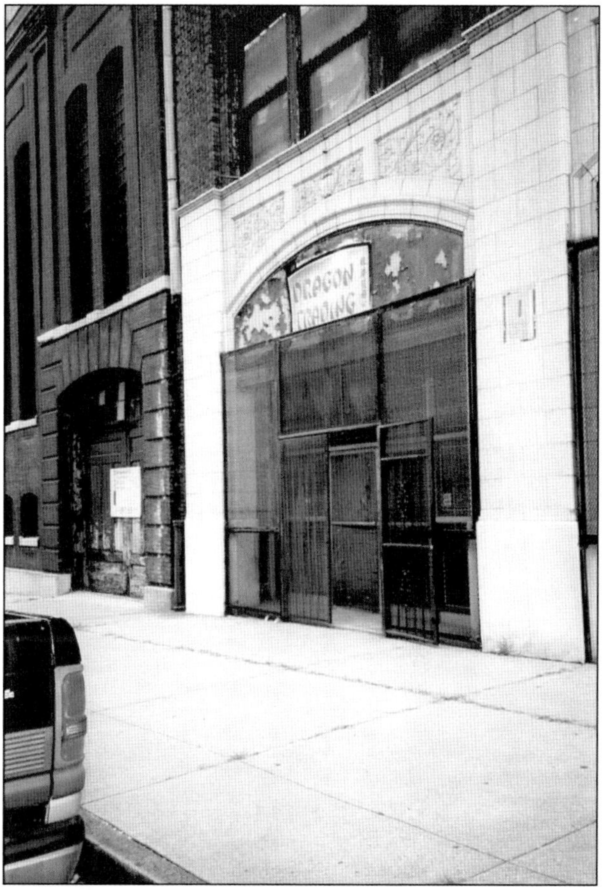

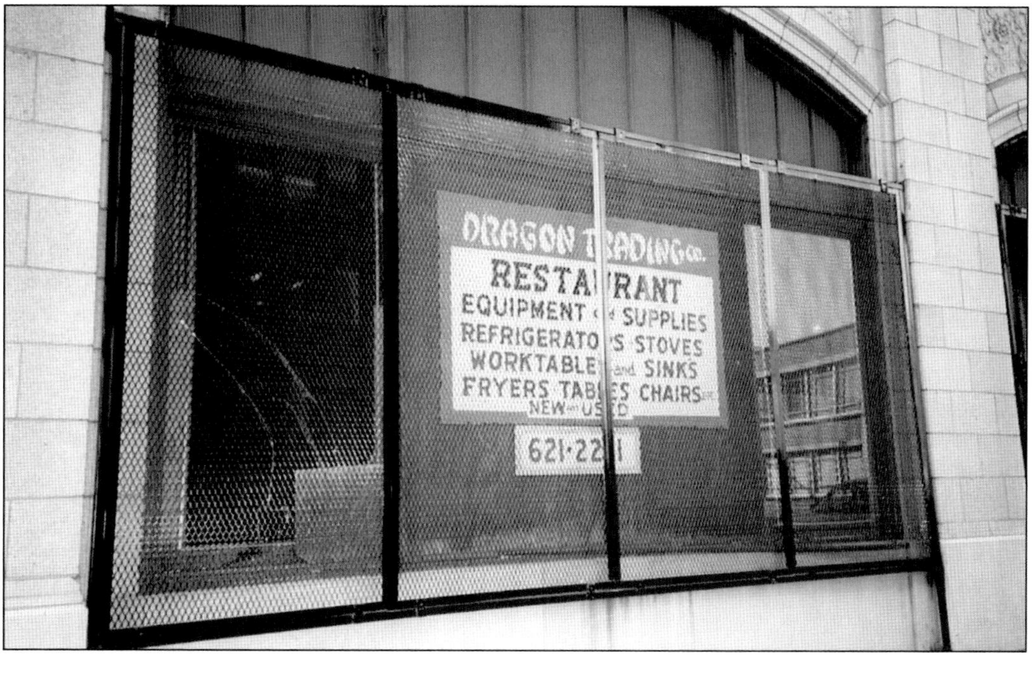

The Dragon Trading Company, a retail/wholesale restaurant equipment store located downtown at 1709 Locust Street, is pictured in 1998. Founded in 1995, it is the first and only restaurant equipment wholesale company in the state. The store is guarded with sturdy metal doors and windows. (Photographs by Huping Ling.)

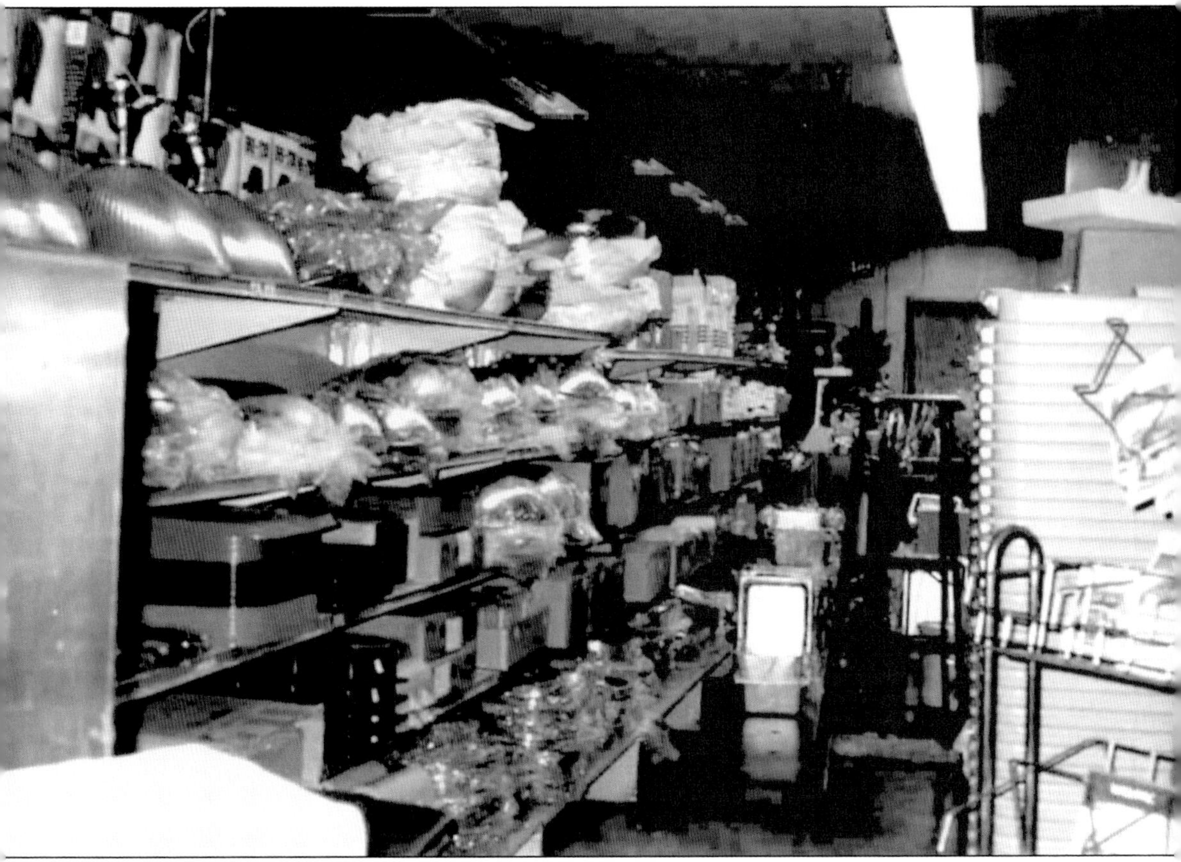

Initially a retail store, under the management of Don Ko (the owner) and his son Tom Ko, the store, pictured in 1998, evolved into a sizeable wholesale company with over 300 types of merchandise for wholesale and retail. (Photograph by Huping Ling.)

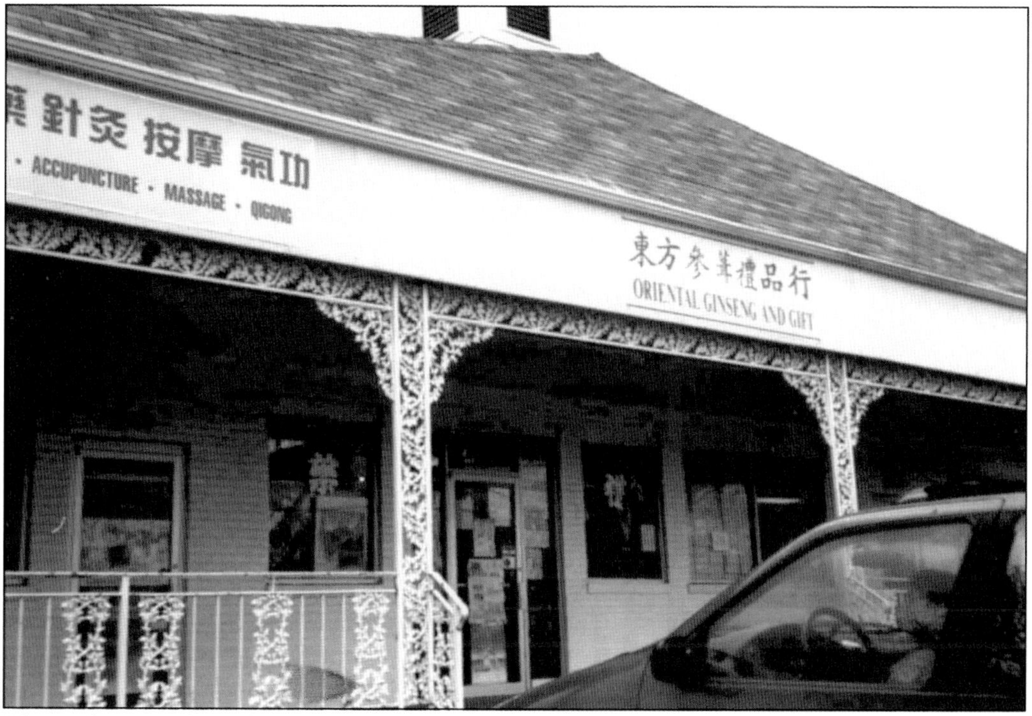

These photographs, taken in 2000, show the exterior and the inside of Oriental Ginseng and Gifts, located at 8144 Olive Boulevard. Owner Zheng Guojin is pictured at work when the author visited for an interview. (Photographs by Huping Ling.)

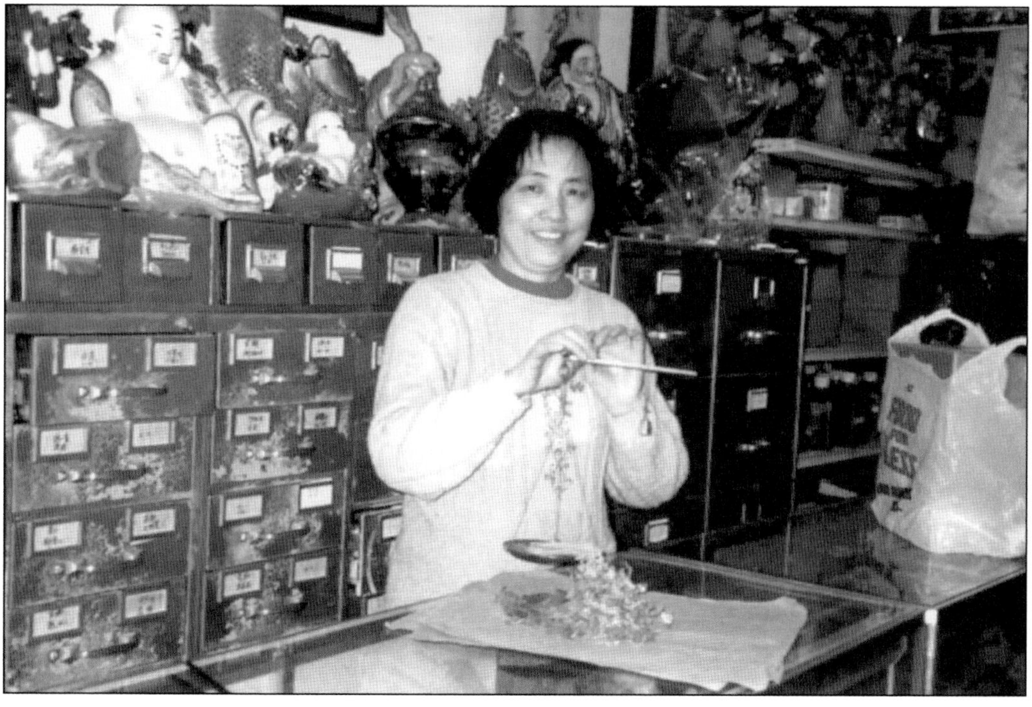

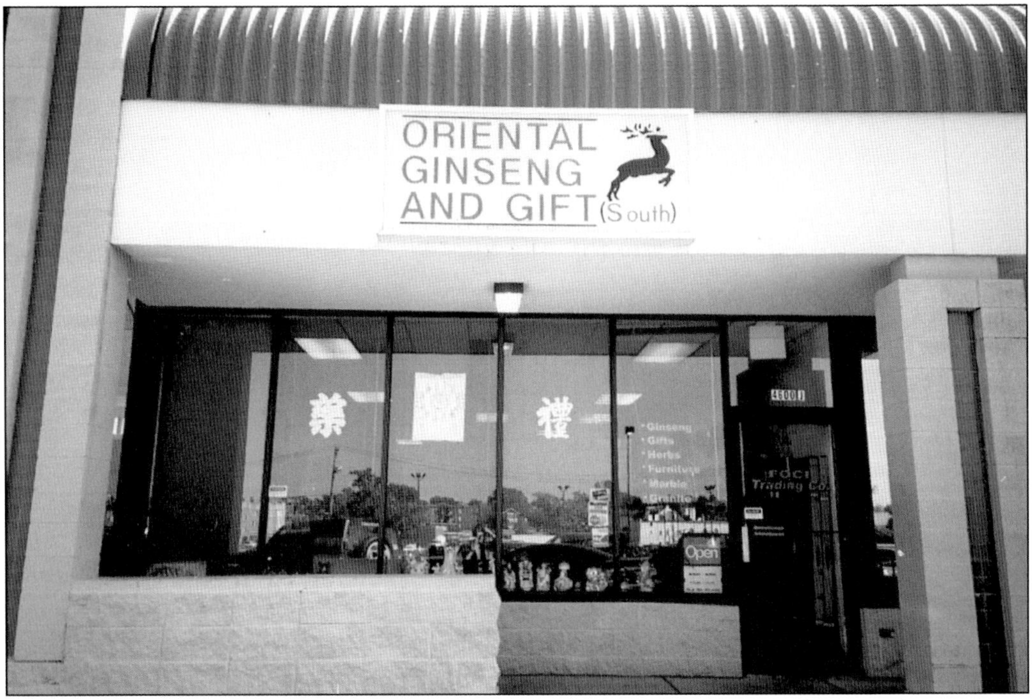

Oriental Ginseng and Gifts (south), located at 4600 Chippewa Street and pictured in 1998, is a branch of the Oriental Ginseng and Gifts that is located at 8144 Olive Boulevard. In addition to Chinese herbs and medicine, the store also carries Chinese furniture, artifacts, and gifts. (Photographs by Huping Ling.)

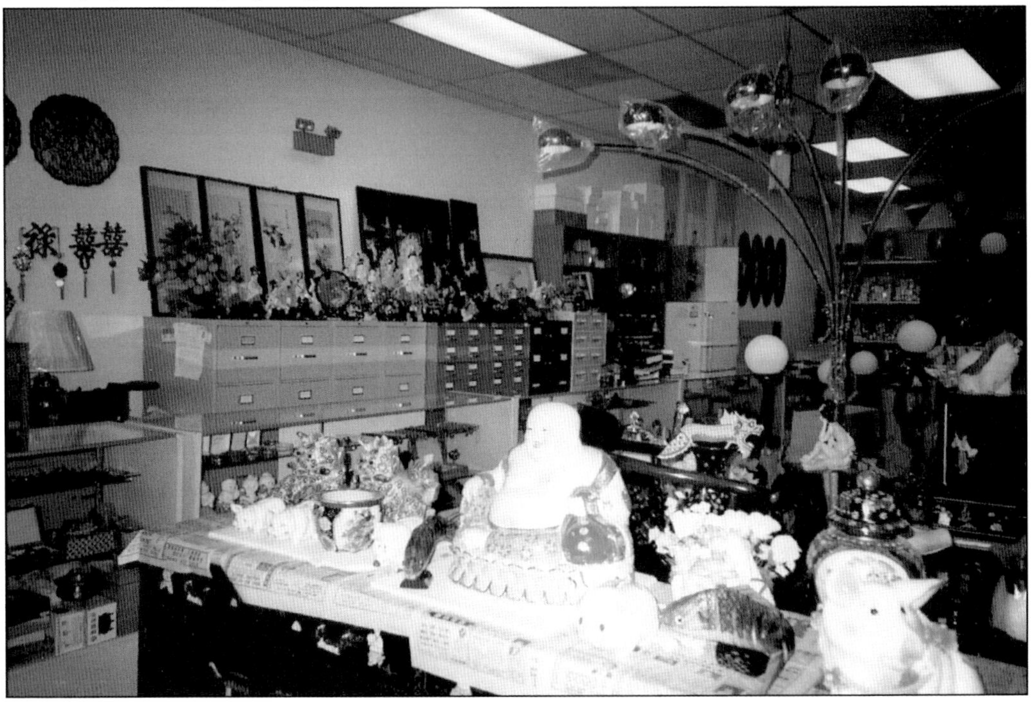

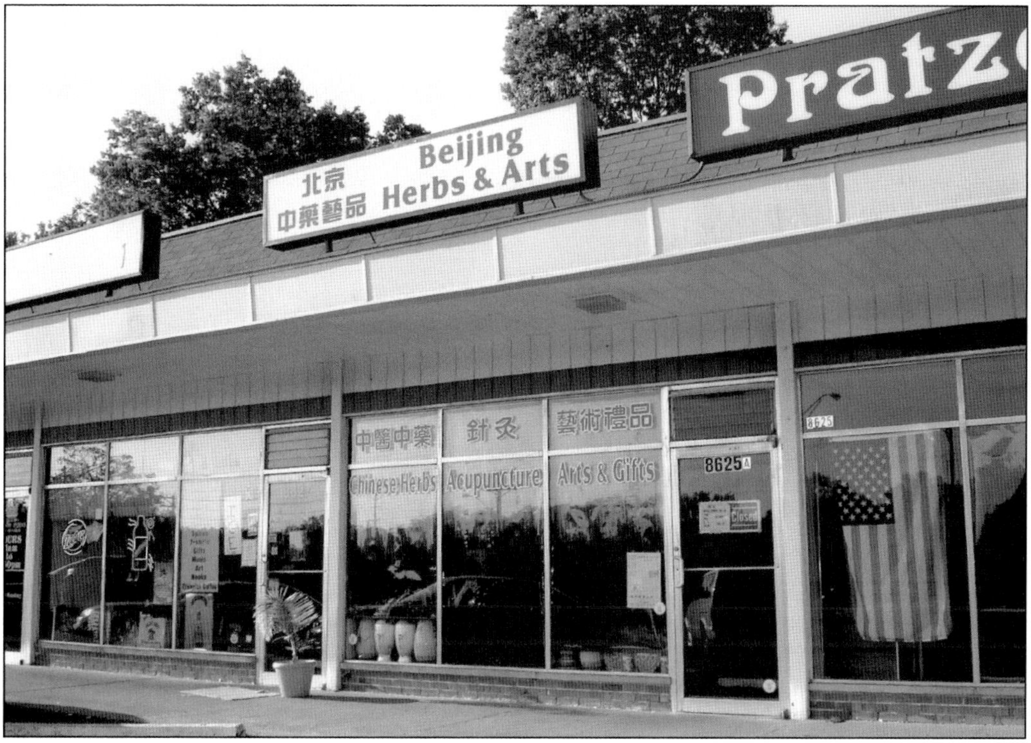

Beijing Herbs and Arts, located at 8625 Olive Boulevard, is pictured in 2006. (Photograph by Huping Ling.)

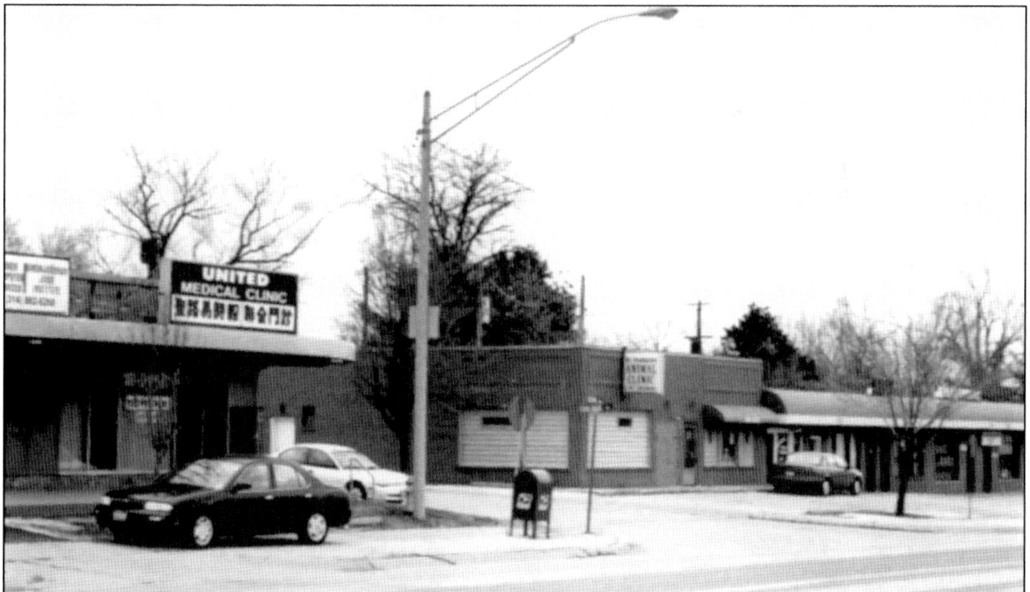

While the traditional food production, and service industries continue to dominate the ethnic economy, other nontraditional service businesses have emerged and are rapidly expanding. The United Medical Clinic, located at 8401 Olive Boulevard, is pictured in 2001. (Photograph by Huping Ling.)

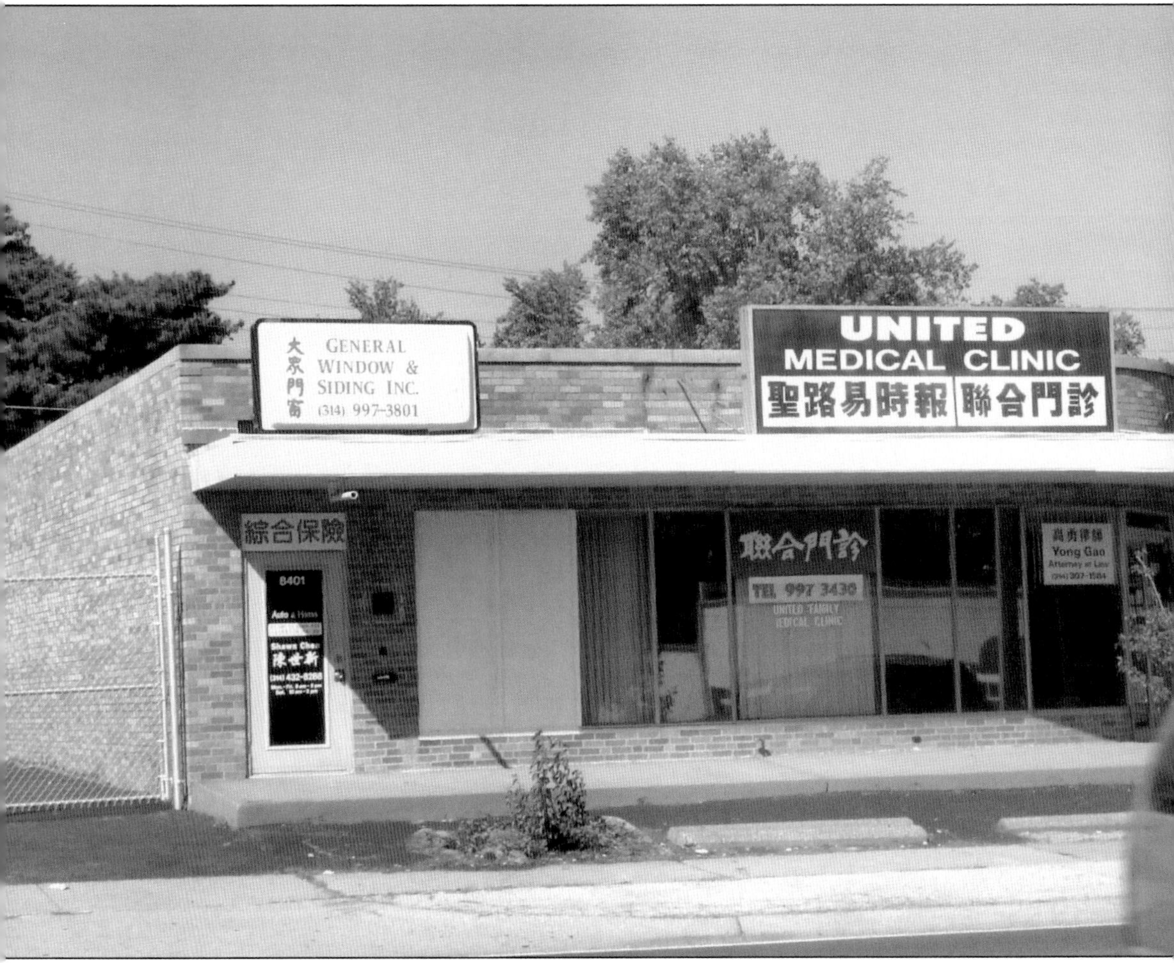

New types of Chinese service businesses in St. Louis with five and more of the same type of businesses in each business category are listed in descending order: real estate (52), medical (23), insurance (16), construction (10), accountancy (7), architecture and design (7), legal (7), health (6), automobile repair (5), gifts (5), jewelry (5), and travel service (5). Auto and Home Insurance, located at 8401 Olive Boulevard, is pictured in 2006, along with General Windows and Siding. The nontraditional Chinese businesses are located mostly in mainstream professional buildings, shopping centers, or plazas. (Photograph by Huping Ling.)

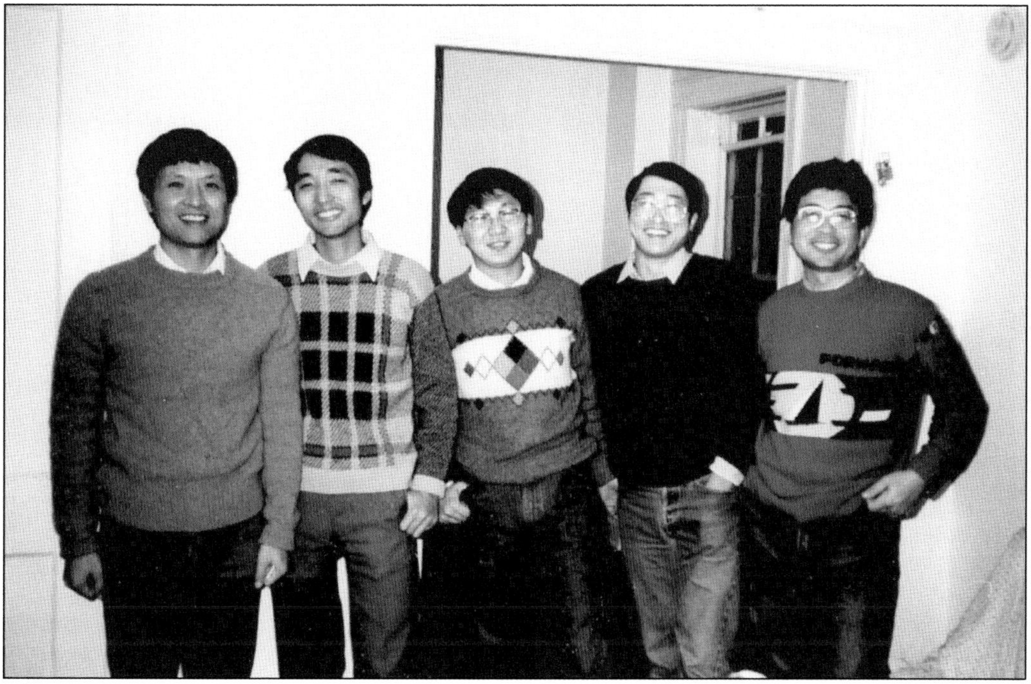

Chris Lu came to St. Louis to study philosophy at Washington University with a scholarship in 1987 and completed the degree two years later. In the image above, Lu and some classmates are in an apartment at 36130 Delmar Boulevard in 1988. Pictured below, Lu graduated with a master of business administration degree from the Southern Illinois University at Carbondale in May 1992. (Chris Lu.)

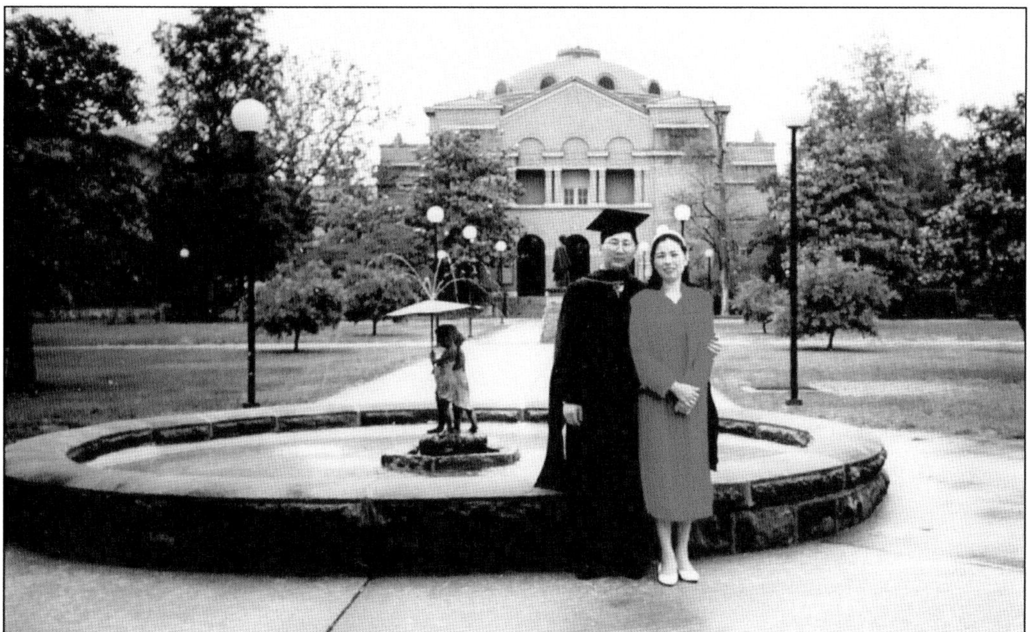

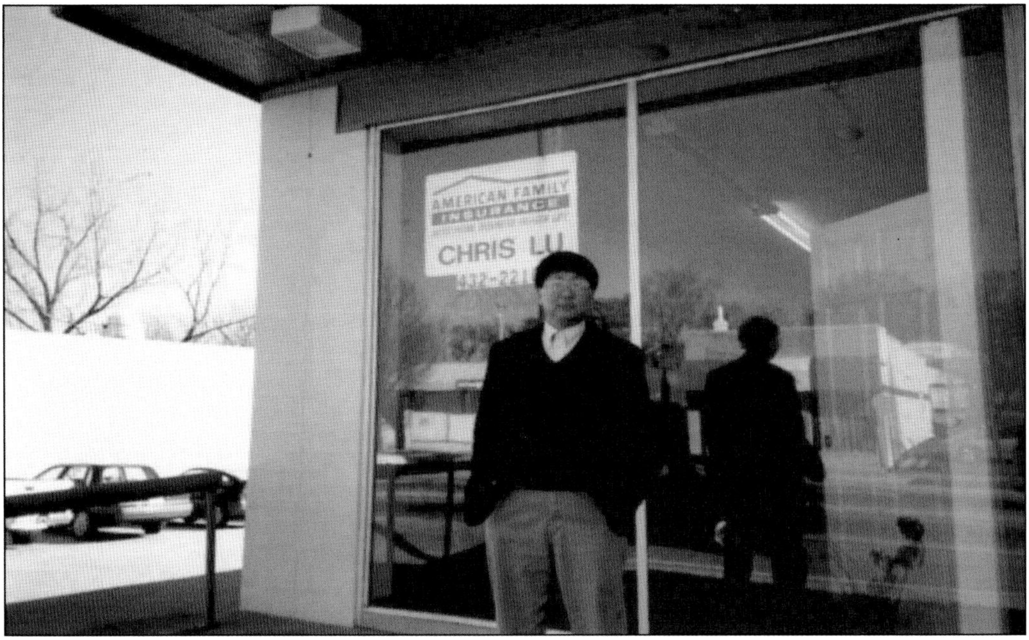

Armed with his master of business administration degree and a realization of the business opportunities resulting from the growing Chinese American population in the area, Chris Lu became an American Family Insurance agent in 1996. A few years later, he initiated his own insurance company, Associated Insurance Brokers, located at 410 Sovereign Court in Manchester, and also started a real estate business, Luhoo Realty. Lu is pictured in front of his office at 8412 Olive Boulevard in 1999. (Photograph by Huping Ling.)

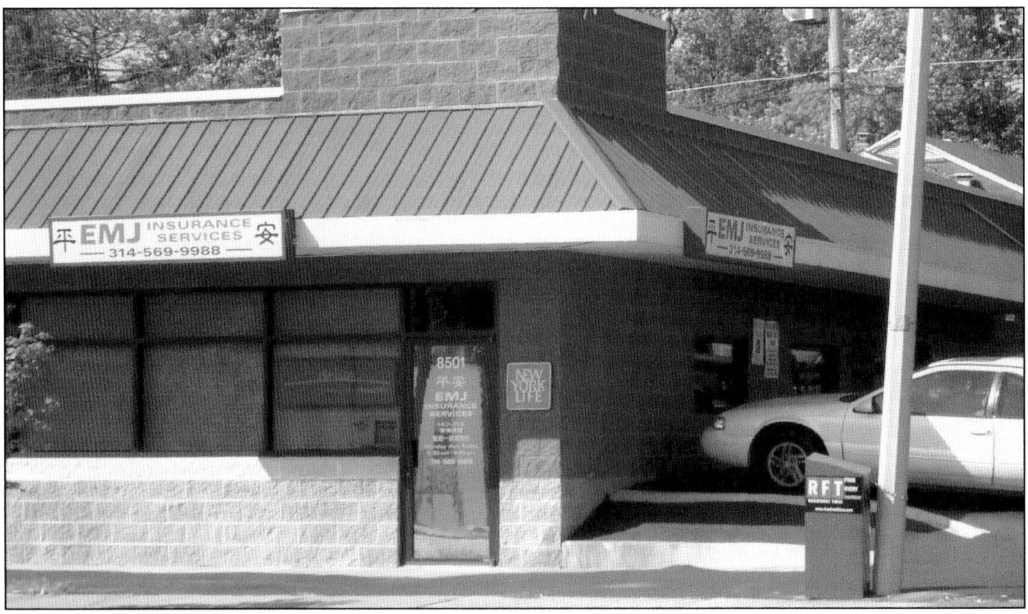

Eric Huang came to America from Taiwan in 1975 and graduated with an accounting degree from the University of Missouri at St. Louis in 1977. He first worked as an accountant and then switched to insurance in 1987. He started his own business in the early years of 2000. EMJ Insurance Services, located at 8501 Olive Boulevard, is pictured in 2006. (Photograph by Huping Ling.)

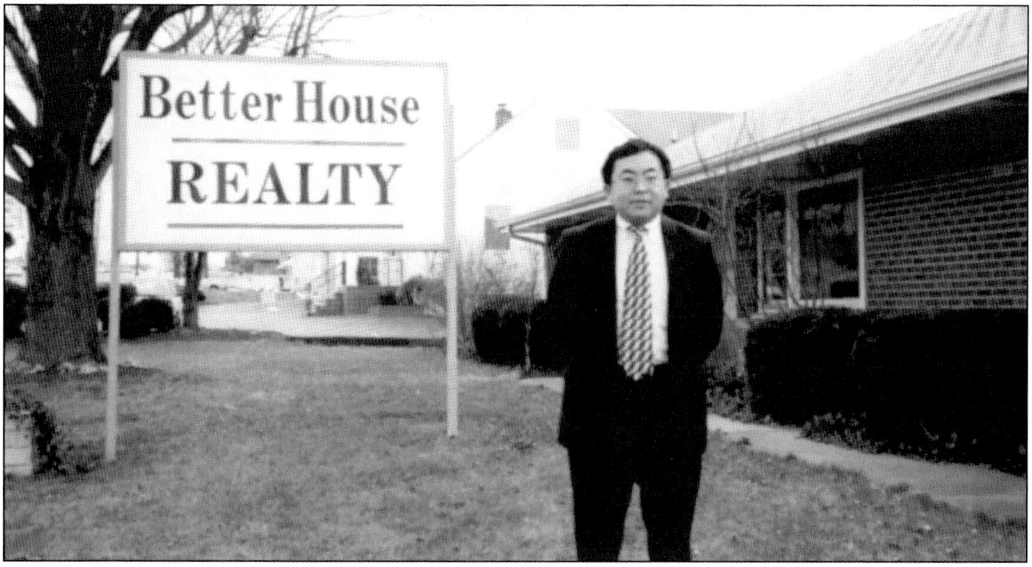

James Zhang, a broker with Better House Realty, is pictured in front of his real estate office at 14567 Manchester Road in Manchester in 1998. Their office is currently located at 85 Nationalway Shopping Center in Balwin. James Zhang came to St. Louis from China in 1987 and graduated with a master's degree in comparative literature from Washington University in 1990. With a master of business administration degree from the University of Missouri at St. Louis, he went into the real estate business in 1992 and launched his own company in 1996, which has grown into one of the major real estate businesses in the area. (Photograph by Huping Ling.)

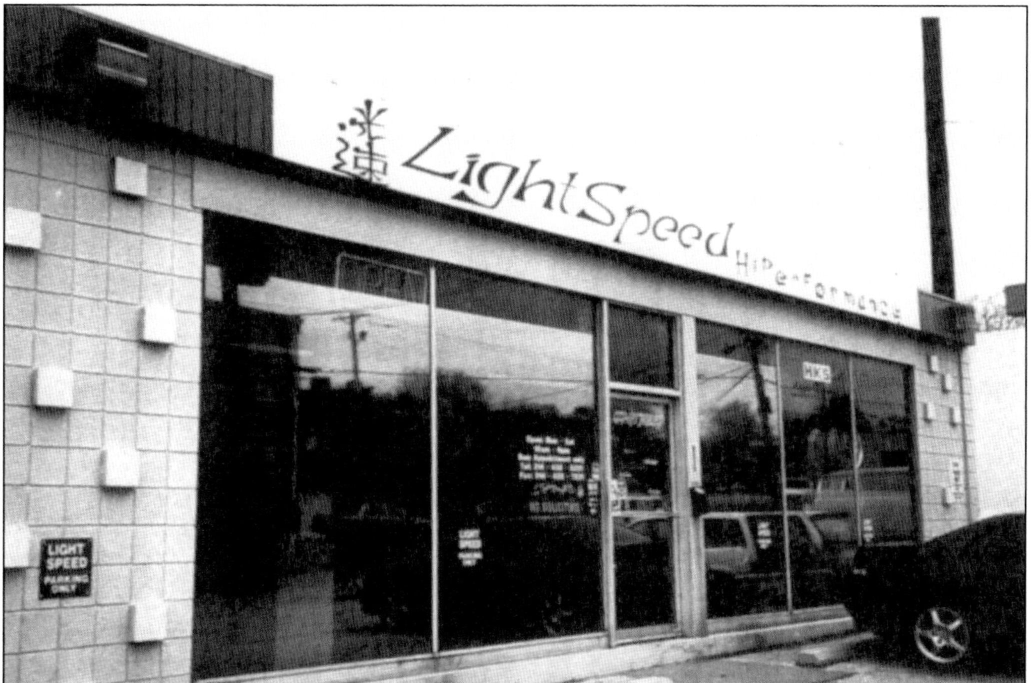

Light Speed: Motorsports, located at 8314 Olive Boulevard, is pictured in 2001. (Photograph by Huping Ling.)

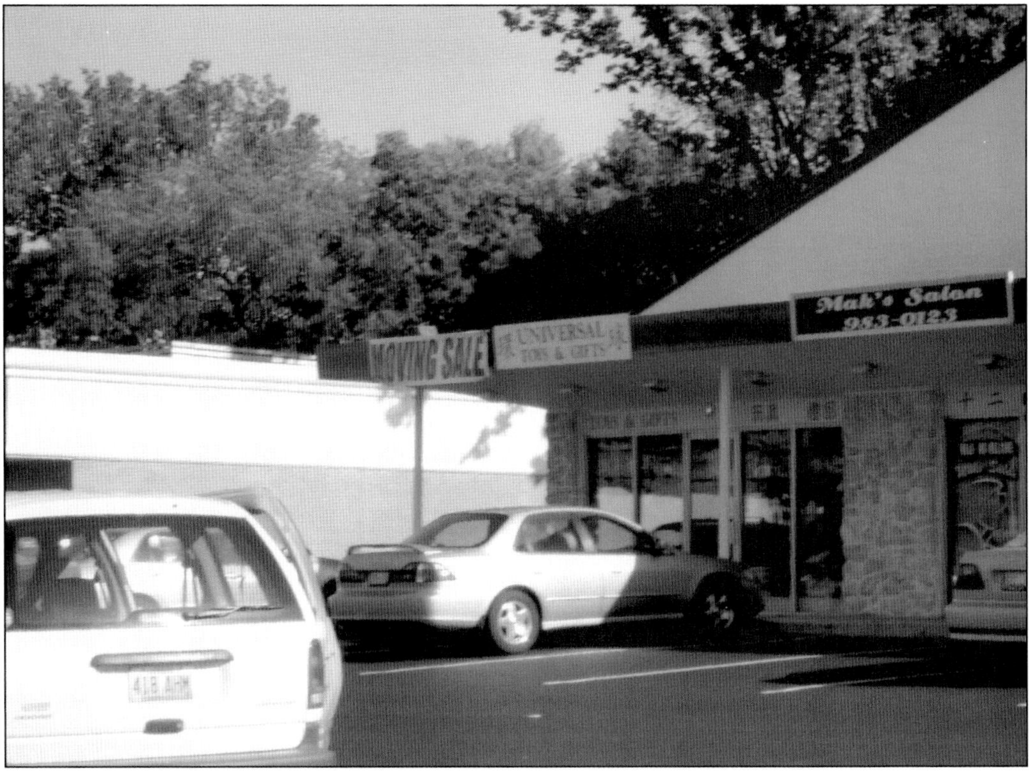

Mak's Salon, located at 8108 Olive Boulevard, is pictured in 2006. (Photograph by Huping Ling.)

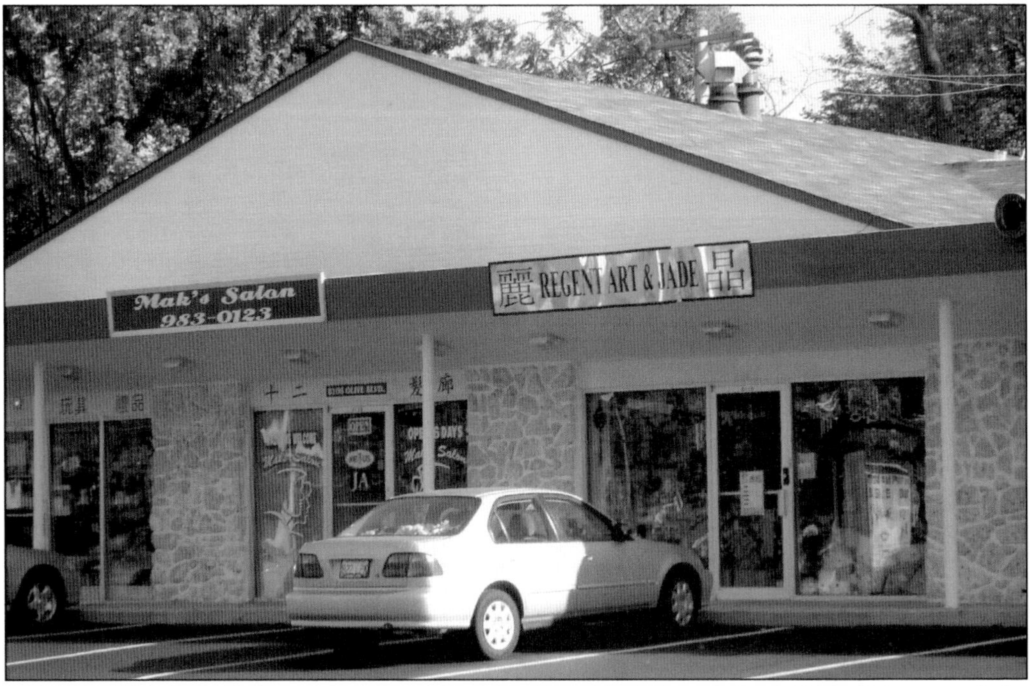

Regent Art and Jewel, located at 8110 Olive Boulevard, is pictured in 2006. (Photograph by Huping Ling.)

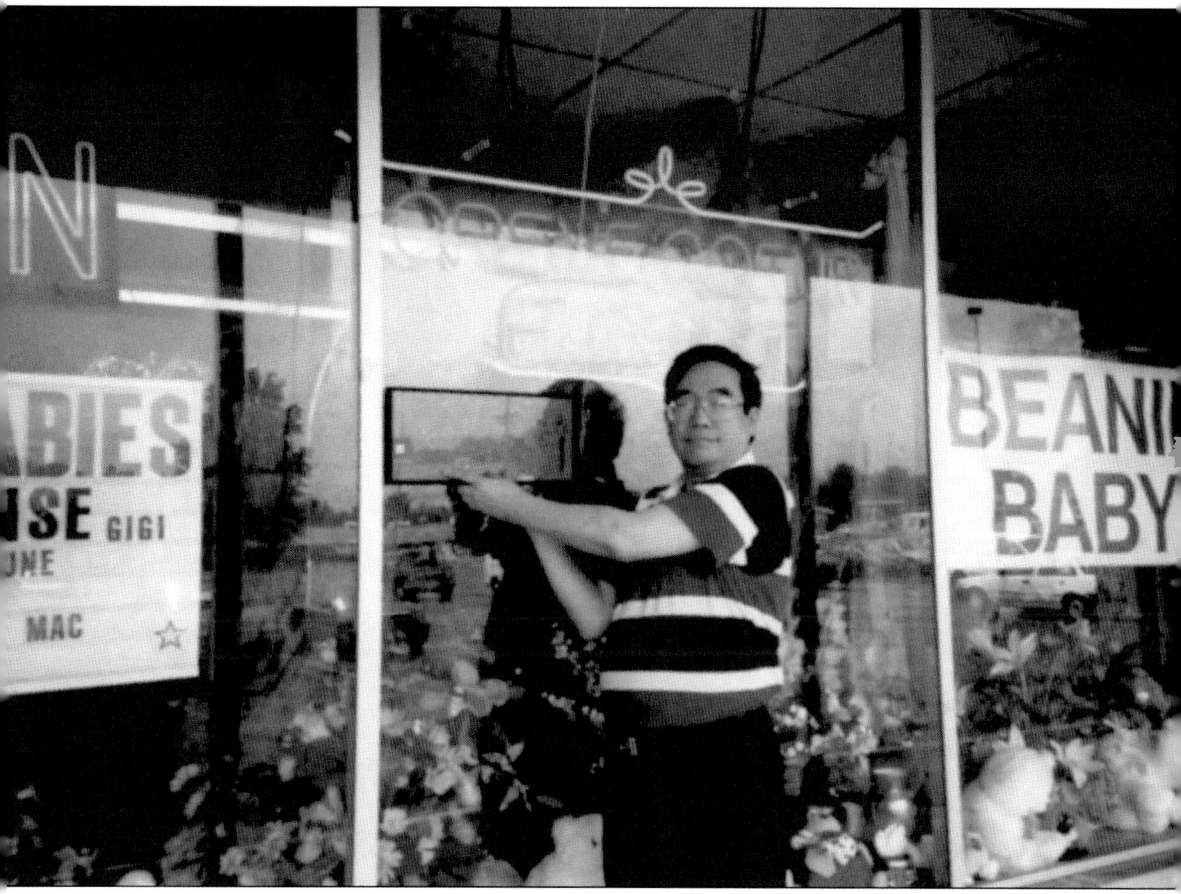

Dachung Pat Peng, owner of Creve Coeur Florist and Gifts, is pictured at the shop, located at 12965 Olive Street, hard at work when interviewed by the author in 1999. Peng came to America in 1969 and earned his doctorate in applied mechanics from Lehigh University. He came to St. Louis in 1976 working at Monsanto Chemical Company. At the height of his career, he decided to take an early retirement and start his own floral business in 1989. (Photograph by Huping Ling.)

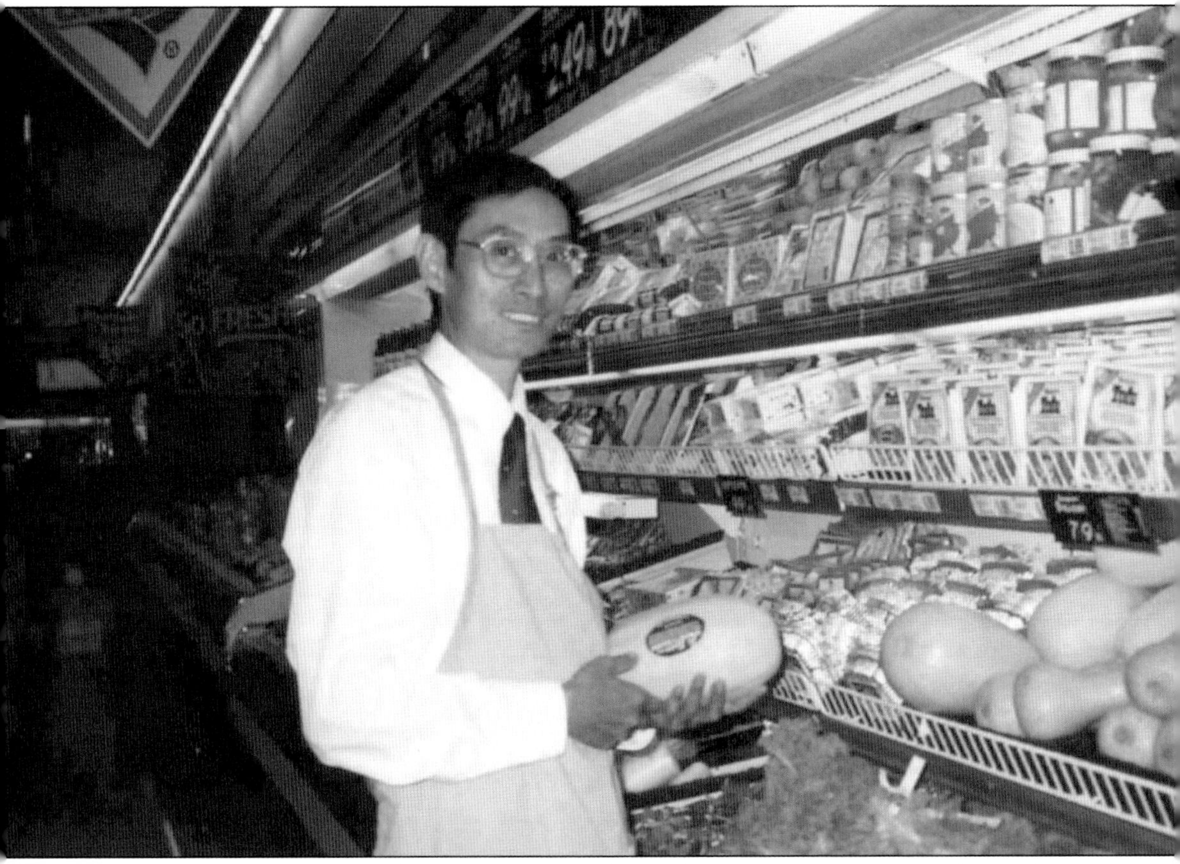

The workers in the back of the stores, normally newly arrived immigrants with less language ability, pack and sort dry goods, prepare fresh vegetables and sea foods, and cut meats. A Chinese employee at Schnucks supermarket in Chesterfield was photographed in 1999. (Photograph by Huping Ling.)

Six

Constructing Cultural Community

As Hop Alley disappeared, On Leong declined, and the suburban-bound professionals increased, a new type of Chinese community, which the author defines as a cultural community, has emerged in the St. Louis area since the 1960s. Different from many of the Chinese American communities throughout the country, the cultural community in St. Louis did not have identifiable physical boundaries. Instead the cultural community was defined within social boundaries of community organizations, Chinese churches and Chinese language schools, as well as the dispersed Chinese restaurants, grocery stores, and other service businesses. Although most elements of the cultural community such as Chinese churches and Chinese language schools did occupy physical structures where they rendered services to the community, these physical structures did not constitute a physical Chinatown since they were scattered throughout the city. Likewise, the dispersed Chinese businesses also failed to create a physical commercial district. However, the cultural activities organized by the community organizations that took place in the cultural institutions generated a sense of community and composed the social/emotional space of the cultural community. Therefore the cultural community can be understood in two dimensions: physical and social/emotional. The facilities of the cultural institutions or community organizations, either owned or rented, constituted the physical space of the cultural community. The activities taking place in these facilities created the social space of the cultural community. The latter depended on the former but was more significant than the former in creating a cultural community. Unlike other types of Chinese communities with geographical boundaries, the physical space of the cultural community was undefined, and often unidentifiable, as the significant part of the community infrastructure possessed no permanent physical space. On the other hand, the social space of the cultural community was visible and easily recognizable when the Chinese language classes were held, the religious congregations were convened, and the cultural activities took place.

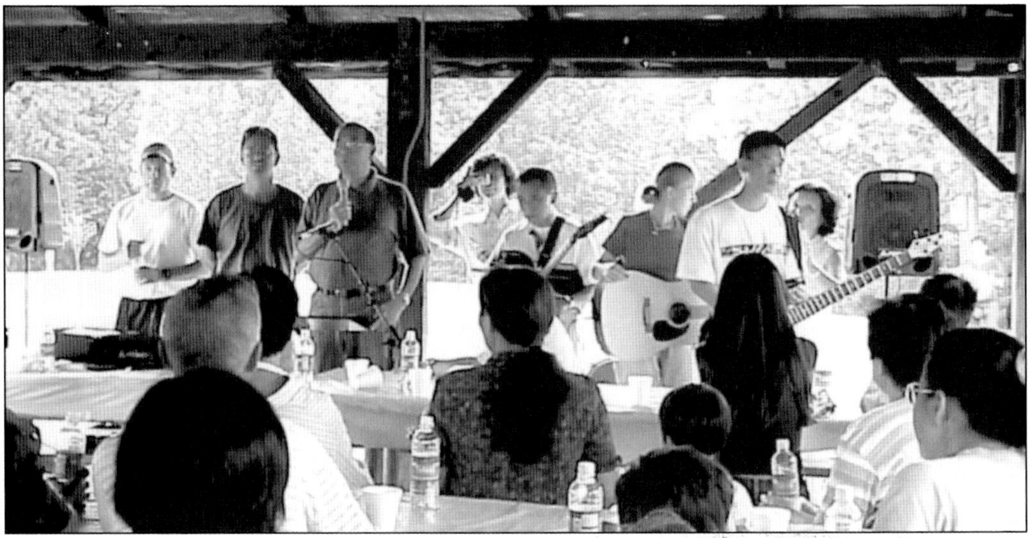

The earliest Chinese church was the St. Louis Chinese Gospel Mission (*Zhonghua Fuyin Jiaohui*), now the St. Louis Chinese Gospel Church. It is one of the largest Chinese Christian churches in St. Louis. The St. Louis Chinese Gospel Church held a Labor Day picnic at Bluebird Park on September 3, 2001. (St. Louis Chinese American News.)

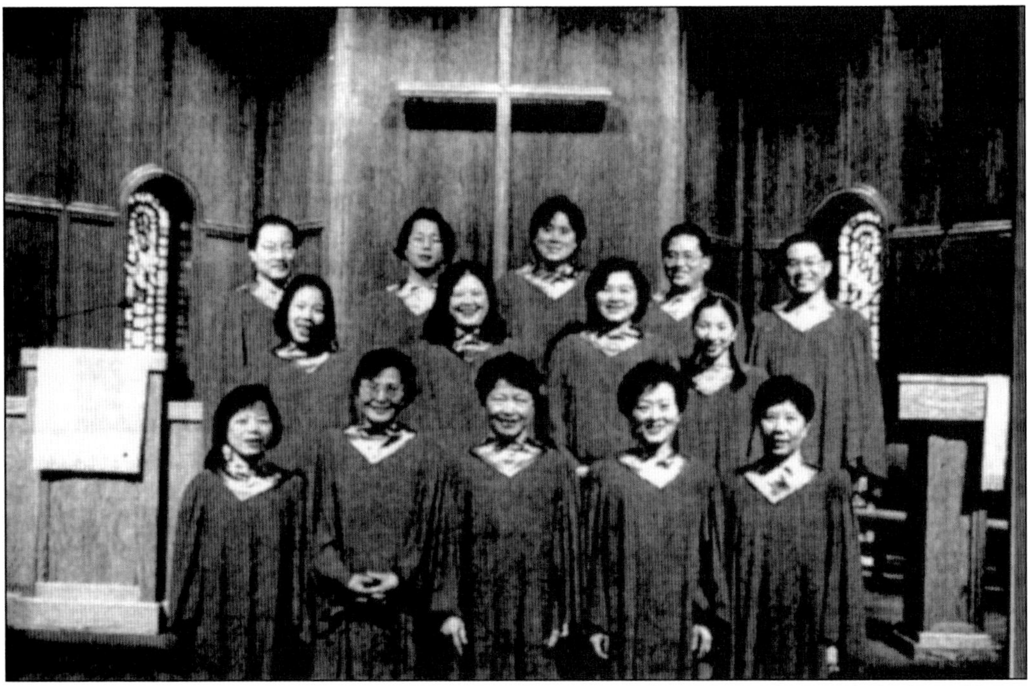

The Chinese in St. Louis embrace many denominations and various religious beliefs and have formed more than 15 religious institutions. The chorus at the Taiwanese Presbyterian Church was photographed on May 15, 1999. (St. Louis Chinese Journal.)

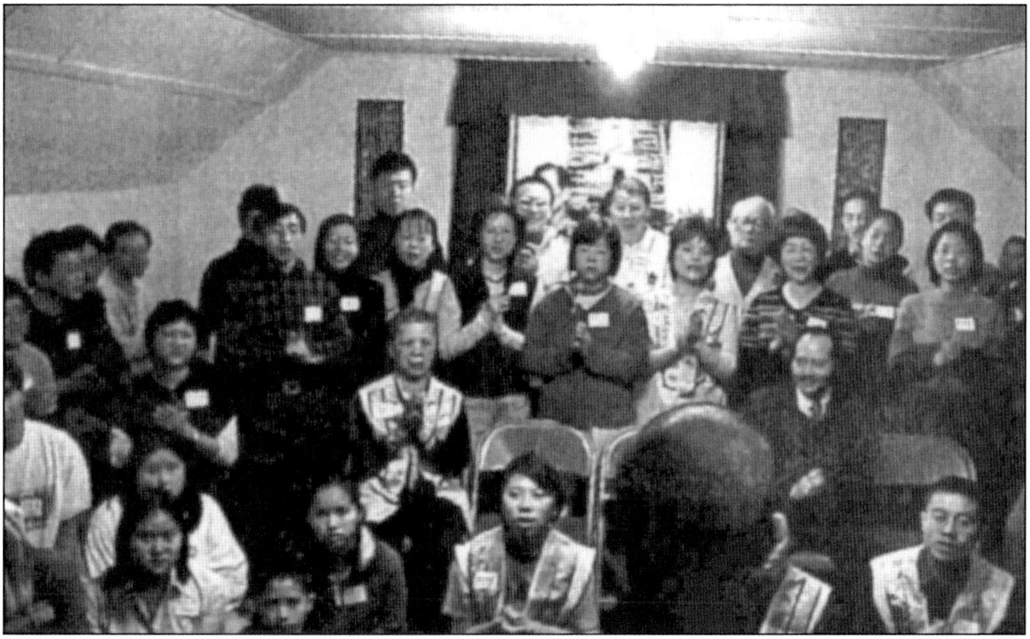

Members of the St. Louis International Buddhist Association were photographed while singing on February 1, 2001. (St. Louis Chinese American News.)

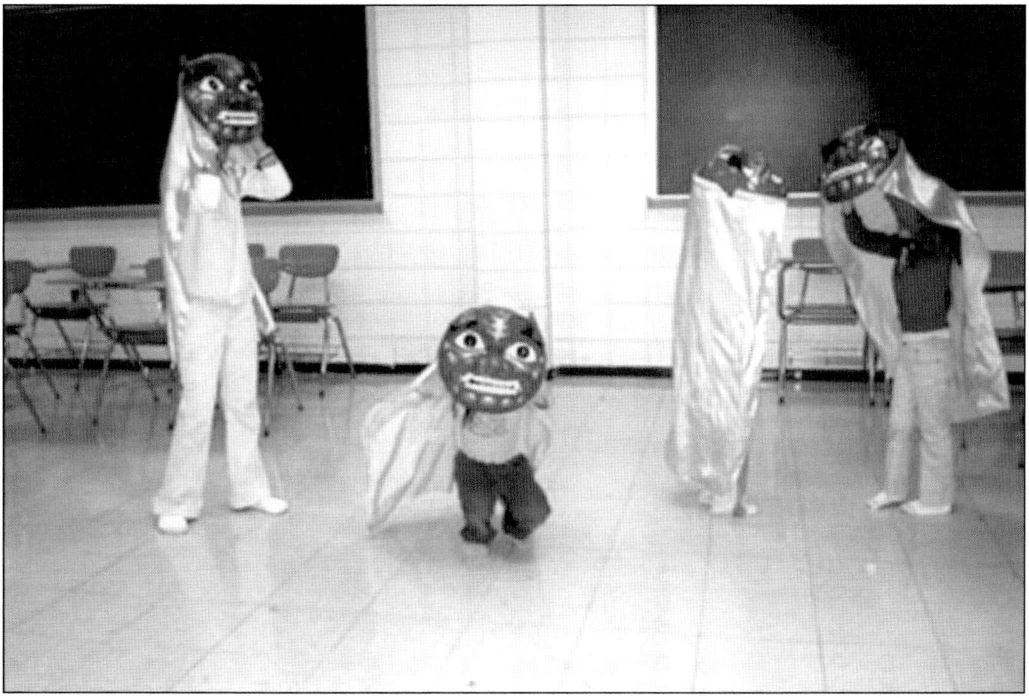

On July 8, 1978, the St. Louis Chinese Academy (*Shengluyi Zhonghua Yuwen Xuexiao*) was founded in a classroom at Washington University. The traditional Chinese characters (*fantizi* or *zhengtizi*) and a phonetic system of *zhuyin fuhao*, prevalent in Taiwan, were taught, and Mandarin Chinese was used as the medium at the school. This photograph shows a dance class at the St. Louis Chinese Academy in 2005. (St. Louis Chinese Academy.)

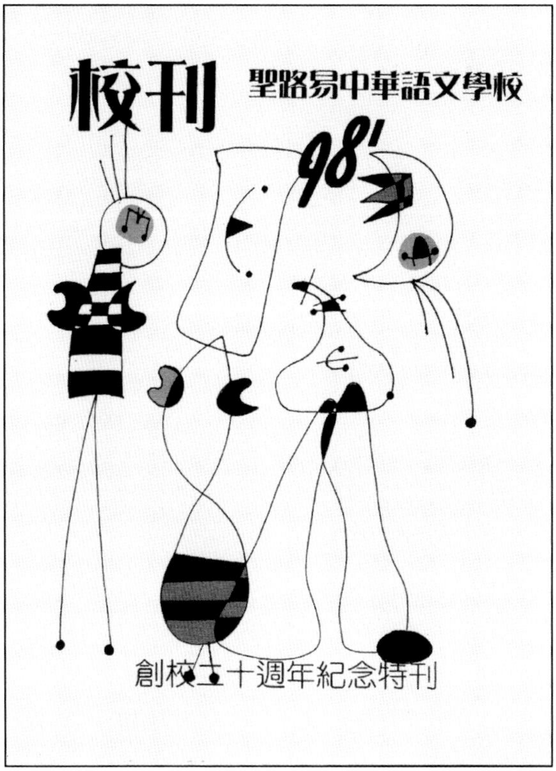

Pictured are the front and back covers of the St. Louis Chinese Academy's school magazine, a special issue commemorating its 20th anniversary in 1998. The back cover lists the school's missions, class offerings and schedules, and tuition and fees. (Photograph by Huping Ling.)

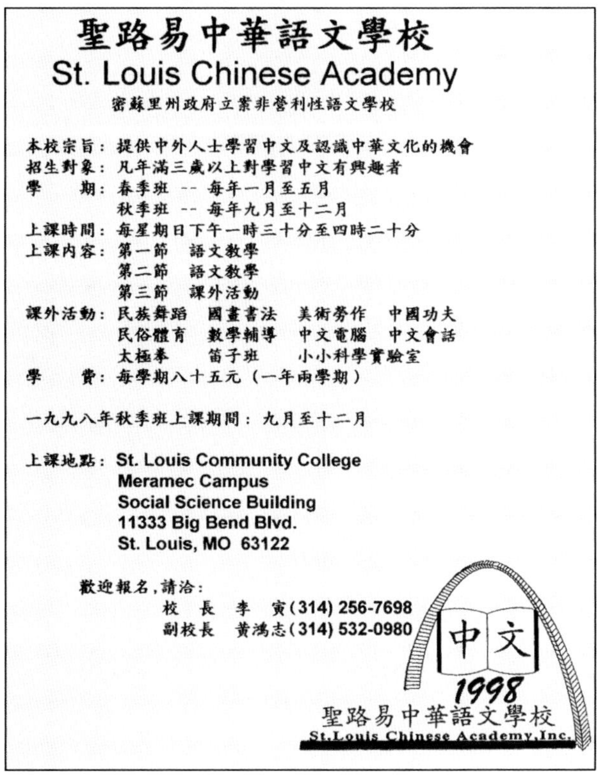
聖路易中華語文學校

St. Louis Chinese Academy

密蘇里州政府立案非營利性語文學校

本校宗旨：提供中外人士學習中文及認識中華文化的機會
招生對象：凡年滿三歲以上對學習中文有興趣者
學　　期：春季班 -- 每年一月至五月
秋季班 -- 每年九月至十二月
上課時間：每星期日下午一時三十分至四時二十分
上課內容：第一節　語文教學
第二節　語文教學
第三節　課外活動
課外活動：民族舞蹈　國畫書法　美術勞作　中國功夫
民俗體育　數學輔導　中文電腦　中文會話
太極拳　笛子班　小小科學實驗室
學　　費：每學期八十五元（一年兩學期）

一九九八年秋季班上課期間：九月至十二月

上課地點：St. Louis Community College
Meramec Campus
Social Science Building
11333 Big Bend Blvd.
St. Louis, MO 63122

歡迎報名，請洽：
校　長　李　寅 (314) 256-7698
副校長　黃鴻志 (314) 532-0980

中文
1998
聖路易中華語文學校
St.Louis Chinese Academy, Inc.

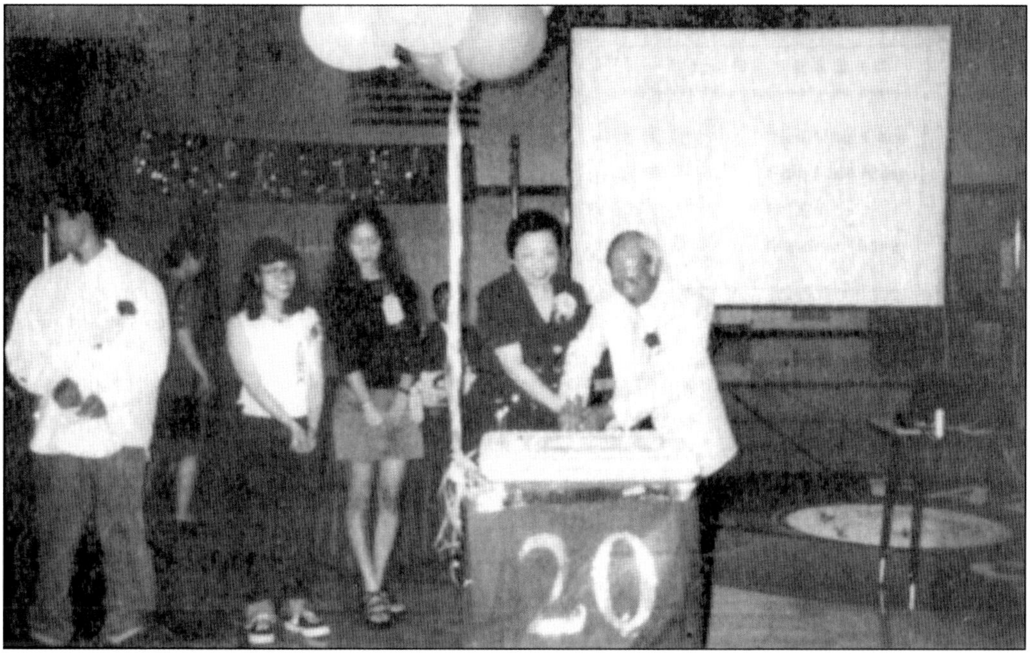

In the fall of 1978, Grace Shen Lo, a biochemist from Taiwan, established the St. Louis Chinese Language School (*Shengluyi Zhongwen Xuexiao*), using space at the St. Louis Chinese Baptist Church. From the initial 12 students to several hundred today, the school has made tremendous progress. In this picture, taken May 6, 1999, founding principal Lo is cutting the cake commemorating the 20th anniversary of the founding of the school. (St. Louis Chinese American News.)

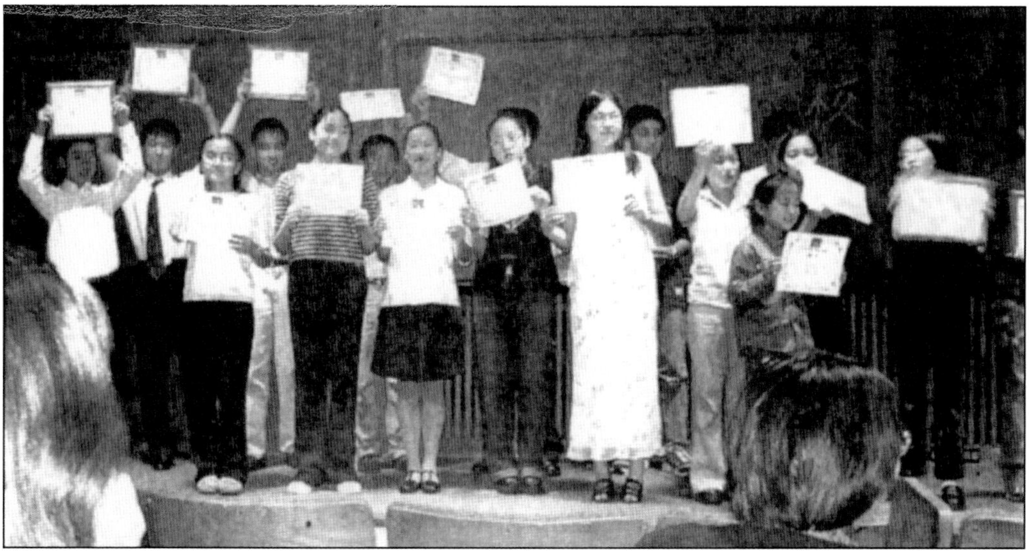

To teach simplified Chinese characters and *pinyin* was the primary motive of the Chinese from the People's Republic of China to start a third school, the St. Louis Modern Chinese School, in 1997. From the initial 40 to several hundred students today, the school has experienced remarkable growth. The winner of the Chinese oratorical contest at the St. Louis Modern Chinese School is pictured November 29, 2001. (St. Louis Chinese American News.)

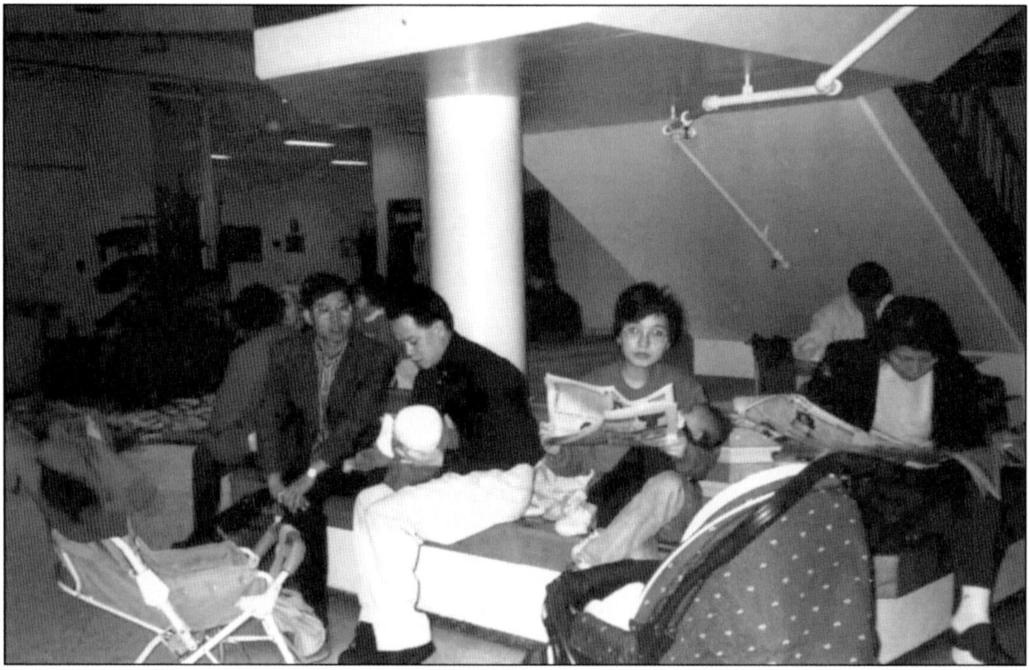

The St. Louis Modern Chinese School not only serves as a place for Chinese children to learn Chinese language and culture, but also as a cultural center for Chinese parents. While offering Chinese language and elective classes to the Chinese children, the school has sponsored lectures for the parents on practical issues of filing tax returns, immigration laws, and Chinese American history, to help them ease the tension caused by cultural adjustment and assimilation to American life. Parents of students at the St. Louis Modern Chinese School are pictured above, chatting while waiting for their children in 2001. Below, parents of students at the St. Louis Modern Chinese School practice Tai Ji Quan while waiting for their children in 2001. (Photographs by Huping Ling.)

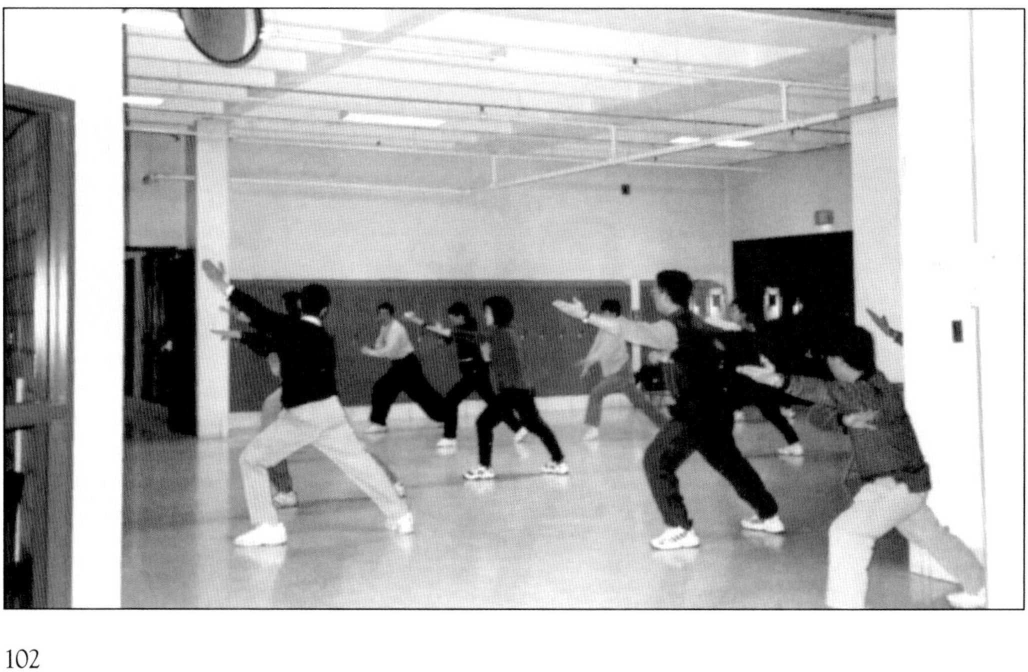

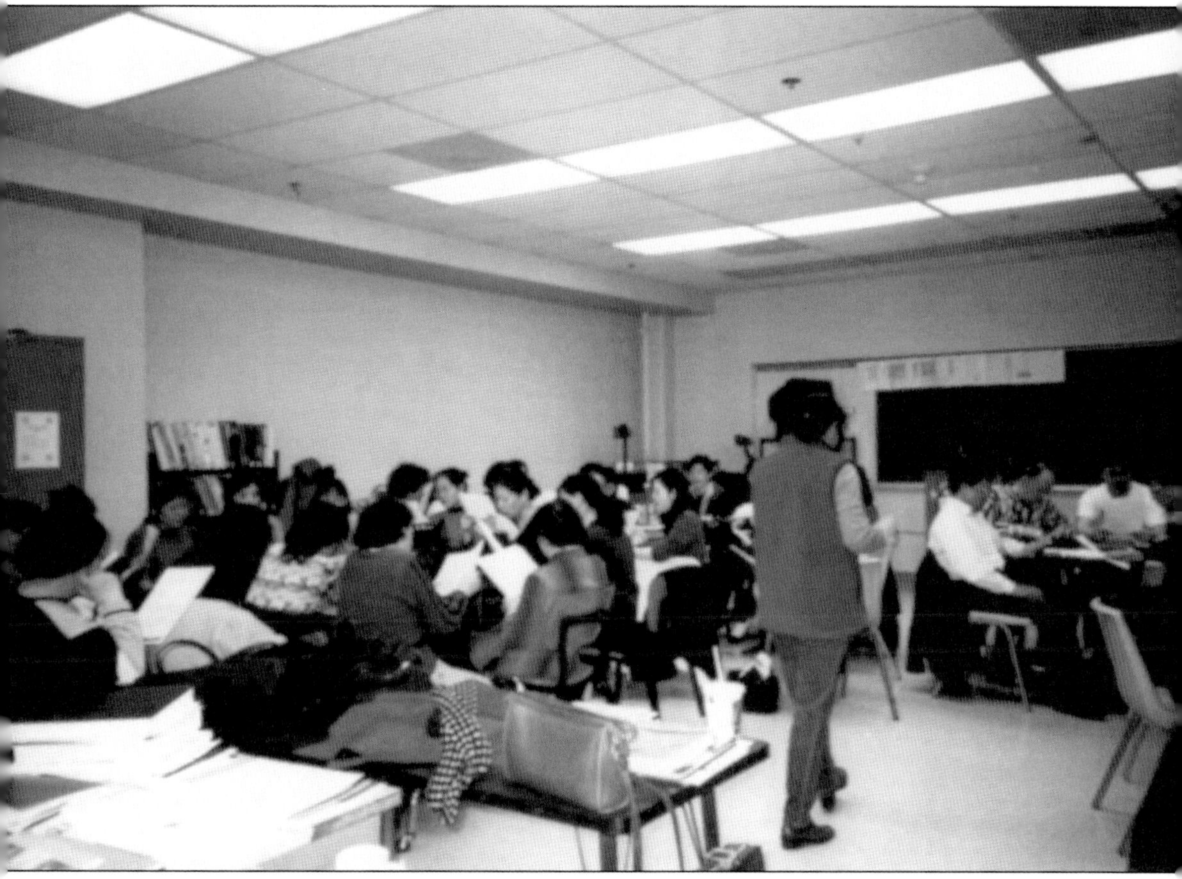

Members of the choir of the St. Louis Chinese Association practiced while their children were taking Chinese language classes at the St. Louis Modern Chinese School in 2001. (Photograph by Huping Ling.)

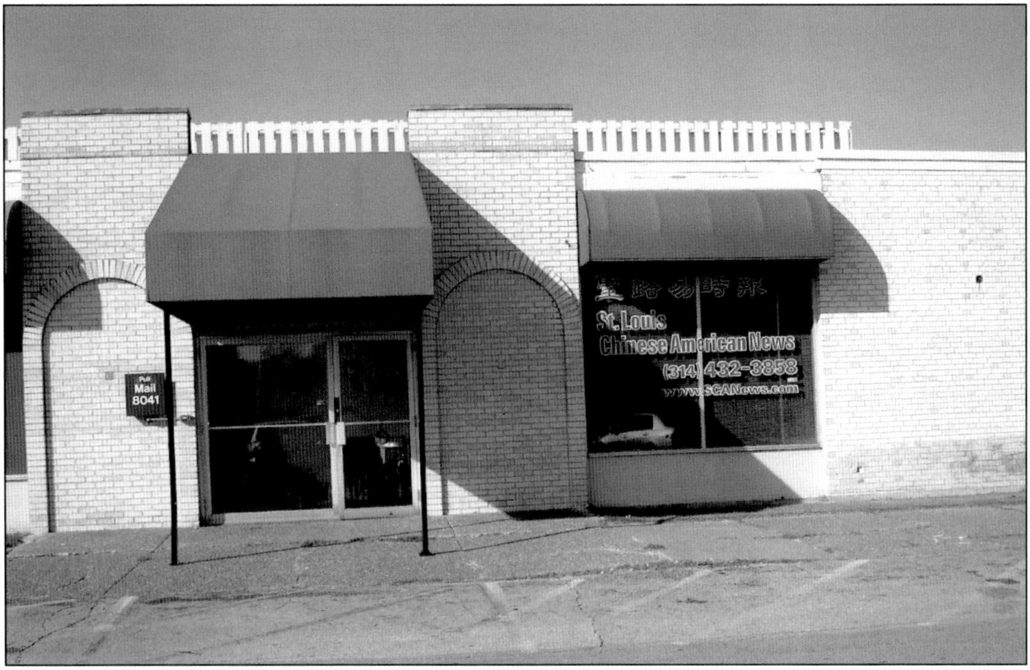

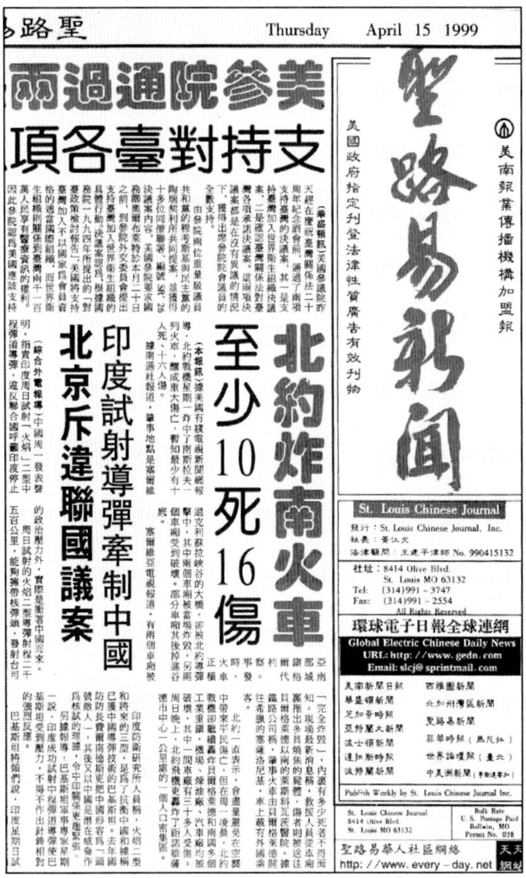
聖路易 Thursday April 15 1999

美參院通過兩

支持對臺各項

北約炸南火車

至少10死16傷

印度試射導彈牽制中國

北京斥違聯國議案

聖路易新聞

美南報業傳播機構加盟報

美國政府指定刊登法律性質廣告有效刊物

St. Louis Chinese Journal

發行：St. Louis Chinese Journal, Inc.

社址：8414 Olive Blvd.
St. Louis MO 63132
Tel: (314)991 - 3747
Fax: (314)991 - 2554
All Rights Reserved

環球電子日報全球連網

Global Electric Chinese Daily News
URL: http: //www. gedn. com
Email: slcj@ sprintmail. com

Publish Weekly by St. Louis Chinese Journal Inc.

St. Louis Chinese Journal
8414 Olive Blvd.
St. Louis MO 63132

Bulk Rate
U. S. Postage Paid
Ballwin, MO
Permit No. 038

聖路易華人社區網絡
http: //www. every - day. net

In 1990, *St. Louis Chinese American News* was established to meet the needs of the people. As the community continued to develop, another Chinese newspaper, *St. Louis Chinese Journal*, entered into the local media in 1996. The establishment and development of the two Chinese language weekly newspapers in St. Louis reflects a trend of resurgence of the Chinese press in the United States and Canada since the 1970s. Both newspapers have experienced the initial difficulty and developed into integral and indispensable parts of the cultural community infrastructure. (Above, photograph by Huping Ling; left, author's collection.)

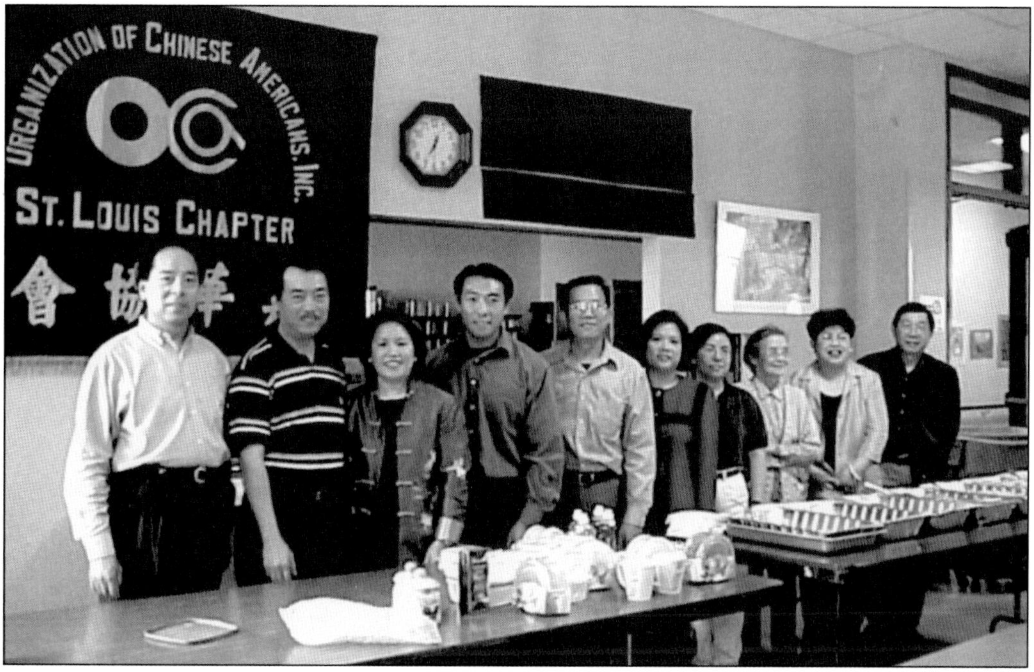

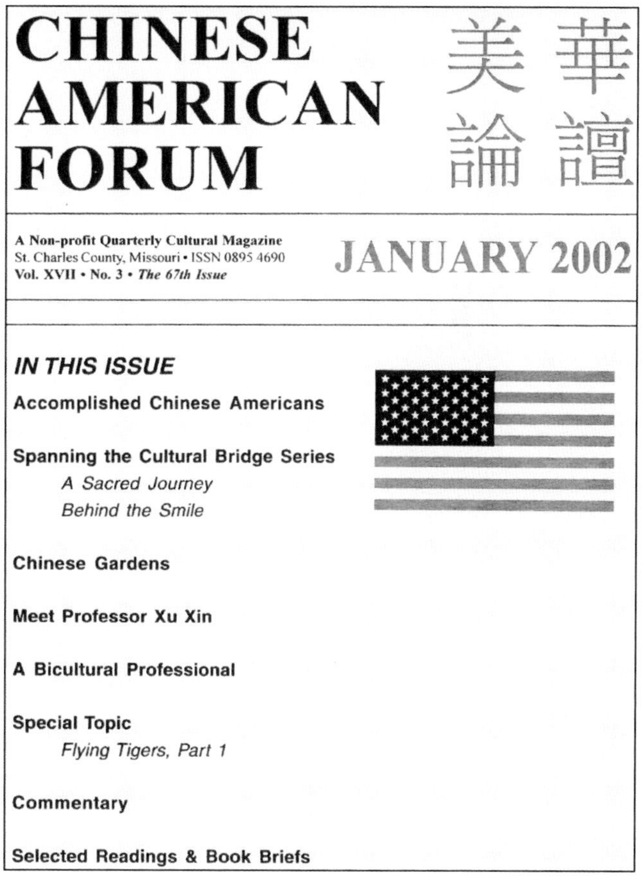
CHINESE AMERICAN FORUM

美華論壇

A Non-profit Quarterly Cultural Magazine
St. Charles County, Missouri • ISSN 0895 4690
Vol. XVII • No. 3 • *The 67th Issue*

JANUARY 2002

IN THIS ISSUE

Accomplished Chinese Americans

Spanning the Cultural Bridge Series
A Sacred Journey
Behind the Smile

Chinese Gardens

Meet Professor Xu Xin

A Bicultural Professional

Special Topic
Flying Tigers, Part 1

Commentary

Selected Readings & Book Briefs

Chinese in St. Louis formed the League of Chinese Americans in 1972, later becoming one of the three founding chapters of the national Organization of Chinese Americans (OCA, *Meihua Xiehui*) in Washington, D.C., in 1973. The St. Louis OCA has emerged as a community leader and replaced On Leong as one of the primary community organizations. As seen above, the St. Louis OCA and Asian American Business Association jointly held a Thanksgiving lunch at Crown Center on Delmar Road, a senior home on November 22, 2001. *Chinese American Forum*, the OCA's quarterly cultural magazine, publishes articles and commentaries pertinent to the causes and interests of the Chinese Americans. (Above, St. Louis Chinese American News; right, author's collection.)

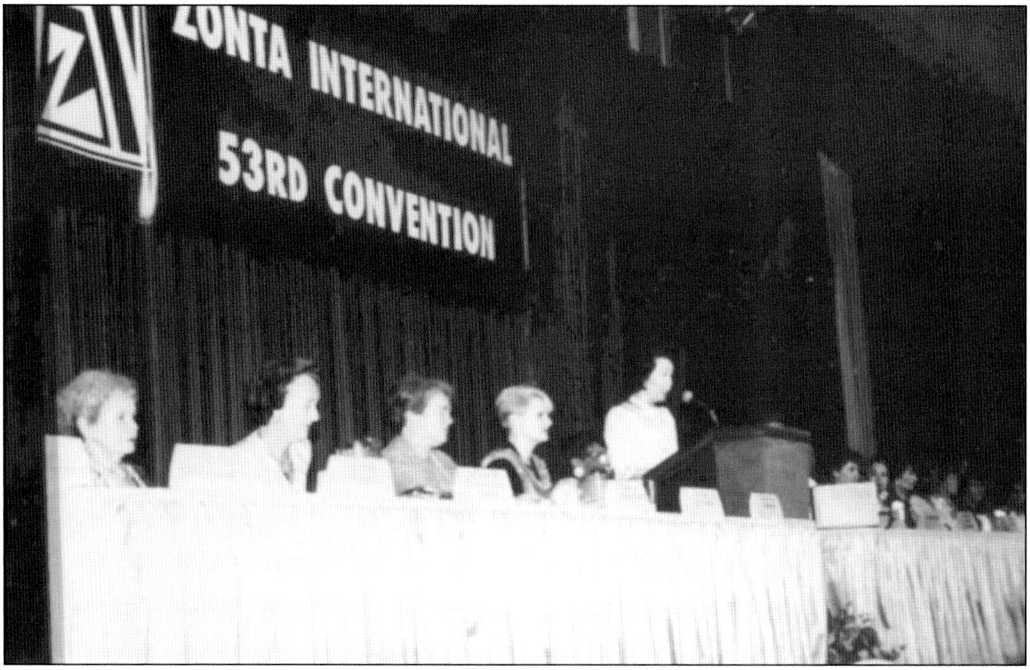

Chinese Americans in St. Louis also branched out to mainstream national and international organizations. Patricia L. Yeh, vice president of Gateway International and Gateway Engineering and Construction, presided over the Zonta International 53rd convention in St. Louis on July 14, 1996. Below, Patricia L. Yeh is pictured at home when interviewed by the author on December 2, 1998. (Above, Patricia L. Yeh; below, photograph by Huping Ling.)

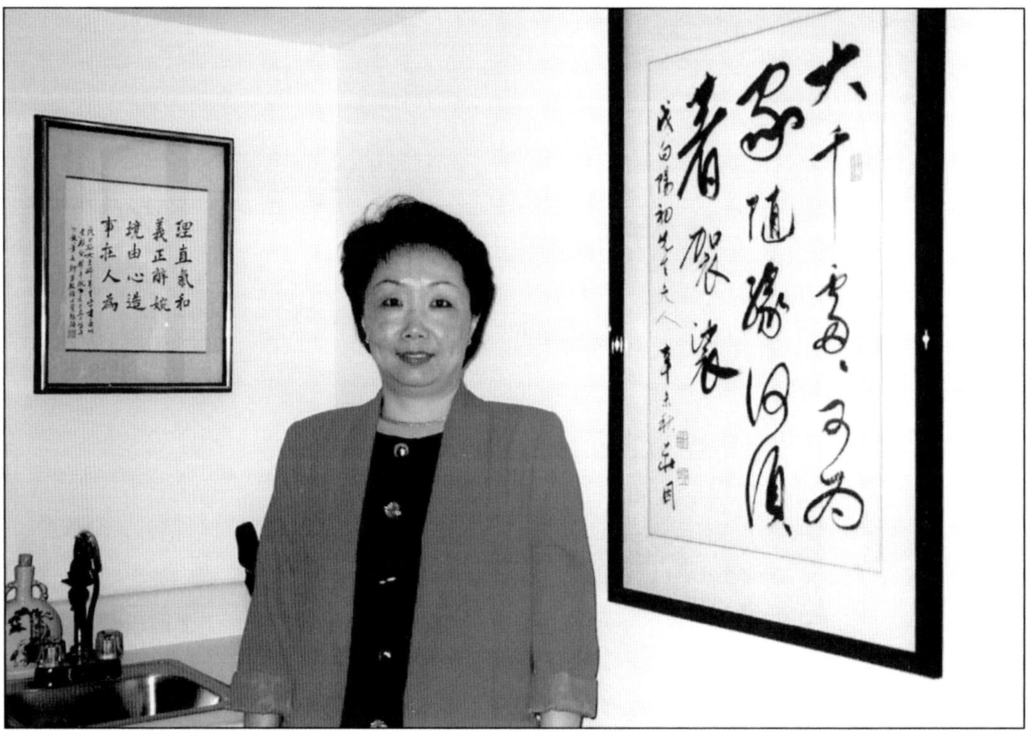

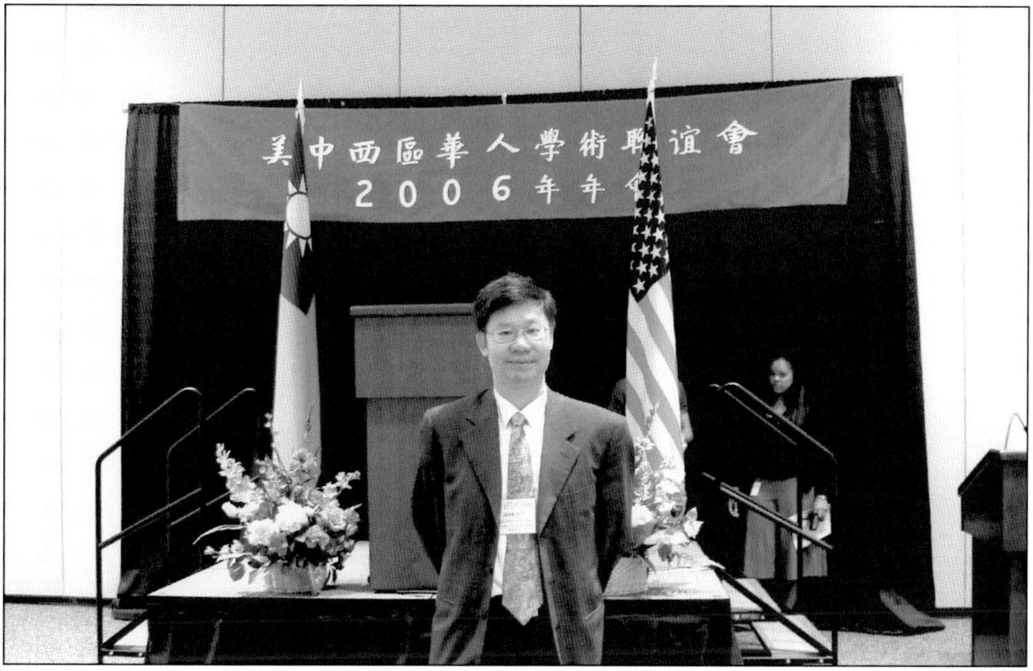

In 1979, a group of politically enthusiastic students from Taiwan formed the St. Louis branch of the Chinese Liberty Assembly (*Zhongguo Ziyouren Xiehui*). In 1998, the Chinese Liberty Assembly changed its name to the Midwest Chinese American Science and Technology Association (MCASTA). Since then, the organization had focused its activities mainly on a flag-rising ceremony on October 10 each year and the annual academic conference. Seen above is Hung-Gay Fung, one of the conference committee members at the MCASTA 23rd Annual Conference at the St. Charles Convention Center on September 16, 2006. In the photograph below are William Li (right) and Helena Chen (center), Steering Committee Chairs of the MCASTA 23rd Annual Conference at the St. Charles Convention Center on September 16, 2006. (Photographs by Huping Ling.)

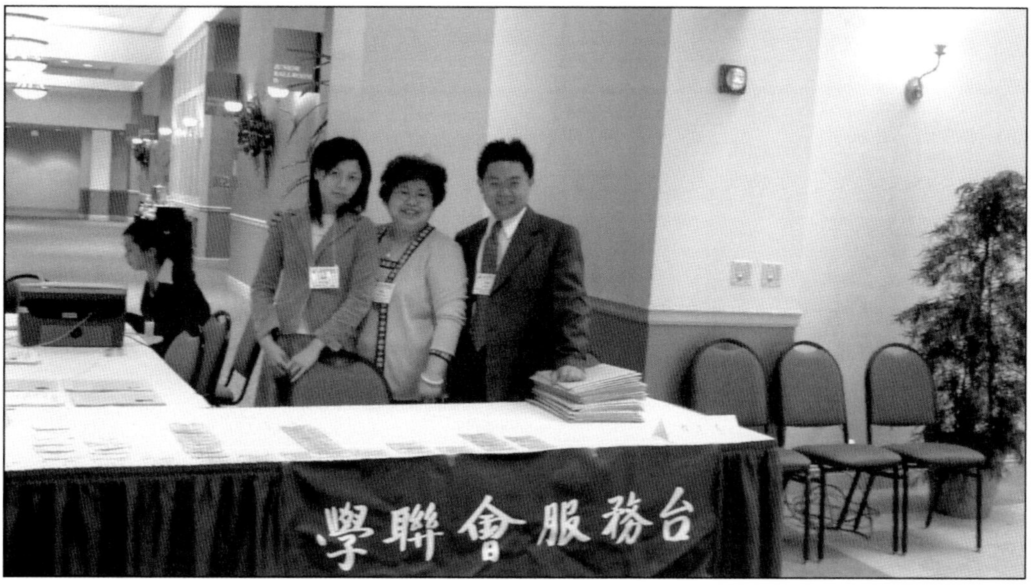

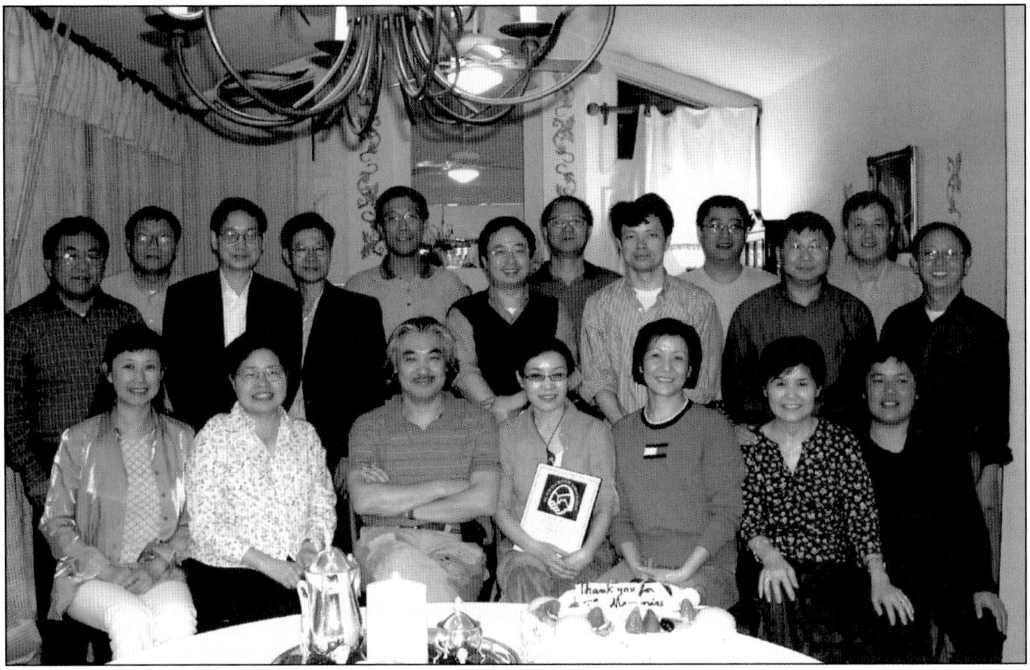

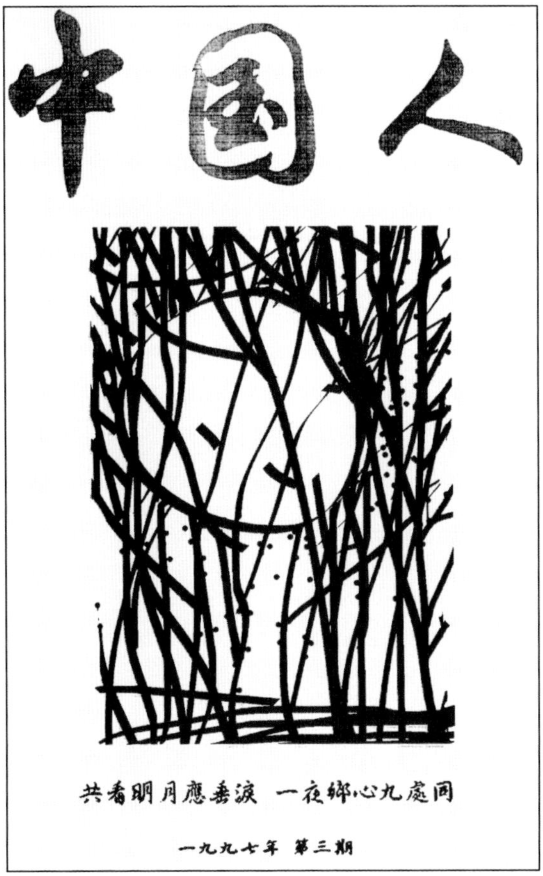

Legal rights and financial security together have enabled the PRC professionals in St. Louis to look beyond personal and familial needs to try to benefit the larger community. Under such circumstances, the St. Louis Chinese Association was formed at the end of 1996. The St. Louis Chinese Association has strengthened the cultural community infrastructure and emerged as one of the leading community organizations. In the top photograph, 2006 board members of the St. Louis Chinese Association present a community service award to Wu Yumei (front center) in March 2006. Pictured at left is the *Chinese*, a literary magazine affiliated with the organization. (Above, St. Louis Chinese Association; left, author's collection.)

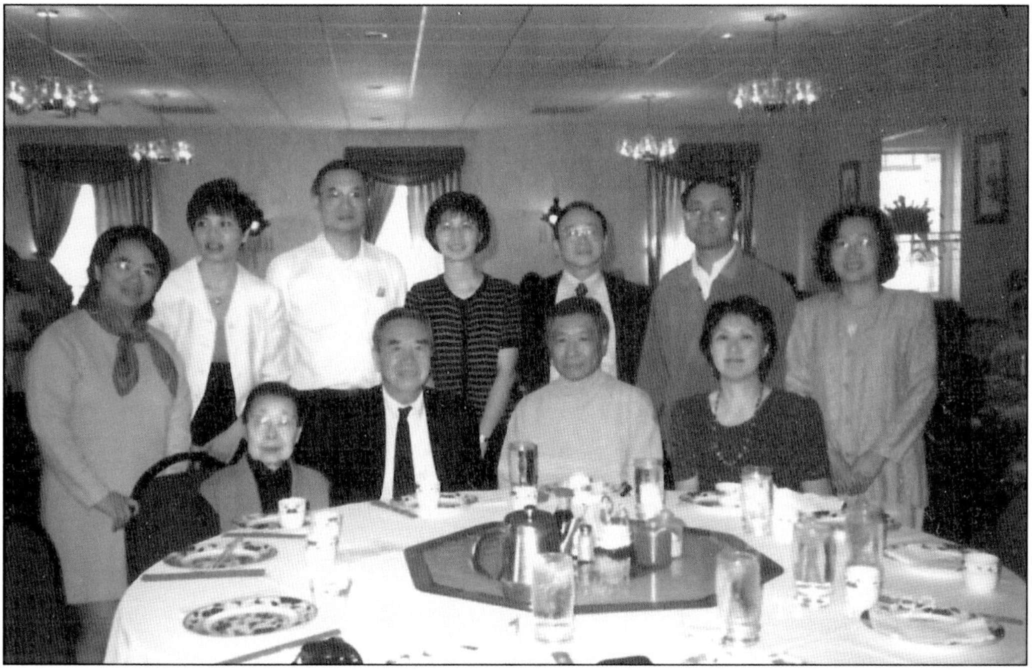

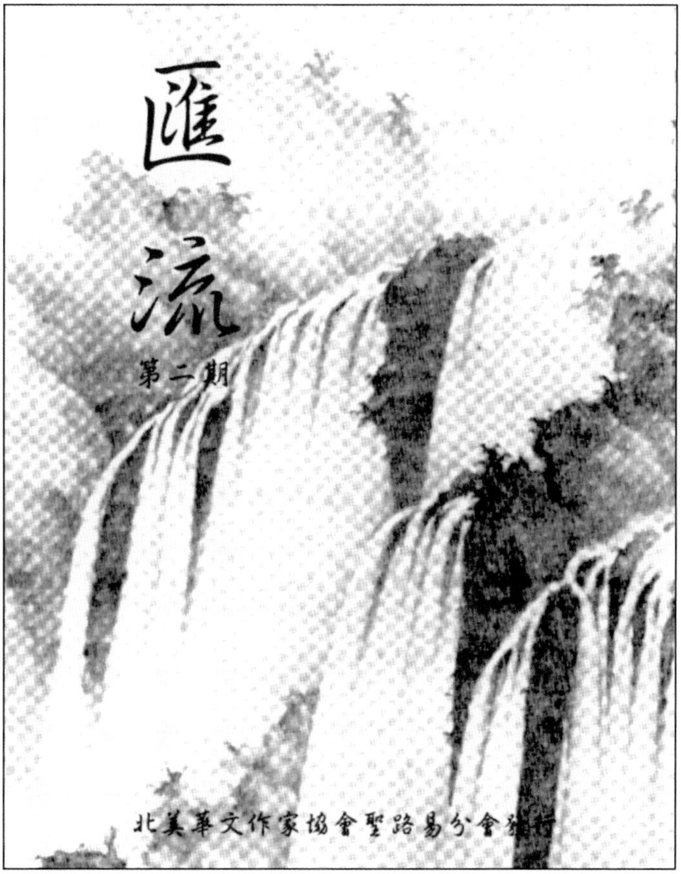

In addition to Chinese churches, language schools, and community organizations, the Chinese in St. Louis also formed groups of cultural interests. The St. Louis Writers Association of North America consists of a group of active and productive writers and poets in the area. Pictured in 2000 in the image above are, from left to right, (first row) Mu-Lien H. Wu, Nelson Wu (1919–2002), poet Zheng Chouyu (from China), and Leslie S. Cheng; (second row) Deh Yung Ling, Wen Hwang, Huey-Sheng Shieh, Shulan Li, Xing Eryuan, Nenger Jinn, and Mimi Chou. Pictured at right, *Huiliu* (converging currents), the association's journal, publishes selected works from members and nonmembers. (Above, Mimi Chou; right, author's collection.)

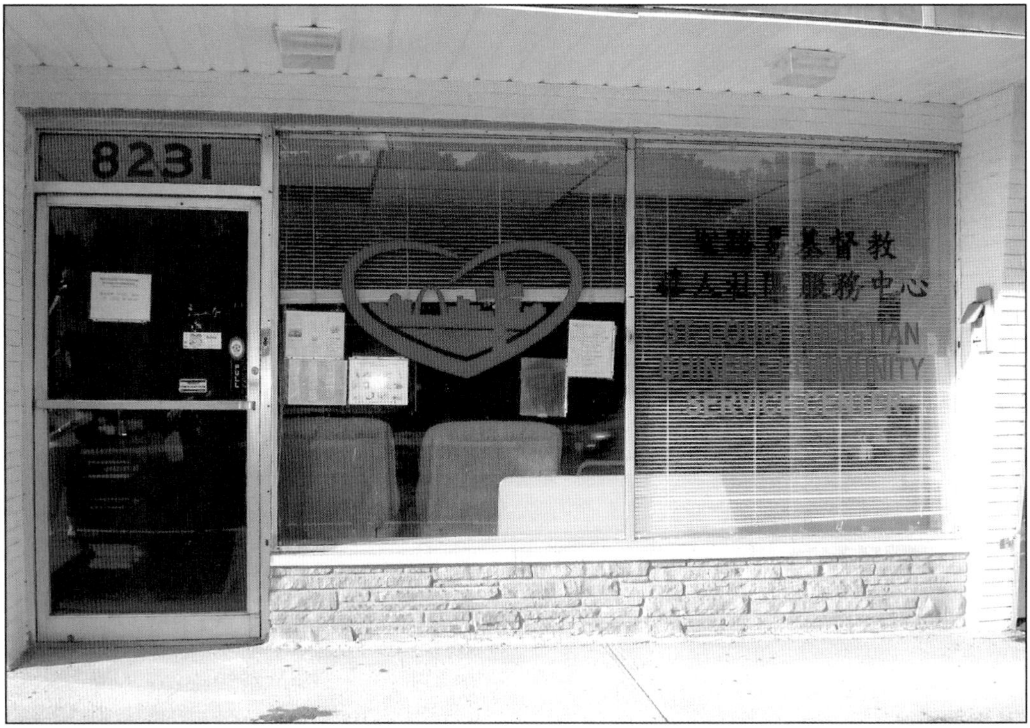

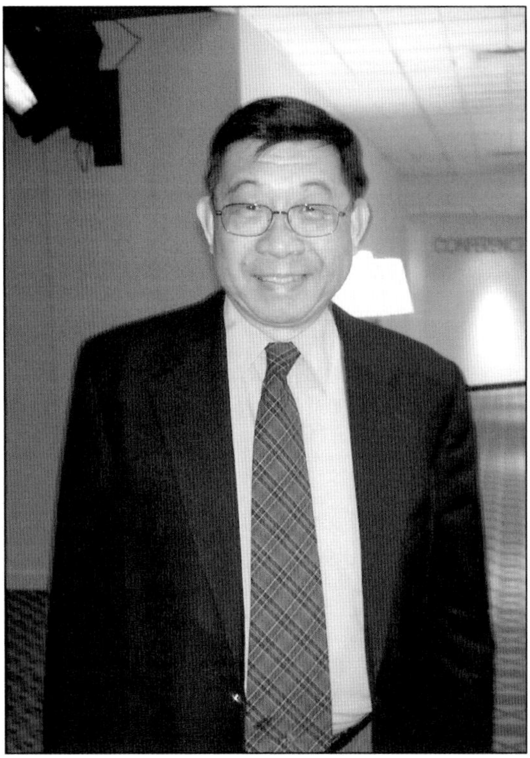

The St. Louis Christian Chinese Community Service Center at 8231 Olive Boulevard, pictured above, is a new community structure founded in 2003. It is funded by government grants and individual donations and staffed primarily by compassionate Chinese Christian volunteers. Its senior center, offering a variety of activities, proves to be very popular among the seniors coming from China, Taiwan, Hong Kong, and Vietnam. Rev. David Cheung serves as the chair of the board, Dr. Gordon Wong as vice chair, and Dr. Harold Law as secretary. Pictured at left, Law has devoted much of his time, money, and energy to the Chinese Christian community in St. Louis and was selected as the winner of the Community Service Award at the 2006 MCASTA annual conference. Law is pictured at the 2005 MCASTA conference when interviewed by the author on October 15, 2005. (Photographs by Huping Ling.)

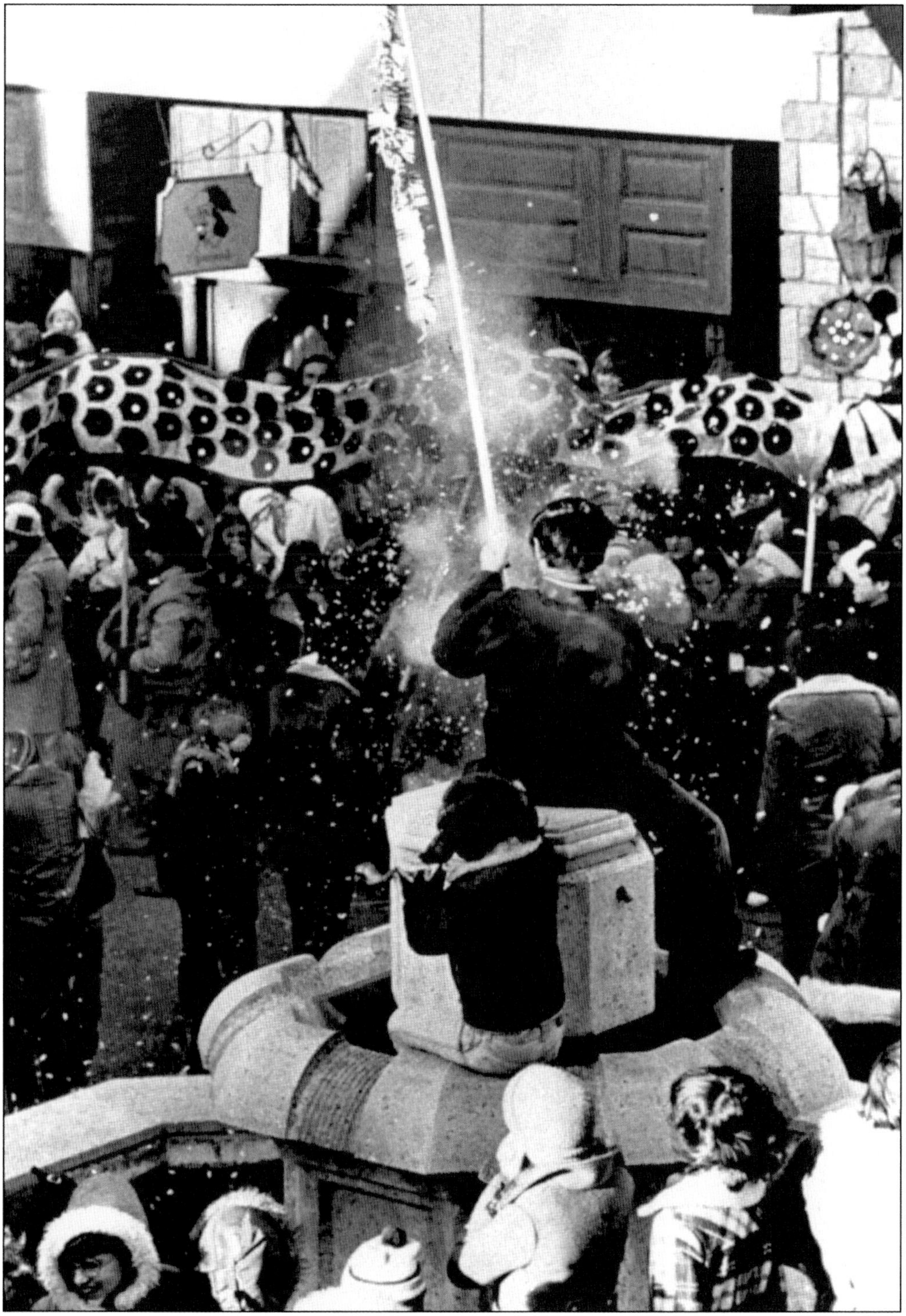

Michael Shun, 12, defies the dragon as he entertains a crowd celebrating the Chinese New Year (Year of the Dragon) at West Port Plaza on February 2, 1976. (Photograph by T. V. Vessell; St. Louis Globe-Democrat, St. Louis Mercantile Library.)

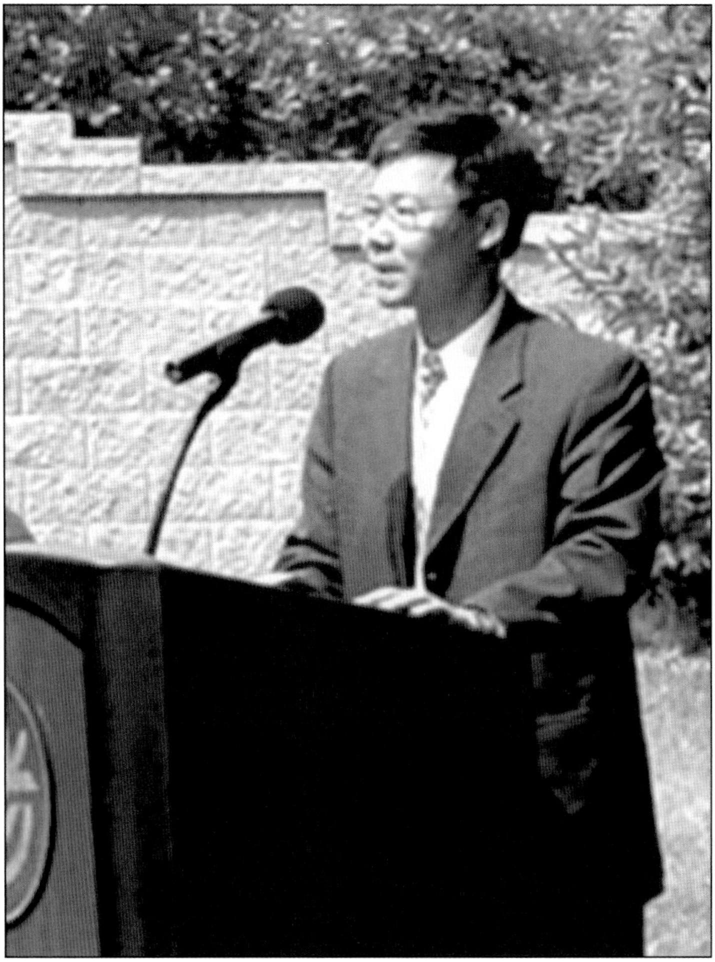

The Chinese Culture Days, initiated by Grace Shen Lo and a group of enthusiastic community activists in the early 1990s, has evolved over the years into a huge annual Chinese cultural display that has drawn thousands of St. Louisans. In the image at left, Hung-Gay Fung, chair of the 2006 committee, opens the event. In the image below, Jenny Lu and staff serve food at China Days in 2006. (St. Louis Chinese American News.)

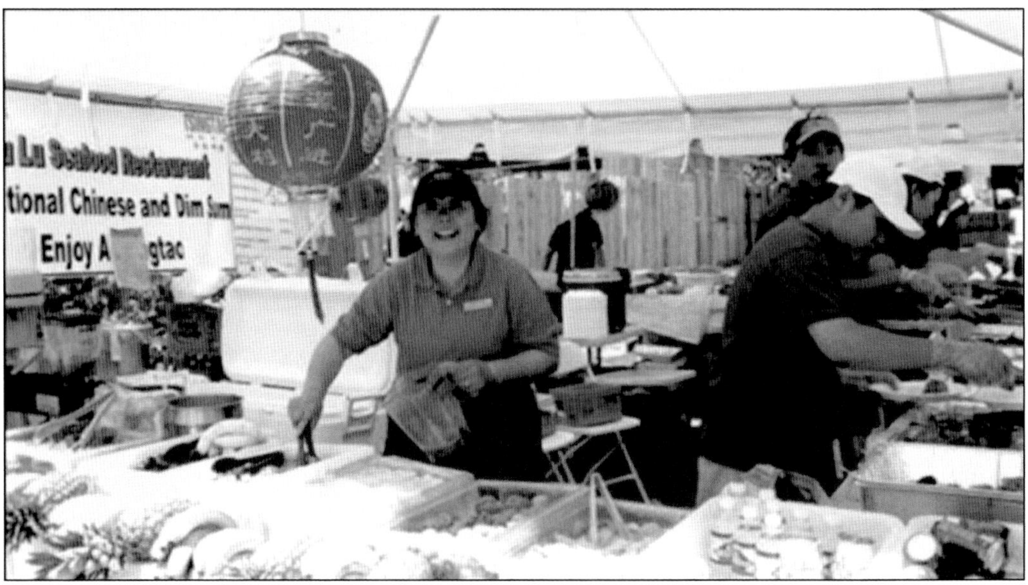

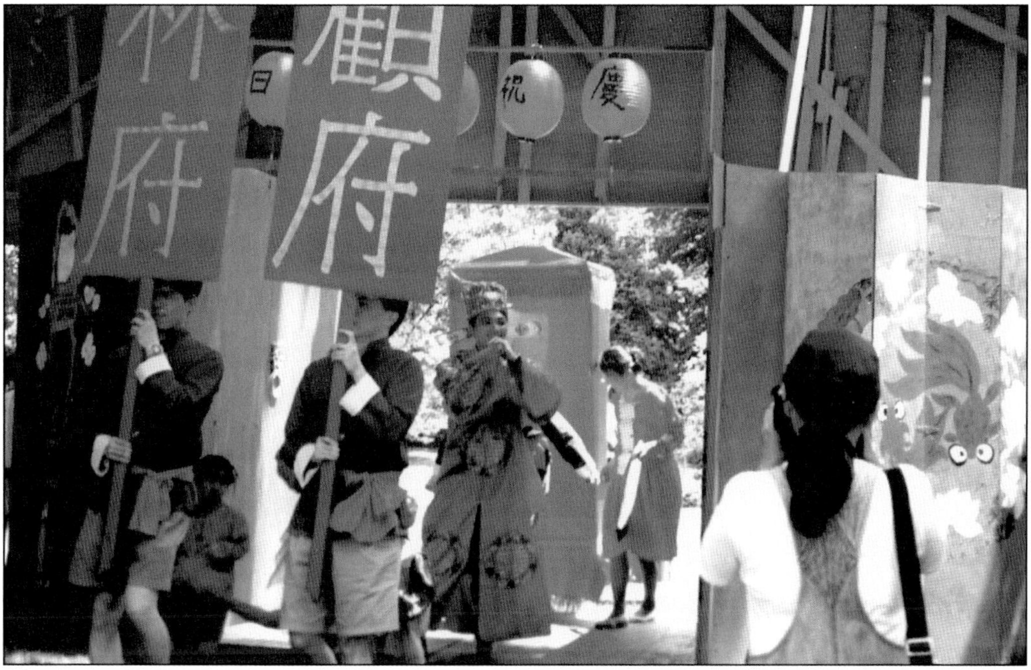

The annual affair, from its planning to execution, involves tremendous human resources and monetary expenses. The preparation of the event usually starts in October of the previous year and continues until the day of the event. The committee organizing the event is constituted by the officers of the major community organizations and includes a number of subcommittees in charge of fund-raising, treasury, food booths, display booths, public relations, entertainment, and costume and design. The continuation and growth of this annual event have effectively demonstrated the community's serious commitment to promoting the diverse Chinese culture and to achieving organizational unity. A Chinese wedding was demonstrated at the Chinese Cultural Days held in the Missouri Botanic Gardens on June 5, 1999. (Photographs by Huping Ling.)

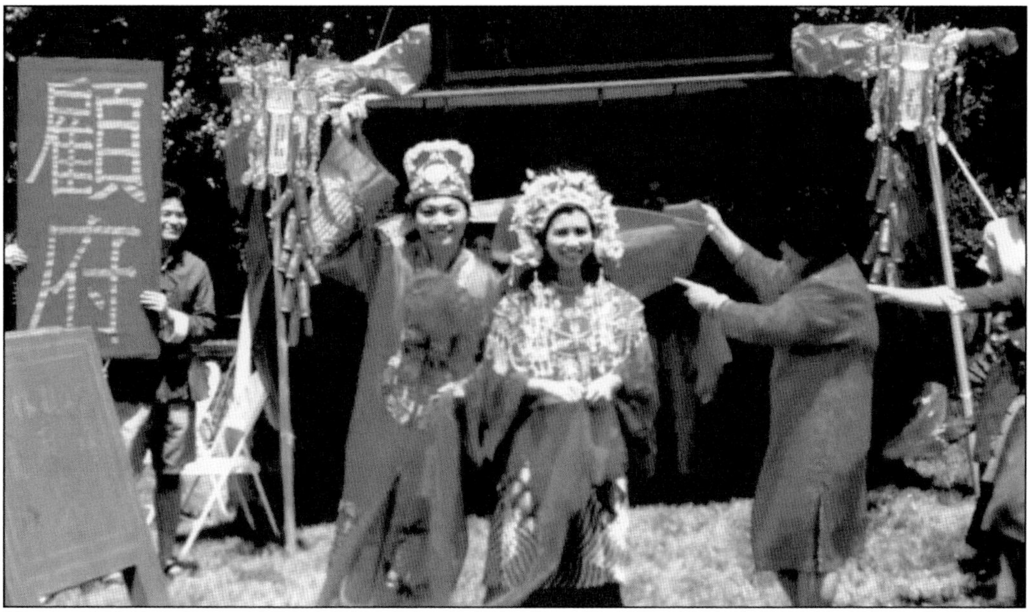

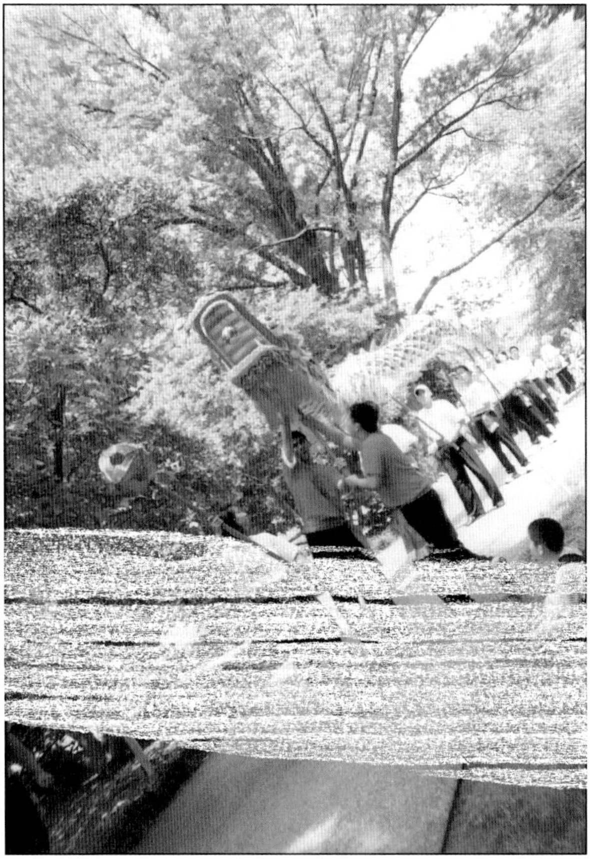

Pictured in 2005, the celebration is normally held for two days in May or June, and features a dragon dance, acrobats, traditional Chinese dance, Beijing opera, stage plays adopted from traditional folktales, a martial arts demonstration, displays of Chinese artifacts, and the sale of Chinese food of various sorts. (Photographs by Huping Ling.)

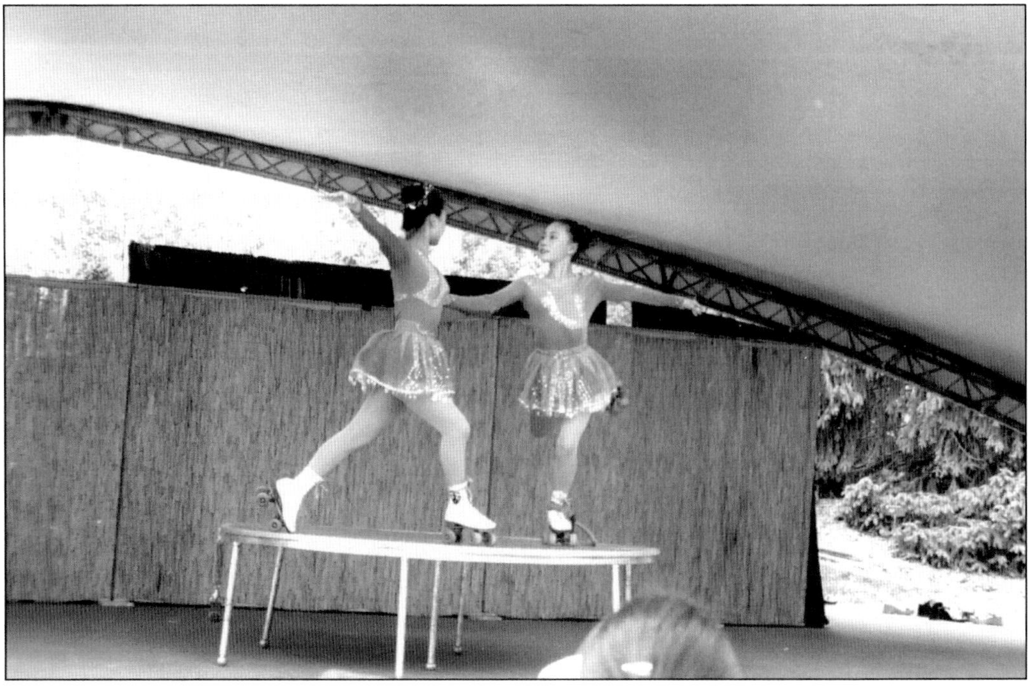

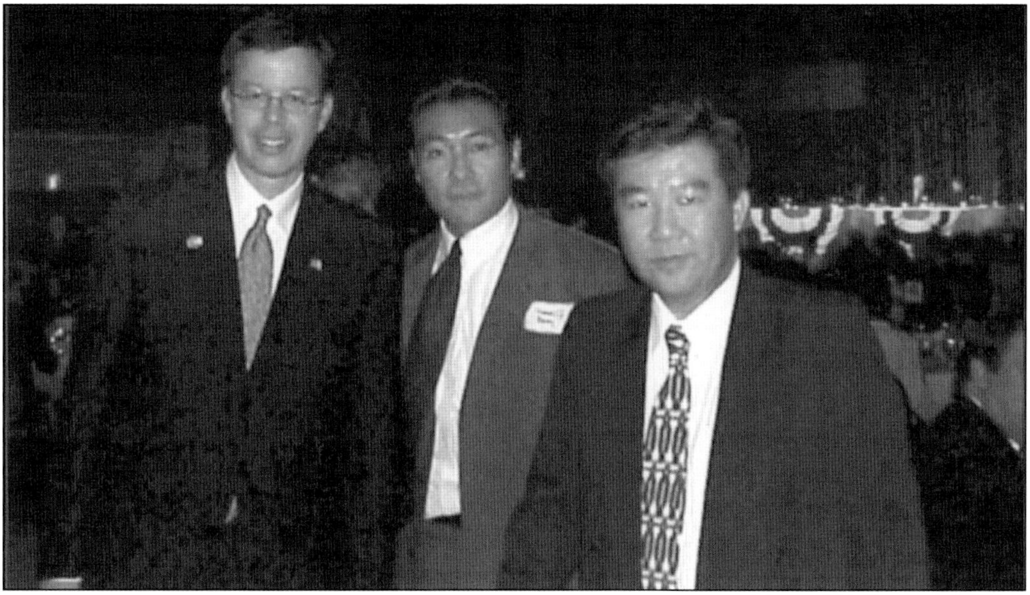

A group of Chinese American business owners and community leaders founded the Pacific-American Campaign Coalition (PACC) in April 2002, in order to seek a greater Asian American political representation and to create more opportunities to voice the needs of the Asian American community in American urban politics. Thomas Wong (center) and Francois Ho (right), president and vice president of the PACC, are pictured with Jim Talent, Republican candidate for Missouri senator, at the dinner/fund-raiser on March 18, 2002. (St. Louis Chinese American News.)

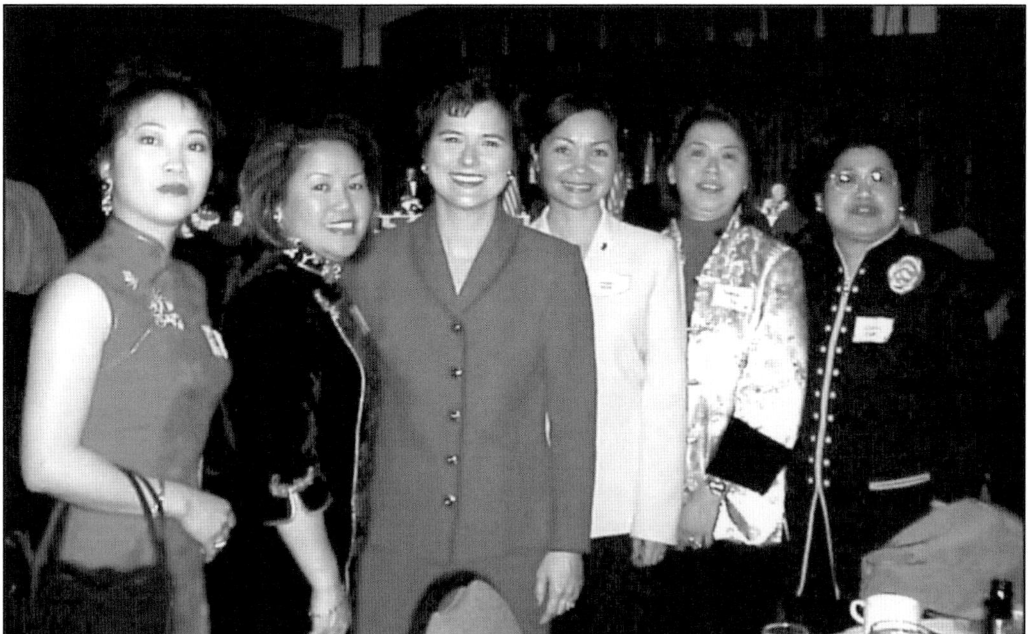

Members of the Asian American Business Association are pictured with Brenda L. Talent, wife of Jim Talent, Republican candidate for Missouri senator, at the dinner/fundraiser on March 18, 2002. (St. Louis Chinese American News.)

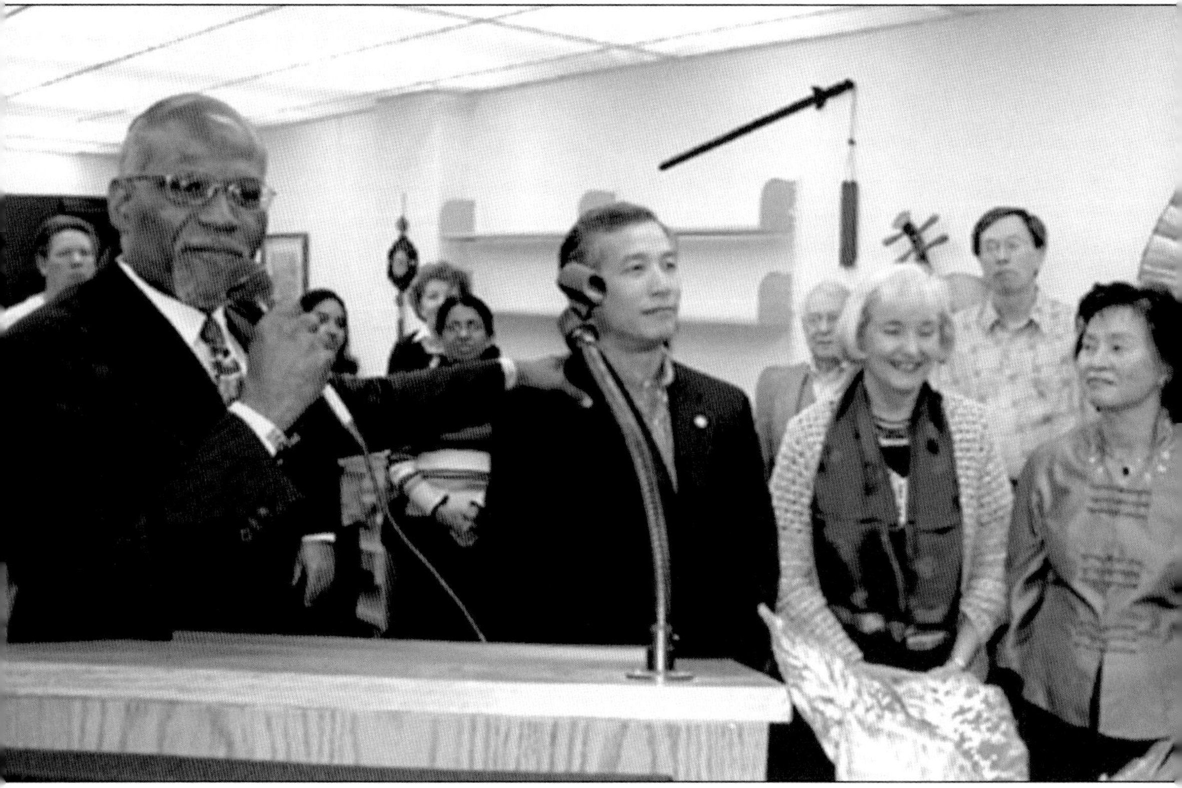

The active participation of the Chinese American community in St. Louis has been recognized by the larger society. Charlie Dooley, St. Louis County commissioner, speaks at the opening ceremony for the new Asian Center at the Daniel Boone Branch of the St. Louis County Library; he is pictured with Ching-Ling Tai (right), the president of the board, on November 12, 2005. (St. Louis Chinese American News.)

The Chinese St. Louisans have also entered the mainstream political process as public appointees serving in state-wide commissions. In May 2001, two female Chinese American St. Louisans, Ching-Ling Tai and Lily Ko, were named by Missouri lieutenant governor Joe Maxwell as commissioners in the Missouri Community Service Commission (MCSC) for a three-year-term from May 11, 2001, to December 15, 2003. Seen on the right is a photograph of Ching-Ling Tai. Seen below are Walter (right) and Lily Ko (second from left) with Missouri governor Bob Holden (second from right) and representative Connie Johnson on Lily Ko's appointment as Missouri Community Service Commissioner in February 2002. (Right, Ching-Ling Tai; below, Walter Ko).

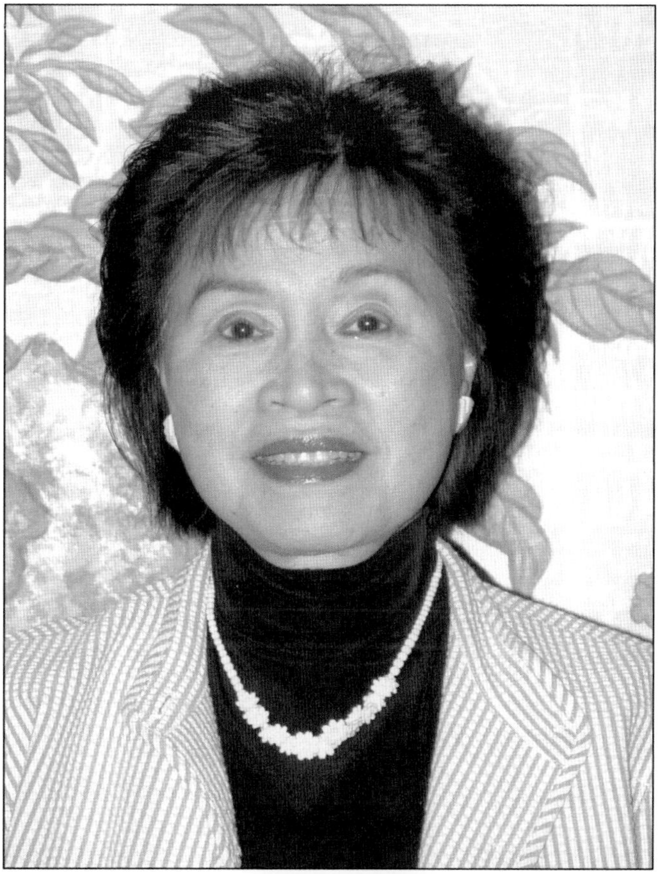

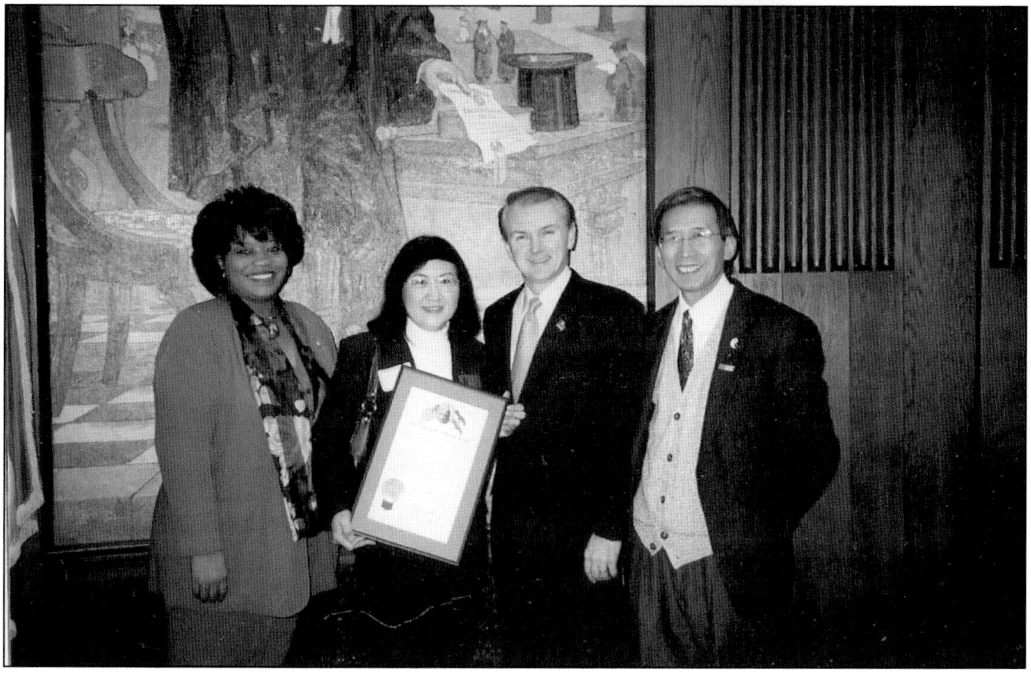

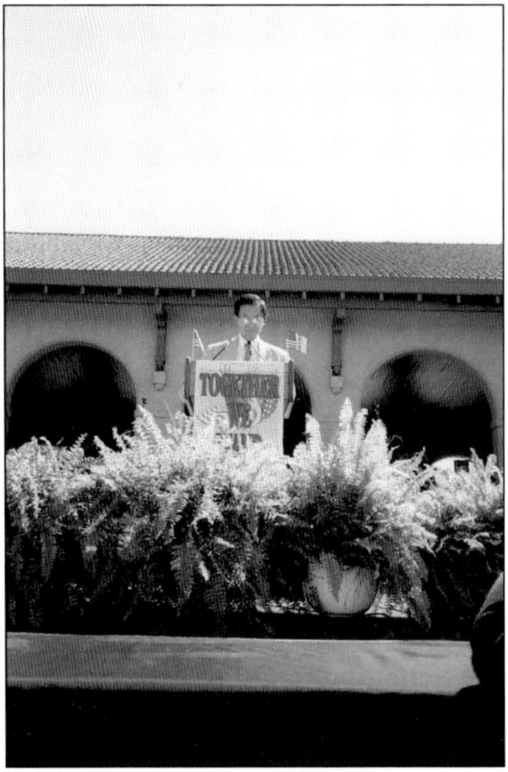

Apart from planned activities such as the Chinese Culture Days, major national events such as the 9/11 terrorist attack in 2001 have also united the community. After the September 11 terrorist attack on the World Trade Center and Pentagon, the St. Louis Chinese community organizations jointly sponsored fund-raising activities. Walter Ko is pictured speaking at the 9/11 Together We Stand rally on September 16, 2001. (Walter Ko.)

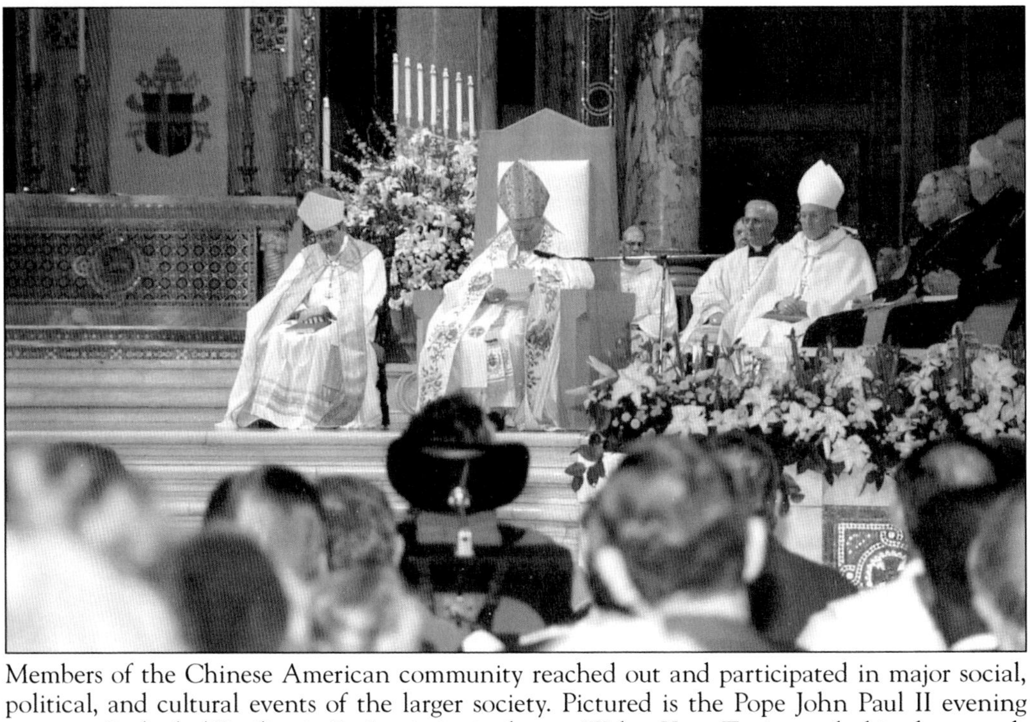

Members of the Chinese American community reached out and participated in major social, political, and cultural events of the larger society. Pictured is the Pope John Paul II evening prayer at Cathedral Basilica in St. Louis; invited guest Walter Ko, a Taoist, took this photograph on January 27, 1999. (Walter Ko.)

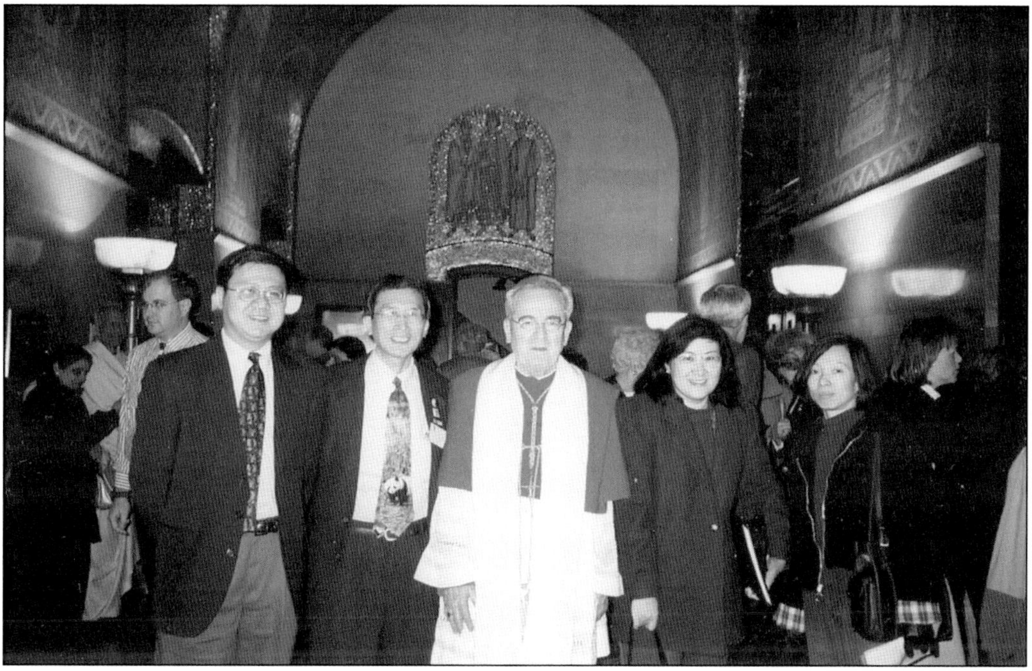

Seen here, from left to right, are Peter Leung, Walter Ko, St. Louis archbishop Justin Rigali, Lily Ko, and Kitty Birch at the Cathedral Basilica where Walter Ko made a speech on January 23, 2002, in joining Pope John Paul II's call of the leaders of the world's religions for an Interfaith Gathering in Prayer for Peace. (Walter Ko.)

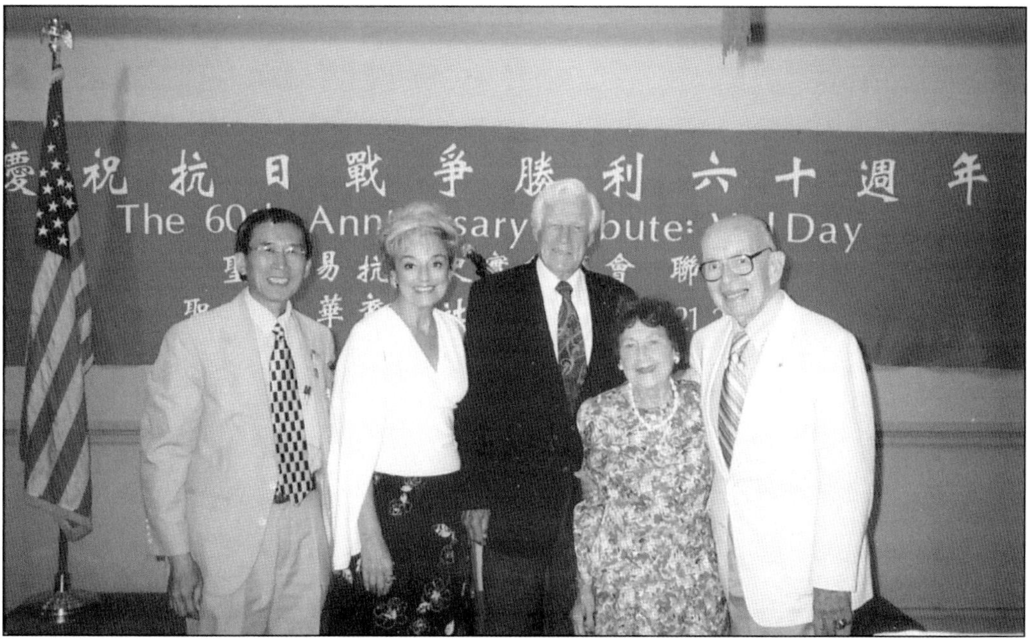

From left to right, Walter Ko, Anna and Whitney Harris (American prosecutor at Nuremburg trial of Nazi Germany), and May and Martin Duggan (KETC television host of *Donnybrook*) are pictured at the commemoration of the 60th Anniversary of V-J Day in St. Louis in August 2005. (Walter Ko.)

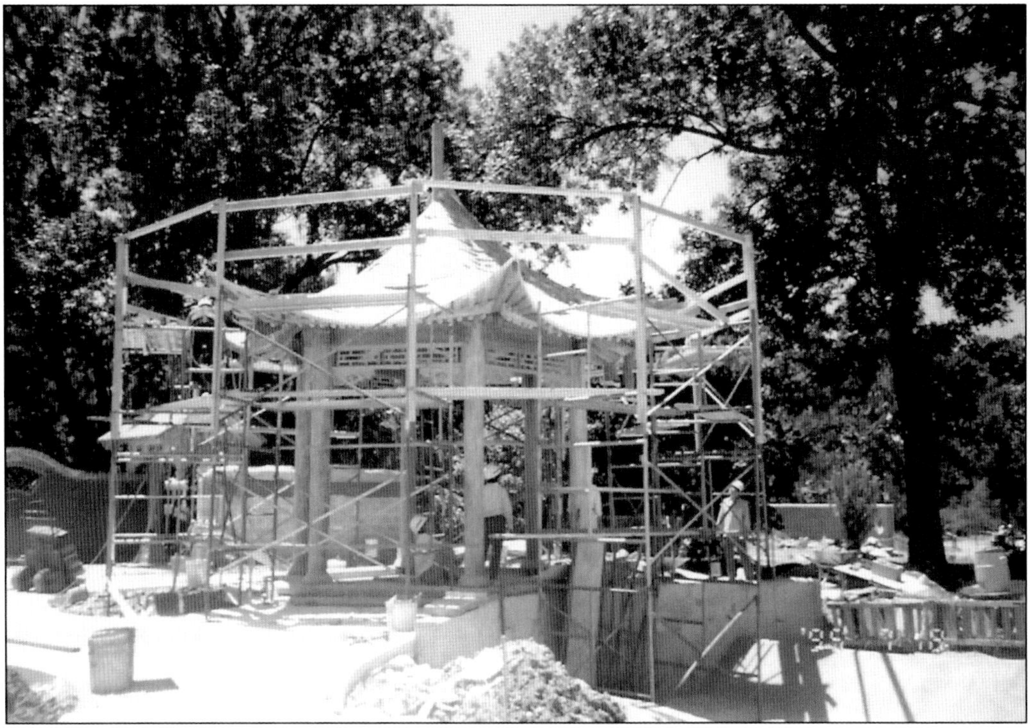

The Chinese Americans in St. Louis help promote the cultural exchange and relationship between St. Louis and Nanjing, China. Construction of the Margret Grigg Nanjing Friendship Garden in the Missouri Botanic Gardens is captured in these photographs from 1995. (Mimi Chou.)

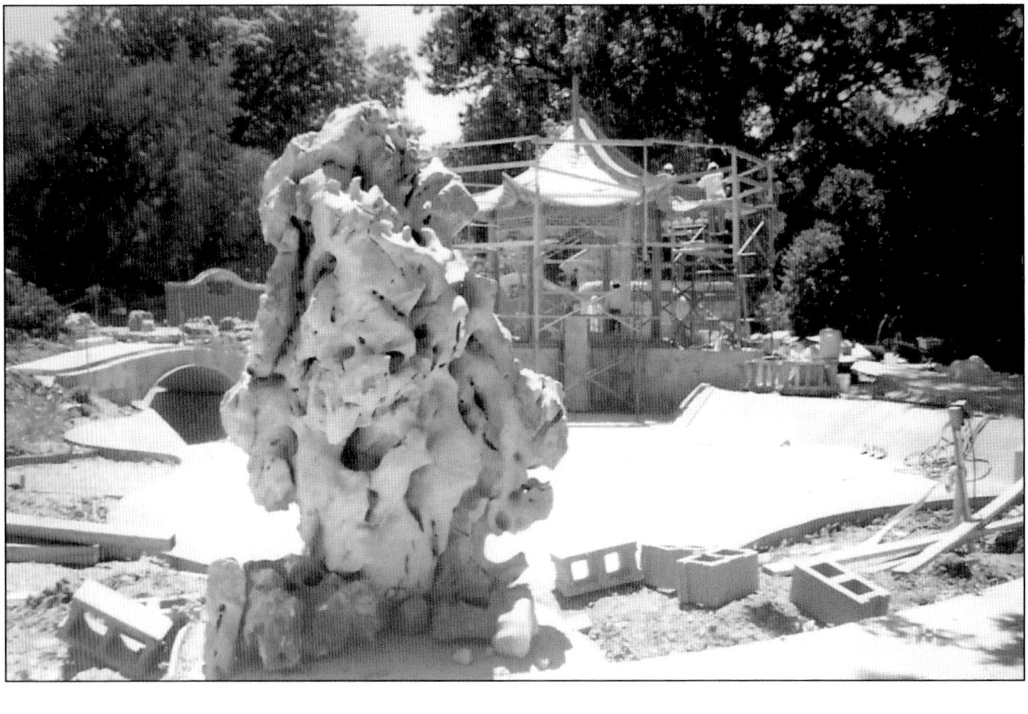

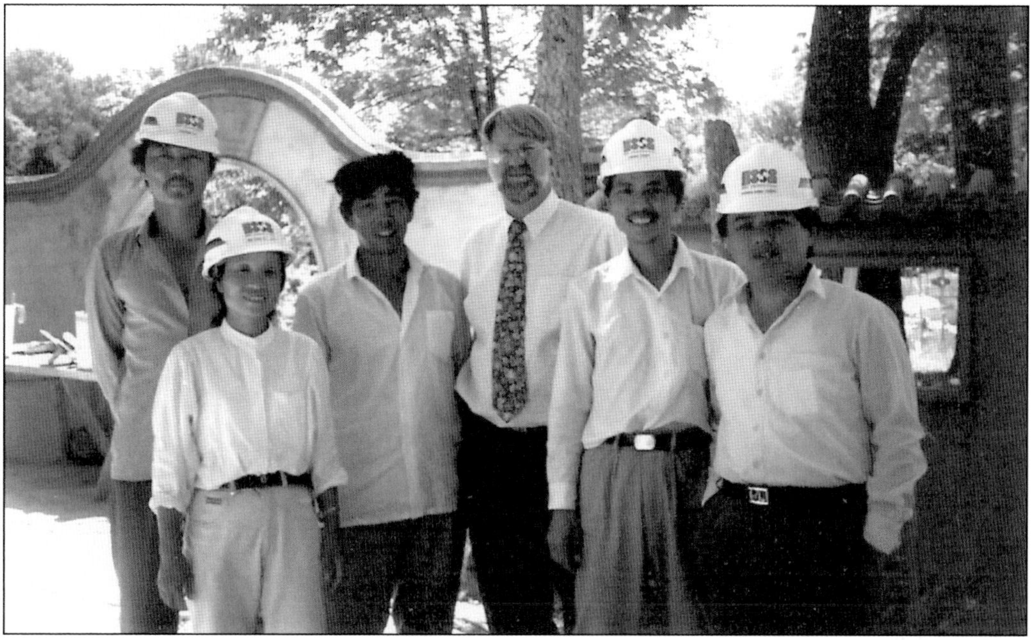

Pictured above, Zhu Daoyu (front left), an engineer from the Nanjing Bureau of Garden, led four Chinese workers to assist in construction. They are, from left to right, Yu Yaoyun, Li Zhihong, Paul Brockmann (director of the Construction Department at Missouri Botanic Gardens), Chen Gang, and Zhou Hongliang. (Mimi Chou.)

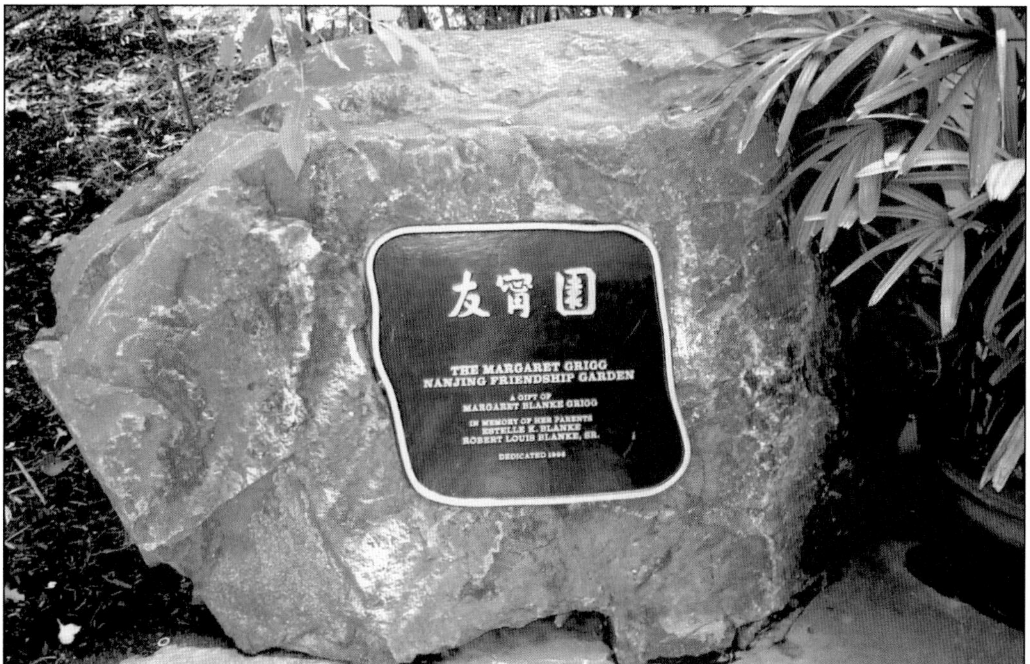

The construction of the garden was made possible thanks to a gift from Margaret Grigg in memory of her parents, Estelle and Robert Blanke. Major features of the garden are gifts from the city of Nanjing, China. (Photograph by Huping Ling.)

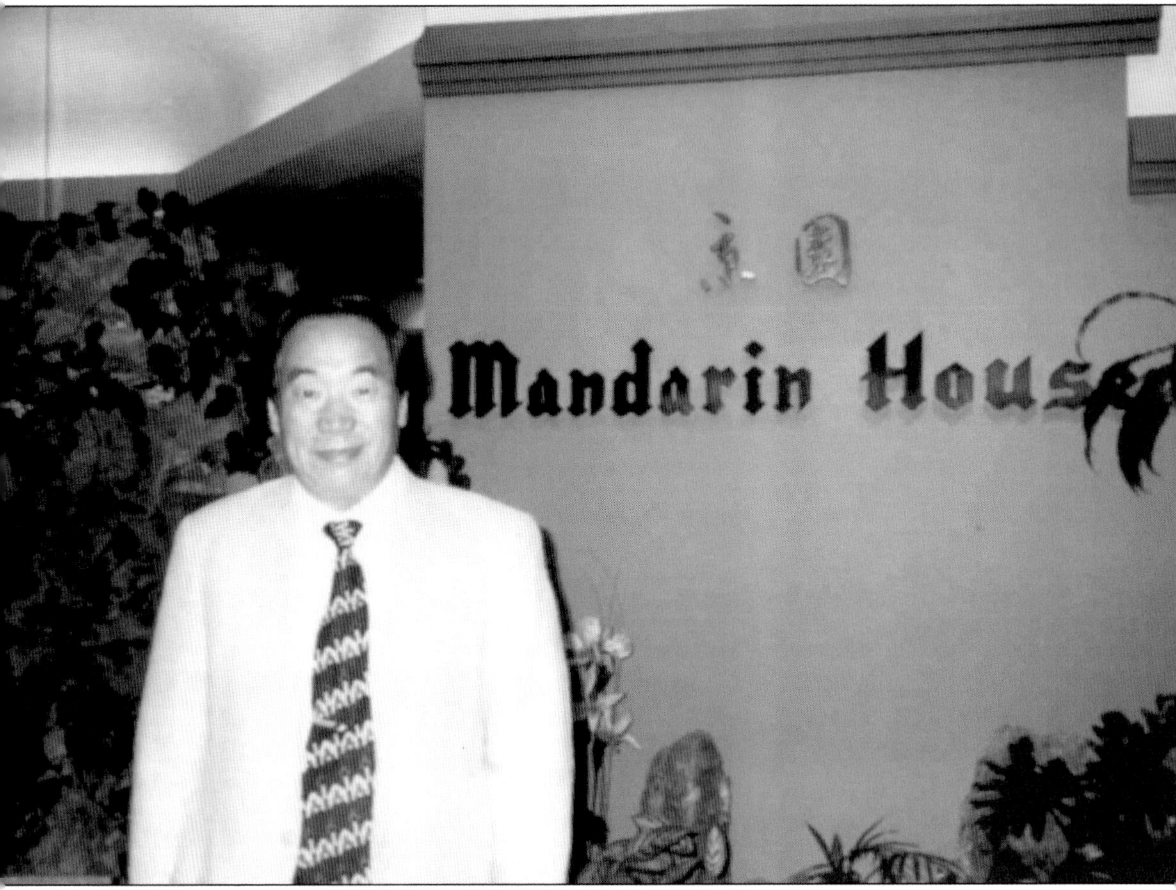

The Chinese American community in St. Louis was strengthened and diversified demographically by the new members from South Korea and Vietnam. In the 1970s and 1980s, a number of Korean Chinese families came to St. Louis working in the food service industry in order to meet the public demand on ethnic Chinese food since the early 1970s. Sherwin Liou, who is Korean Chinese and owner of the Mandarin House restaurant located at 9150 Overland Plaza, is pictured in 1999. (Photograph by Huping Ling.)

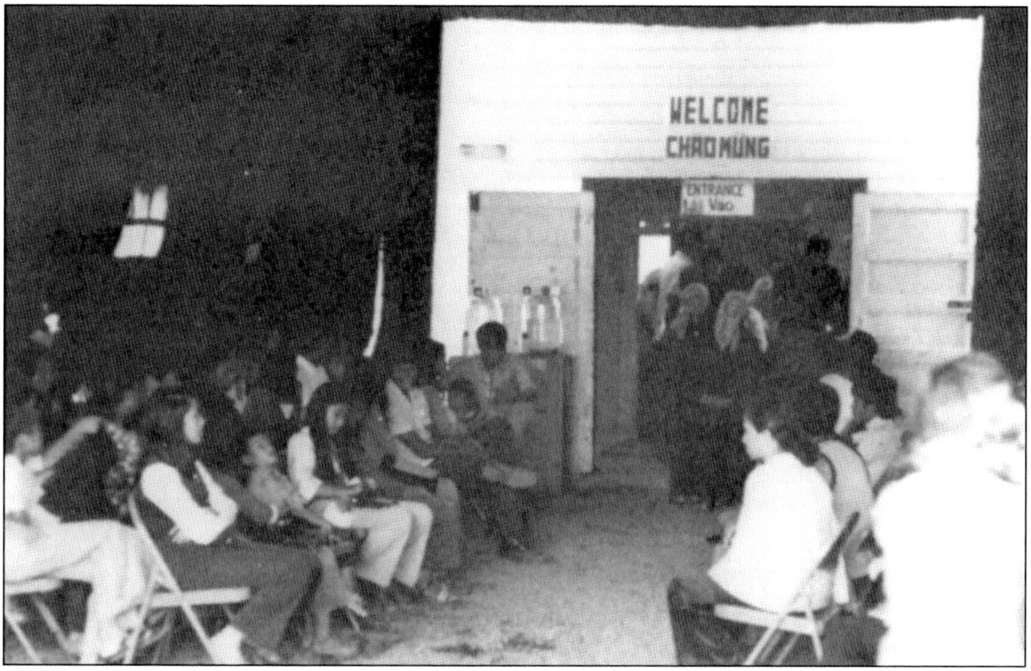

The Vietnamese Chinese came to St. Louis as refugees following the fall of Vietnam to Communists in 1975. In the spring of 1975, the United States and many other countries opened themselves to the war refugees from Indochina. St. Louis had its share of the refugees, receiving about 10,000 since 1975. Vietnamese refugees wait in tent shelters outside the Immigration and Naturalization Service processing center in Fort Indiantown Gap, Pennsylvania, in 1975. (Immigration and Naturalization Service Annual Report, 1975.)

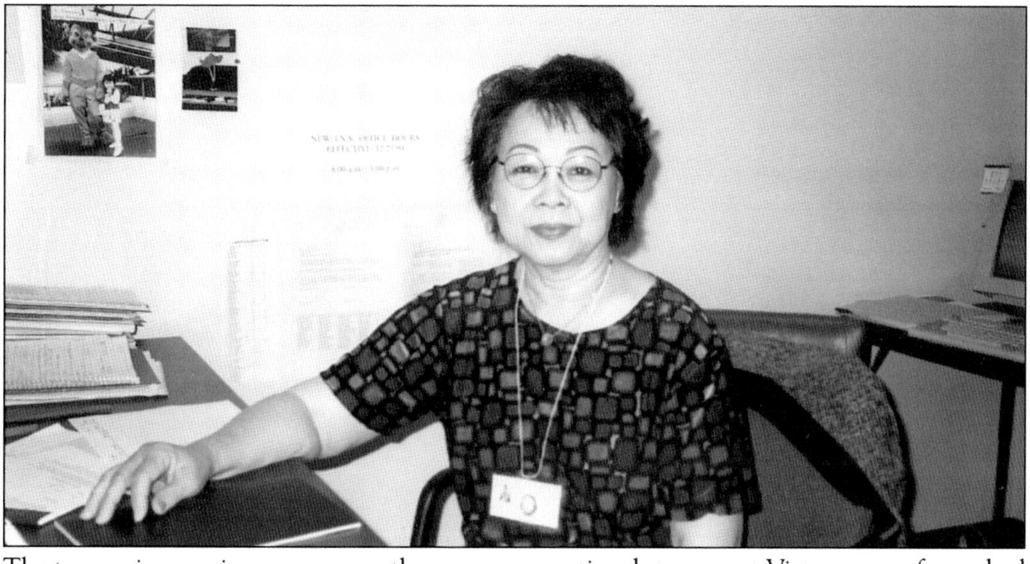

The trauma in escaping passage was the common emotional stress most Vietnamese refugees had to deal with first. Ha's story typifies the refugee experience in escaping Vietnam and in settlement in their new homes. Ha (pseudonym), case management coordinator at the International Institute of Metro St. Louis, helps with the Vietnamese elderly cope with the trauma. Ha is pictured at work when interviewed by the author on June 14, 1999. (Photograph by Huping Ling.)

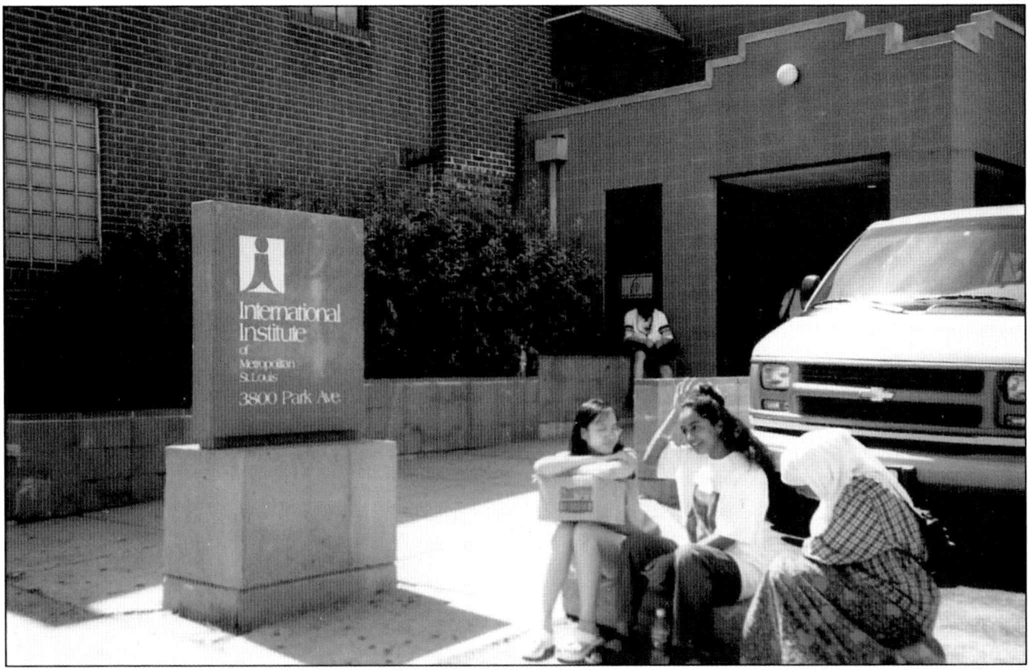

The work of settlement and relocation of Vietnamese refugees was carried out by the International Institute of Metro St. Louis. New immigrants are pictured in 1999 outside of the institute, located at 3800 Park Avenue. (Photograph by Huping Ling.)

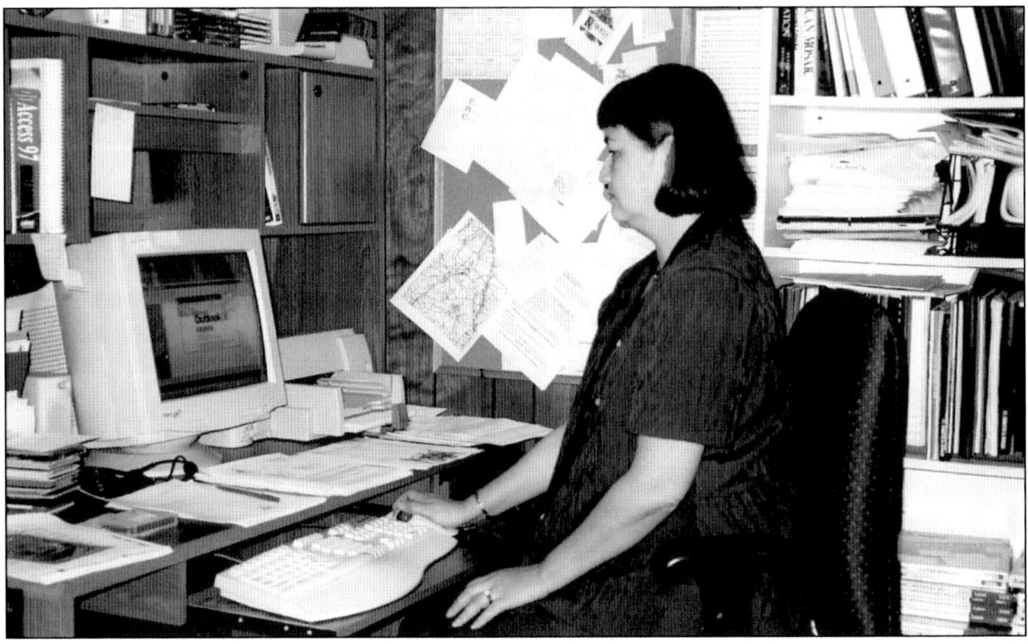

Founded in 1919, the institute has been helping newcomers from around the world become self-sufficient St. Louisans. The staff and volunteers of the institute annually helped about 6,000 immigrants and refugees from more than 40 countries. Anna Crosslin, president of the International Institute of Metro St. Louis, was photographed at work when interviewed by the author on May 28, 1999. (Photograph by Huping Ling.)

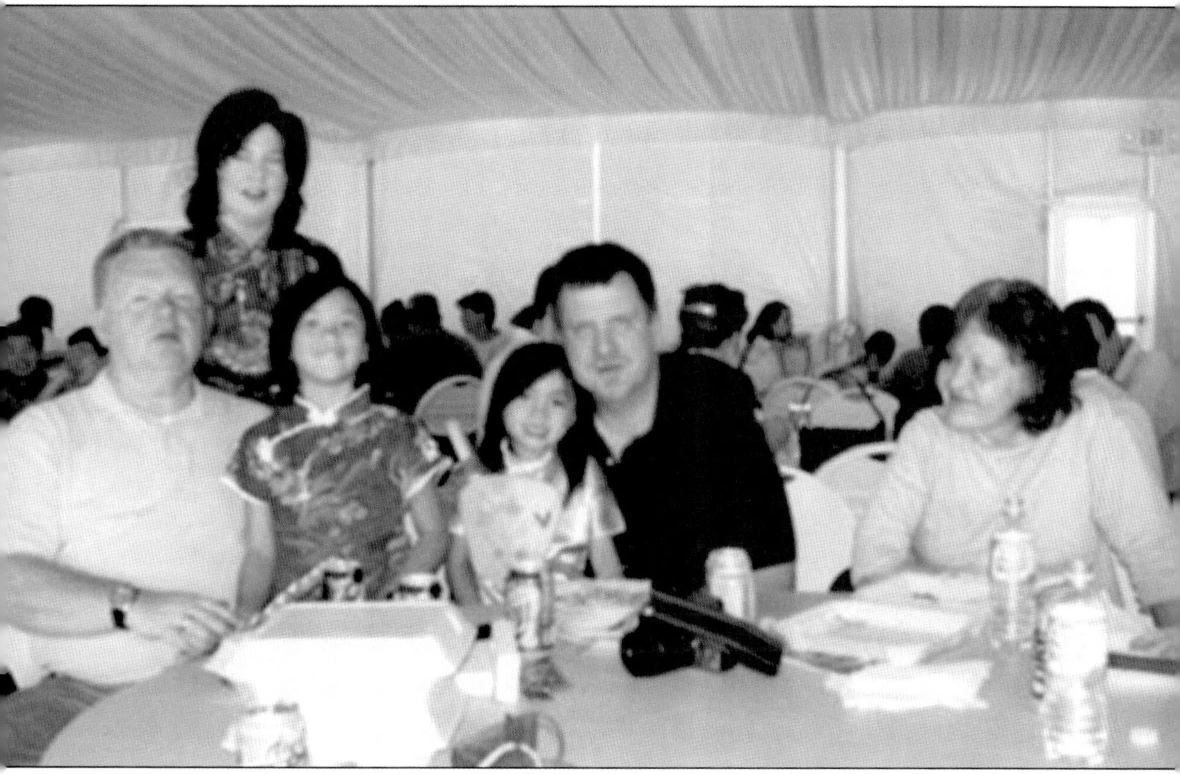

American families with adopted children from China have formed the St. Louis Families with Children from China (FCC), which has been an integral part of the St. Louis Chinese American cultural community. FCC members are pictured at the 2006 China Days. (St. Louis Chinese American News.)

BIBLIOGRAPHY

Bennitt, Mark, ed. *History of the Louisiana Purchase Exposition.* New York: Arno Press, 1976.

Blake, C. Fred. "The Chinese of Valhalla: Adaptation and Identity in a Midwestern American Cemetery." *Markers X, Journal of the Association for Gravestone Studies.* 1993: 53–89.

Burnett, Betty. *St. Louis at War: The Story of a City 1941–1945.* St. Louis: The Patrice Press, 1987.

Choi, Kyung. "The Assimilation of Korean Immigrants in the St. Louis Area." Ph.D. diss., St. Louis University, 1984.

Christensen, Lawrence Oland. "Black St. Louis: A Study in Race Relations, 1865–1916." Ph.D. diss., University of Missouri, 1972.

Cortinovis, Irene E. "China at the St. Louis World's Fair." *Missouri Historical Review* Vol. 77 (1977–1978): 59–66.

Dreer, Herman. "Negro Leadership in St. Louis: A Study in Race Relations." Ph.D. diss., University of Chicago, 1955.

Early, Gerald, ed. *Ain't But a Place: An Anthology of African American Writings about St. Louis.* Columbia, MO: University of Missouri Press, 1998.

Ehrlich, Walter. *Zion in the Valley, the Jewish Community of St. Louis.* Vol. I, 1807–1907. Columbia, MO: University of Missouri Press, 1997.

Hurley, Andrew, ed. *Common Fields: An Environmental History of St. Louis.* St. Louis: Missouri Historical Society Press, 1997.

Iglauer, Henry S. "The Demolition of the Louisiana Purchase Exposition of 1904." *Missouri Historical Society Bulletin.* Vol. 22, no. 4 (1965–1966): 457–467.

Inoue, Miyako. "Japanese-Americans in St. Louis: From Internees to Professionals." *City and Society.* Vol. 3, no. 2 (December 1989): 142–152.

Ling, Huping. *Chinese St. Louis: From Enclave to Cultural Community.* Philadelphia: Temple University Press, 2004.

———. "New Perspectives on Chinese American Studies—Cultural Community Theory." *Overseas Chinese History Studies* No. 1 (2007).

———. "Reconceptualizing Chinese American Community in St. Louis: From Chinatown to Cultural Community." *Journal of American Ethnic History.* Vol. 24, no. 2 (Winter 2005): 65–101.

———. "Hop Alley: Myth and Reality of the St. Louis Chinatown, 1860s–1930s." *Journal of Urban History* Vol. 28, no. 2 (January 2002): 184–219.

———. "Growing up in 'Hop Alley:' The Chinese American Youth in St. Louis during the Early-Twentieth Century." In *Asian American Children,* ed. Benson Tong, 65–81. Westport, CT: Greenwood Press, 2004.

———. "Governing 'Hop Alley:' On Leong Chinese Merchants and Laborers Association, 1906–1966." *Journal of American Ethnic History*. Vol. 23, no. 2 (Winter 2004): 50–84.
———. *Ping Piao Mei Guo: New Immigrants in America*. Shanxi, China: Beiyue Literature and Art Publishing House, 2003.
———. "Lu Qiao Qi Ren." *St. Louis Chinese American Journal*, October 19, 2000.
———. *Chinese St. Louisans. The St. Louis Chinese American News*. December 21, 2000 to July 19, 2001.
———. *Surviving on the Gold Mountain: A History of Chinese American Women and Their Lives*. Albany, NY: State University of New York Press, 1998.
Lipsitz, George. *The Sidewalks of St. Louis: Places, People, and Politics in an American City*. Columbia, MO: University of Missouri Press, 1991.
Long, Suzanna Maupin. "'I Made It Mine Tho the Queen Waz Always Fair': The St. Louis Black Clubwomen Movement, 1931–1946." Thesis, University of Missouri at St. Louis, 1988.
Mormino, Gary Ross. *Immigrants on the Hill, Italian-Americans in St. Louis, 1882–1982*. Urbana: University of Illinois Press, 1986.
Olson, Audrey L. *St. Louis Germans, 1850–1920: The Nature of an Immigrant Community and Its Relation to the Assimilation Process*. New York: Arno Press, 1980.
Primm, James Neal. *Lion of the Valley: St. Louis, Missouri*. Boulder, CO: Pruett Publishing Company, 1990.
Rudwick, Elliott M. *Race Riot at East St. Louis July 2, 1917*. Carbondale, IL: Southern Illinois University Press, 1964.
Rynerson, Ann M., and Pamela A. DeVoe. "Refugee Women in a Vertical Village: Lowland Laotians in St. Louis." *Social Thought*. Vol. 10, no. 3 (summer 1984): 33–48.
St. Louis Chapter of the Organization of Chinese Americans. *Ironing Out the Fabric of Our Past: An Oral History of Five Chinese Americans in St. Louis, the Early 1900s*. St. Louis: 1993.
Sit, Hong. *My View from a Bridge*. Houston: Blessing Books, 1999.
Sobel, Irwin, Werner Z. Hirsch, and Harry C. Harris. *The Negro in the St. Louis Economy, 1954*. St. Louis: The Urban League of St. Louis, 1954.
The St. Louis Chapter of the Organization of Chinese Americans. *Ironing Out the Fabric of Our Past: An Oral History of Five Chinese Americans in St. Louis, The Early 1900s*. St. Louis: 1993.
Sullivan, Margaret Lo Piccolo. "Hyphenism in St. Louis, 1900–1921: The View from the Outside." Ph.D. diss., St. Louis University, 1968.
Washington University. *A Partial Bibliography of Resources on the History of Saint Louis Ethnic Cultures*. St. Louis: Sociology Department, Washington University.
Wright, John A. *Discovering African-American St. Louis: A Guide to Historic Sites*. St. Louis: Missouri Historical Society Press, 1994.